250 Amazing Coffee Cake Recipes

(250 Amazing Coffee Cake Recipes - Volume 1)

Angela Haas

Copyright: Published in the United States by Angela Haas/ © ANGELA HAAS

Published on October, 12 2020

All rights reserved. No part of this publication may be reproduced, stored in retrieval system, copied in any form or by any means, electronic, mechanical, photocopying, recording or otherwise transmitted without written permission from the publisher. Please do not participate in or encourage piracy of this material in any way. You must not circulate this book in any format. ANGELA HAAS does not control or direct users' actions and is not responsible for the information or content shared, harm and/or actions of the book readers.

In accordance with the U.S. Copyright Act of 1976, the scanning, uploading and electronic sharing of any part of this book without the permission of the publisher constitute unlawful piracy and theft of the author's intellectual property. If you would like to use material from the book (other than just simply for reviewing the book), prior permission must be obtained by contacting the author at author@bisquerecipes.com

Thank you for your support of the author's rights.

Content

250 AWESOME COFFEE CAKE RECIPES 7

1. 1 Dish Caramel Pecan Coffee Cake Recipe 7
2. 1959 CITY SCHOOL SOUR CREAM COFFEE CAKE Recipe 7
3. Almond Zucchini Babka Recipe 8
4. Almond Lemon Coffeecake Recipe 9
5. Any Fruit Coffee Cake Recipe 9
6. Apple Cinnamon Coffee Cake Recipe 10
7. Apple Coffee Cake Recipe 10
8. Apple Ginger And Hazelnut Coffee Cake Recipe 11
9. Apple Oatmeal Coffee Cake Recipe 11
10. Apple Rum Custard Coffeecake Recipe 12
11. Apple Sour Cream Coffeecake Recipe 12
12. Apple Streusel Coffeecake Recipe 13
13. Apple Walnut Oatmel Coffee Cake Recipe 13
14. Apple Cream Cheese Coffee Cake Recipe 14
15. Apple Nut Ring Recipe 14
16. Apple Topped Cake Recipe 15
17. Apricot Almond Coffee Cake Recipe 15
18. Apricot Lemon Coffeecake Recipe 16
19. Apricot Chocolate Ring Recipe 16
20. Asian Pear And Ricotta Coffee Cake Recipe 17
21. Banana Coffee Cake Recipe 17
22. Banana Coffee Cake With Chocolate Chip Streusel Recipe 17
23. Banana Coffee Cake With Chocolate Chip Streusel Recipe 18
24. Banana Coffeecake Recipe 18
25. Banana Crumb Coffee Cake Recipe 19
26. Banana Walnut Coffee Cake Recipe 19
27. Banana Sour Cream Coffee Cake From The Bent Creek Lodge Recipe 20
28. Banana Nana Pecan Bread Recipe 20
29. Basic Coffee Cake Recipe 21
30. Best Of The West Blackberry Coffeecake Recipe 21
31. Bisquick Coffee Cake Recipe 22
32. Blackberry Crunch Coffeecake Recipe 22
33. Blackberry Streusel Coffeecake Recipe 22
34. Blueberry Applesauce Coffeecake Recipe. 23
35. Blueberry Buckle Coffee Cake Recipe 23
36. Blueberry Buckle With Cream Cheese Whipped Cream Recipe 24
37. Blueberry Coffee Cake Recipe 25
38. Blueberry Cream Cheese Brunch Buckle Recipe 26
39. Blueberry Crumb CoffeeCake Recipe 26
40. Blueberry Monkey Pull Apart Bread Recipe 27
41. Blueberry Ricotta Cheese Streusel Coffeecake Recipe 27
42. Blueberry N Cheese Coffee Cake Recipe .. 28
43. Blueberry Streusel Bread Recipe 28
44. Blums Coffee Crunch Cake Recipe 28
45. Brandied Coffee And Honey Cake Recipe 29
46. Butter Crumb Coffee Cake With Cranberries Recipe 29
47. Buttercup Squash Coffeecake Recipe 30
48. Buttermilk Cinnamon Bread Recipe 31
49. Butternut Squash Coffeecake Recipe 31
50. CHRISTMAS BREAD Recipe 32
51. COCONUT CHOCOLATE CHIP COFFEE CAKE Recipe 32
52. CREAM CHEESE COFFEE CAKE DIABETIC FRIENDLY Recipe 33
53. Cafe Au Lait Breakfast Cake Recipe 34
54. Canadian Banana Coffee Cake Recipe 34
55. Captains Raspberry Almond Coffee Cake Recipe 35
56. Caramel Nut Twisted Sweet Potato Coffee Cake Recipe 35
57. Cheaters Puff Pastry Pinwheels Recipe 36
58. Cheesecake Coffee Cake Recipe 36
59. Cherry Sourdough Coffee Cake Recipe 37
60. Cherry Cashew Coffeecakes Recipe 37
61. Cherry Coffee Cake Recipe 38
62. Cherry Cream Coffeecake Recipe 39
63. Cherry Rhubarb Coffee Cake Recipe 39
64. Childhood Cinnamon Cake Recipe 40
65. Choc Chip Pound Cake Recipe 40
66. Chocolate Chip Pumpkin Spice Bread Recipe 40
67. Chocolate Chunk Coffee Cake Recipe 41
68. Chocolate Chunk Ricotta Cake Recipe 42
69. Chocolate Coffee Fudge Cake Recipe 42
70. Chocolate Hazelnut Nutella Coffee Ring Recipe 42

71. Chocolate Macadamia Sock It To Me Cake Recipe 43
72. Chocolate Nut Bread Recipe 44
73. Chocolate Peanut Butter Coffee Cake Muffins Recipe 44
74. Chocolate Peanut Butter Cup Bread Recipe 45
75. Chocolate Raspberry Quick Bread Recipe 45
76. Chocolate Sticky Buns Recipe 46
77. Chocolate Tea Bread Recipe 46
78. Chocolate Chip Coffee Cake Recipe 47
79. Chocolate Coffee Bean Ice Cream Cake ... 47
80. Cinnamon Walnut Coffee Cake Recipe 48
81. Cinnamon Bread Recipe 48
82. Cinnamon Chip Pumpkin Bread Recipe ... 49
83. Cinnamon Cream Cheese Spirals Recipe .. 49
84. Cinnamon Streusel Coffeecake Recipe 50
85. Cinnamon And Raisins Swirl Recipe 51
86. Cinnamon Coffee Pecan Cake Recipe 51
87. Coconut Coffee Liqueur Cake Recipe 52
88. Coffee Almond Cake Recipe 52
89. Coffee Cake Muffins Recipe 53
90. Coffee Cake Recipe 53
91. Coffee Crisp Coffee Cake Recipe 54
92. Coffee Lover's Coffee Cake 54
93. Coffee Marshmallow Icebox Cake Recipe 55
94. Coffee N Cream Strusel Cake Recipe 55
95. Coffee Chocolate Cake 56
96. Coffee Chocolate Layer Cake With Mocha Mascarpone Frosting Recipe 56
97. Coffee Orange Fudge Cake Recipe 57
98. Country Blueberry Coffee Cake Recipe 58
99. Cowboy Coffee Cake Recipe 58
100. Cranberry Pecan Coffeecakes Recipe 58
101. Cranberry Sauce Coffee Cake Recipe 59
102. Cranberry Vanilla Coffee Cake Recipe 60
103. Cream Cheese Braids Recipe 60
104. Cream Cheese Coffee Cake Recipe 61
105. Creamy Blueberry Coffeecake Recipe 62
106. Creamy Mascarpone And Raspberry Coffee Cake Recipe 62
107. Creamy Peach Kuchen Recipe 63
108. Crescent Carmel Swirl Recipe 63
109. Crunch Topped Spice Cake Recipe 64
110. Danish Pastry Dough Recipe 64
111. Delicious N Healthy Amish Rolled Oats Cake Recipe 65

112. Easy Caramel Pecan Coffee Cake Recipe .65
113. Easy Delicious Apple Coffee Cake Recipe 66
114. Easy Raspberry Cheese Danish Recipe 66
115. Emilys Half In And Half Out Coffee Cake Recipe 66
116. Filled Coffee Ring Recipe 67
117. Four Seaons Chocolate Cake With Coffee Cream Frosting Recipe 68
118. French Roast Coffee Cake Recipe 68
119. Fruit Filled Coffee Cake Recipe 69
120. Fruity Coffee Cake Recipe 69
121. GORILLA BREAD Recipe 70
122. Ginger Ale Pumpkin Bread Recipe 70
123. Ginger Strawberry Raspberry Coffee Cake Recipe 71
124. Gooey Butter Coffee Cake Recipe 71
125. Grandma Janes Buttery Cinnamon Rolls Made With A Cake Mix Recipe 72
126. Grandmothers Coffee Buns Or Coffee Cake Recipe 72
127. Great Grandma Bailey's Coffee Cake Recipe 73
128. Hills And Valleys Coffee Cake Recipe 73
129. Holiday Coffee Cake Recipe 74
130. Holy Mole Granola Crunch Bread Recipe 75
131. Honey Lemon Coffee Cake Recipe 75
132. Honey Glazed Buttermilk Oatmeal Coffee Cake Recipe 75
133. Hungarian Coffee Cake Recipe 76
134. Irenes Famous Carrot Coffee Cake Recipe 77
135. Java Calypso Loaves Recipe 77
136. Jetts Cinnamon Swirl Tube Coffee Cake Recipe 77
137. Jetts Party Coffee Cake Recipe 78
138. Jewish Coffee Cake Recipe 78
139. Joys Easy Apple Raisin Cake Recipe 79
140. LEMON COCONUT BREAD With Cheese Filling Recipe 79
141. Land Of Nod Recipe 80
142. Lemon Coffee Cake Recipe 80
143. Lemon Cream Cheese Coffee Cake Recipe 81
144. Lemon Nut Bread Recipe 81
145. Louisiana Butter Pecan Coffee Cake Recipe 82
146. Low Fat Vegan Coffee Cake Recipe 82

147. MINCEMEAT COFFEE CAKE Recipe 82
148. Make Ahead Orange Coffee Cake Recipe 83
149. Mamon Filipino Sponge Cake Recipe 83
150. Mandarin Chocolate Chip Coffee Cake Recipe 84
151. Maritime Coffee Cake Recipe 85
152. Mississippi Chocolate And Coffee Cake Recipe 85
153. Mochiko Cake Recipe 86
154. Monkey Tail Bread Recipe 86
155. Nana Annas Blueberry Sour Cream Coffee Cake Recipe 87
156. No Knead Coffee Cake Loaf Recipe 87
157. Nutty Apricot Coffeecakes Recipe 88
158. Oatmeal Banana Bread Recipe 89
159. Oh I Knew You Were Coming So I Baked An Almond Cream Cheese Bundt Recipe 89
160. Old Fashioned Cinnamon Brown Sugar Coffee Cake Recipe 90
161. Old Fashioned Pumpkin Bread Recipe 90
162. Orange Chocolate Coffee Cake Recipe 91
163. Out With The Old Tea Cake Recipe 91
164. Overnight Berry Coffee Cake Recipe 92
165. Overnight Coffee Cake Recipe 92
166. PULL APART COFFEE CAKE Recipe . 93
167. Party Size Coffee Cake Supreme Recipe ... 93
168. Party Size Polish Style Coffee Cakes Recipe 94
169. Party Size Sour Cream Chocolate Chip Coffee Cake Recipe 95
170. Party Size Strawberry Rhubarb Coffee Cake Recipe 96
171. Peaches And Cream Coffee Cake Recipe . 96
172. Peachy Morning Coffeecake Recipe 97
173. Peanut Butter Coffee Cake Recipe 97
174. Pecan Coffee Cake Recipe 98
175. Pecan Roll Monkey Bread Recipe 98
176. Pecan Streusel Coffee Cake Recipe 100
177. Peek A Boo Fig Coffeecake Recipe 100
178. Perfect Apple Cream Coffee Cake Recipe 101
179. Pineapple Macadamia Coffeecakes Recipe 101
180. Pioneer Ladies Coffee Cake Recipe 102
181. Polish Coffee Cake Recipe 103
182. Praline Apple Bread Recipe 103
183. Pull Apart Or Monkey Coffee Cake Recipe 104
184. Pull Apart Coffee Cake Recipe 105
185. Pull Apart Caramel Coffee Cake 105
186. Pumpkin Coffeecake Recipe 105
187. Pumpkin Spice Coffee Cake Recipe 106
188. Quick Bread Dry Mix Recipe 106
189. Quickie Sticky Buns Recipe 107
190. RASPBERRY CREAM CHEESE COFFEE CAKE Recipe 107
191. RICH COFFEE CAKE DOUGH Recipe 108
192. Rage Of The Town Raspberry Coffeecake Recipe 110
193. Ramona Cafe Cinnamon Rolls Recipe 110
194. Raspberry Cheese Coffee Cake Recipe ... 111
195. Raspberry Coffee Cake Recipe 111
196. Raspberry Cream Cheese Coffee Cake Recipe 112
197. Raspberry Crunch Coffeecake Recipe 112
198. Raspberry Marzipan Coffee Cake Recipe 113
199. Raspberry Almond Coffee Cake Recipe . 113
200. Raspberry Marzipan Coffee Cake Recipe 114
201. RaspberryCheese Coffee Cake Recipe 114
202. Reillys Monkey Bread Recipe 115
203. Rhubarb Coffee Cake Recipe 115
204. Roses Overnight Coffee Cake Recipe 116
205. Russian Honey Coffee Cake Loaf Recipe 116
206. Russian Nut Roll Bread Recipe 117
207. SOUR CREAM COFFEE CAKE Recipe 117
208. Save The Day Quick Cake Recipe 118
209. Sinfully Delicious Strawberry Coffeecake Recipe 118
210. Sour Cream Apple Coffee Cake Squares Recipe 119
211. Sour Cream Coffee Cake Recipe 119
212. Sour Cream Coffee Cake Trifle Recipe .. 120
213. Sour Cream Coffee Cake With Brown Sugar Pecan Streusel Recipe 120
214. Sour Cream Coffee Cake With Pears And Pecans Recipe 122
215. Sour Cream Coffee Cake With Apples Recipe 122
216. Sour Cream Coffeecake Recipe 123
217. Sour Cream Pumpkin Coffeecake Recipe 123

218. Sour Cream Rhubarb Coffee Cake Recipe 124
219. Spiced Brown Sugar Pecan Coffee Cake Recipe ... 124
220. Starbucks Blueberry Coffee Cake Recipe 125
221. Strawberry Coffee Cake With Crumb Topping Recipe ... 125
222. Strawberry Cream Coffeecake Recipe ... 126
223. Strawberry Delight Coffee Cake Recipe .. 126
224. Strawberry Poppy Seed Coffeecake Recipe 127
225. Strawberry Rhubarb Coffee Cake Recipe 128
226. Strawberry Rhubarb Filled Coffee Cake Recipe ... 128
227. Streusel Coffee Cake A Delectable Cake For Tea Or Dessert Recipe ... 129
228. Super Moist Pumpkin Bread Recipe ... 130
229. Swedish Scorpa Recipe ... 130
230. Sweet Lemon Coffeecake Recipe ... 131
231. Sweet Potato Caramel Coffee Cake Recipe 132
232. Sweet Potato Coffee Cake With Pecan Topping Recipe ... 132
233. Sweet Potatoe Praline Coffee Cake Recipe 133
234. Sweetly Cinnamon Coffee Cake Recipe .. 133
235. Tea Braised Beef With Apples Recipe 134
236. The Best Pumpkin Bread Ever Recipe 134
237. The Manly Coffee Cake Recipe ... 134
238. Triple Chocolate Coffee Cake Recipe 135
239. Turkish Coffee Cake Recipe ... 135
240. Unbelievable Coffee Cake Recipe ... 136
241. VELVET DEVILS FOOD LAYER CAKE WITH COFFEE BUTTERCREAM FROSTING Recipe ... 136
242. Vegan Rhubarb Cake Recipe ... 137
243. Vegan Sour Creme Coffeecake Recipe 138
244. White Chocolate Banana Bread Recipe ... 138
245. Cheese And Apricot Coffee Cake Recipe 139
246. Choco Choco Coffee Dream Cake Recipe 139
247. Chocolate Cinnamon Nut Filled Coffee Cake Recipe ... 140
248. Cup Of Coffee Cake Recipe ... 140
249. Mango Coffee Cake Recipe ... 140
250. Traditional Cape Koeksisters Recipe ... 141

INDEX ... 143
CONCLUSION ... 146

250 Awesome Coffee Cake Recipes

***

1. 1 Dish Caramel Pecan Coffee Cake Recipe

Serving: 68 | Prep: | Cook: 25mins | Ready in:

Ingredients

- Batter:
- cooking spray
- 1 3/4 cups flour
- 2 envelopes yeast
- 2 tbsp. sugar
- 1/2 salt
- 3/4 cup very warm water (120 to 130F)
- 2 tbsp. butter, melted
- caramel pecan Topping:
- 1/3 cup Light or dark corn syrup
- 1/3 cup brown sugar
- 2 tbsp. butter, melted
- 1/2 cup Chopped pecans
- cinnamon sugar Topping:
- 1/4 cup sugar
- 1 tsp. Ground Saigon cinnamon

Direction

- Mix batter ingredients in a pre-sprayed 9 1/2 inch deep dish pie plate.
- Stir together corn syrup, brown sugar and butter in a small bowl.
- Add pecans and mix well.
- Combine cinnamon sugar topping ingredients in a small bowl.
- Top batter evenly with cinnamon sugar topping.
- Spoon the caramel pecan topping evenly over the batter.
- Bake by placing in a cold oven; set temperature to 350F.
- Bake 25 minutes, until lightly browned and firm in center.
- Cool slightly; serve warm.

2. 1959 CITY SCHOOL SOUR CREAM COFFEE CAKE Recipe

Serving: 8 | Prep: | Cook: 45mins | Ready in:

Ingredients

- 1 1/2 c cake flour
- 1/2 c flour
- 1 ts baking soda
- 1 ts baking powder
- 1/2 c butter
- 1 c sugar
- 1 egg, lightly beaten
- 1 ts vanilla
- 1 c sour cream
- ----------------------------------TOPPING---------------------------------
- 1/4 c flour
- 3/4 c Brown sugar; packed
- 1/4 ts salt
- 1 c Chopped walnuts
- 1/4 c butter

Direction

- All ingredients should be at room temperature. In bowl mix together flours, soda and baking powder.
- In another bowl cream together butter with sugar until fluffy and light.
- Add egg and vanilla and mix well. Add half of dry ingredients, mixing just until flour is

blended. Blend in sour cream, then remaining dry ingredients.
- Spread half of batter lightly into a 10-inch tube pan. Sprinkle with half of Topping and spread with remaining batter. Sprinkle with remaining Topping. Bake at 350 degrees 40 to 45 minutes.
- TOPPING: Mix together flour, sugar, salt and nuts. Add butter in small pieces. Rub in by hand until mixture is crumbly. Be careful not to overmix.

3. Almond Zucchini Babka Recipe

Serving: 20 | Prep: | Cook: 50mins | Ready in:

Ingredients

- 1 cup unsweetened almond milk, warmed
- 1/4 cup brown sugar
- 1 tsp active dry yeast
- 4 cups all purpose flour
- 2 cups whole wheat flour
- 1/4 tsp nutmeg
- 1/4 cup sugar
- Zest of 1 orange
- 2 tbsp ground flaxseeds
- 1/2 tsp salt
- 12 oz shredded zucchini, squeezed dry (about 2 cups or 2 medium)
- 1 tsp vanilla
- 1/2 Cup Earth Balance (or other vegan) margarine, cubed, room temperature
- --Filling--
- 3/4 cup almond butter, warmed until very runny
- 2 tbsp Earth Balance (or other vegan) margarine, melted
- 3 oz miniature, bittersweet chocolate chips
- 3 oz dried cranberries
- 2 tbsp ground almonds
- 1 tbsp cinnamon

Direction

- In a large bowl (or stand mixer), combine almond milk and brown sugar.
- Sprinkle the yeast overtop and let stand 5 minutes, until foamy.
- Combine flours, nutmeg, sugar, orange zest, flaxseeds and salt in a medium bowl. Set aside.
- To the foamed yeast mixture, add the zucchini and vanilla, stirring well.
- Add 3 cups of the dry mixture to the bowl and begin mixing (on low speed), until the dry ingredients are incorporated.
- Add in remaining dry mixture, and allow the mixer to begin kneading the dough.
- Continue working the dough with the dough hook, slowly beating in margarine cubes one at a time. It should become very shiny and soft.
- Continue kneading for 10 minutes.
- Turn into an oiled bowl, cover and allow to rise 1 1/2 hours, until doubled in volume.
- Lightly grease two loaf pans, set aside.
- Punch down the dough, divide in half and roll one portion out into a rectangle on a (very) well-floured surface. Roll it out lengthwise as far as possible- The longer the dough, the more spirals you will get in the finished bread.
- Beat together the almond butter and Earth Balance in a small bowl until very fluid.
- Spread the rectangle with half the almond butter, leaving 1/2" on one long side clear.
- Mix together the chocolate chips, cranberries, ground almonds and cinnamon, then sprinkle half evenly over the dough.
- Starting with the long edge that is completely covered, roll up the dough as tightly as possible.
- Arrange the log with the two ends next to each other (like a squashed horse shoe), then twist together.
- Carefully fit the twist into one pan.
- Repeat with the remaining half of the ingredients.
- Cover and let rise 1 hour, until just about doubled.
- Preheat oven to 350F.

- Bake for 40 – 50 minutes, until golden and hollow sounding when tapped.

4. Almond Lemon Coffeecake Recipe

Serving: 6 | Prep: | Cook: 35mins | Ready in:

Ingredients

- 1 cup brown sugar firmly packed
- 1 cup almonds sliced
- 1/4 cup flour
- 3 tablespoon butter melted
- 1 teaspoon lemon zest grated
- 1/2 cup butter softened
- 1/2 cup sugar
- 3 large eggs
- 1 teaspoon lemon zest grated
- 1/2 teaspoon vanilla extract
- 2 cups flour
- 1 teaspoon baking powder
- 1 teaspoon baking soda
- 2/3 cup lemon juice
- 1/2 cup powdered sugar
- 2-1/2 teaspoons lemon juice

Direction

- Preheat oven to 350.
- Grease a tube pan.
- In medium bowl mix together brown sugar, nuts and flour then stir in butter and zest.
- Using an electric mixer set on medium speed beat together butter and sugar until fluffy.
- Add eggs 1 at a time beating well after each addition then beat in zest and vanilla.
- In large bowl mix together flour, baking powder and baking soda.
- Reduce mixer speed to low.
- Beat flour mixture and lemon juice into egg mixture beginning and ending with flour.
- Spoon half the batter into prepared pan then sprinkle with half of the streusel.
- Top with remaining batter and streusel then bake 35 minutes.
- Transfer pan to a wire rack to cool completely.
- Stir together confectioners' sugar and lemon juice until smooth.
- Turn cake out onto a serving plate placing it right side up then drizzle with glaze.

5. Any Fruit Coffee Cake Recipe

Serving: 9 | Prep: | Cook: 45mins | Ready in:

Ingredients

- 1 1/2 cups chopped, peeled apples, apricots, peaches, or pineapple; or 1 1/2 cups blueberries or raspberries
- 1 cup sugar
- 2 tbsp cornstarch
- 1 1/2 cups unbleached flour
- 1/2 tsp baking powder
- 1/4 tsp baking soda
- 6 tbsp olive oil
- 1 beaten egg
- 1/2 cup buttermilk or sour milk
- 1/2 tsp vanilla
- 1/4 cup unbleached flour

Direction

- In a saucepan combine choice of fruit and 1/4 cup water. Bring to boiling; reduce heat.
- (Do not simmer raspberries.)
- Cover and simmer about 5 minutes or till tender. Combine 1/4 cup of the sugar and the cornstarch. Stir into fruit mixture. Cook and stir till thickened and bubbly. Cook and stir 2 minutes more. Set aside.
- In a mixing bowl stir together 1/2 cup of the sugar, the 1 1/2 cups flour the baking powder, and baking soda. Add 4 tbsp. till it is mixed. Combine egg, buttermilk, or sour milk, and vanilla. Add to flour mixture. Stir just till moistened. Spread half of the batter in an 8 x 8 x 2-inch baking pan. Spread fruit mixture over

batter. Drop remaining batter in small mounds atop filling.
- Combine the remaining 1/4 cup sugar and the 1/4 cup flour. Add remaining 2 tbsp. oil and mix. Sprinkle over batter.
- Bake in a 350 degrees oven for 40 to 45 minutes or till golden brown. Serve warm.
- Makes 9 servings
- Rhubarb-Strawberry Coffee Cake:
- Prepare as above, except substitute 3/4 cup fresh or frozen cup-up rhubarb and 3/4 cup frozen unsweetened whole strawberries for the fruit.
- ~Enjoy~

6. Apple Cinnamon Coffee Cake Recipe

Serving: 10 | Prep: | Cook: 40mins | Ready in:

Ingredients

- 5 cups tart apples, cored, peeled, chopped
- 1 cup sugar
- 1 cup dark raisins (soaked in boiling water and a shot of rye and drained)
- 1/2 cup pecans or walnuts, chopped
- 1/4 cup vegetable oil
- 2 tsp. vanilla extract
- 1 egg, beaten
- 2 cups all-purpose flour, sifted
- 1 tsp. baking soda
- 2-1/2 tsp. ground cinnamon

Direction

- Preheat oven to 350 degrees F.
- Lightly oil a 13 x 9 x 2 inch baking pan.
- In large mixing bowl, combine apples with sugar, raisins, and nuts. Mix well and let stand for 30 minutes.
- Stir in oil, vanilla and egg.
- Sift together flour, soda and cinnamon, and stir into apple mixture about a third at a time, just enough to moisten dry ingredients.
- Turn batter into prepared pan.
- Bake 35 to 40 minutes.
- Cool cake slightly before serving.
- Note: Apples and raisins keep this cake moist, which means less oil used.

7. Apple Coffee Cake Recipe

Serving: 5 | Prep: | Cook: 25mins | Ready in:

Ingredients

- 1 cup flour
- 1 teaspoon baking powder
- 1/2 teaspoon salt
- 2/3 cup sugar
- 1 teaspoon ground cinnamon
- 5 1/2 Tbsp unsalted butter, room temperature
- 1 egg, beaten
- 1/2 cup whole milk
- 1 medium Cortland or other baking apple, peeled and sliced

Direction

- Set the oven to 375°F. Grease a 9-inch square baking dish with or pie pan a 4-cup capacity.
- Sift the flour, baking powder, and salt.
- In a bowl, combine 1/3 a cup of the sugar with the cinnamon, set aside.
- In the bowl of an electric mixer, cream the butter with the remaining 1/3 cup sugar. Beat in the egg until blended. Add the flour mixture in three additions, alternating with the milk, beating until just combined.
- Spread half the batter in the baking dish. Lay the apple slices on the batter so they just cover the batter (you may have to overlap some slices). Sprinkle the apples with half of the cinnamon-sugar mixture. Spread the rest of the batter over the apples. Sprinkle the remaining cinnamon-sugar on top.
- Bake the cake for 25 minutes or until it is golden brown and apples start to bubble at the edges.

8. Apple Ginger And Hazelnut Coffee Cake Recipe

Serving: 6 | Prep: | Cook: 45mins | Ready in:

Ingredients

- 1/3 cup dried cherries (I used cherry flavored dried cranberries)
- 1/3 cup dark rum
- 1/4 cup butter, softened
- 1 1/2 cups brown sugar, packed
- 1 egg
- 1 tbsp freshly grated ginger
- 2 1/3 cups flour
- 2 tsp ground ginger
- 1 tsp baking soda
- 1 tsp salt
- 3 cups peeled and diced apples (2 large)
- 1 cup sour cream
- Topping:
- 1/3 cup brown sugar
- 1 tsp ground ginger
- 1/2 cup toasted hazelnuts, coarsley chopped

Direction

- Soak dried cherries in rum for at least 20 minutes.
- Beat butter and brown sugar. Add egg and fresh ginger and blend until mixed.
- Sift together the flour, 2 tsp. ground ginger, baking soda, and salt. Stir into butter mixture. Stir in diced apple, cherries and rum, and sour cream. Mix until well incorporated.
- Spread batter in a greased 9" x 13" pan.
- Stir together topping ingredients and sprinkle over batter.
- Bake for 40 minutes at 350F, or until a toothpick inserted in the middle comes out clean. Cool and cut into squares.

9. Apple Oatmeal Coffee Cake Recipe

Serving: 15 | Prep: | Cook: 35mins | Ready in:

Ingredients

- 1 cup flour (all purpose or whole wheat or half/half)
- ¾ tsp baking soda
- ½ tsp salt
- ½ tsp cinnamon
- 1/2 cup sugar (even less if you don't like it too sweet)
- 1 cup rolled oats
- ½ cup cooking oil (you could use a bit less if you like)
- 1 egg
- 1 tsp vanilla extract
- 1 apple, peeled and chopped (about ¾ cup more or less)
- ¼ cup orange juice
- ¼ cup raisins

Direction

- Preheat oven to 350F.
- Grease an 8"x8" pan or similar (I use a 6.5"x10"-I think that it is a brownie pan).
- Put the raisins into small bowl and pour the orange juice over it and let them plump a bit while you peel and chop the apple.
- Mix all the dry ingredients together. Add the chopped apples and toss around so that they get coated with flour. Measure the oil into a cup and add the egg and vanilla and mix a bit with a fork then add it all at once to the dry mixture. Fold together till mixed and then add the raisins and orange juice. The mixture will be fairly thick. Put it into the prepared pan and spread evenly. Bake at 350 for about 30-35 minutes; it should be a nice colour and a tester will come out clean. Let it cool for a bit and serve. This is great at room temperature and also served slightly warm.

- *Just a note on the oil-use a good cooking oil like vegetable or canola or corn oil-not olive oil*

10. Apple Rum Custard Coffeecake Recipe

Serving: 8 | Prep: | Cook: 50mins | Ready in:

Ingredients

- 1-1/2 cups unbleached flour
- 5 tablespoons granulated sugar
- 1 tablespoon lemon rind grated
- 2/3 cup butter
- 1 large egg yolk
- 1 tablespoon milk
- 1/2 cup soft bread crumbs
- 2 tablespoon butter melted
- 4 cups sliced tart apples
- 1 tablespoon lemon juice
- 1/4 cup granulated sugar
- 1/4 cup raisins
- 1/4 cup rum
- 3 large eggs beaten
- 1/3 cup granulated sugar
- 1-3/4 cup milk

Direction

- Soak raisins in 1/4 cup rum for 1/2 hour before using.
- Mix flour, sugar and lemon rind then cut in butter until mixture resembles coarse crumbs.
- Add egg yolk and 1 tablespoon milk then mix gently to form a dough.
- Pat into bottom of a tube pan that has sides only greased.
- Press dough up sides of pan 1".
- Toss together bread crumbs and melted butter then spread evenly over pastry crust.
- Toss apple slices, lemon juice and 1/4 cup of sugar then spread apple mixture over crumbs.
- Drain raisins reserving rum then sprinkle raisins over apples.
- Bake in a preheated 350 oven for 15 minutes.
- Beat eggs and sugar until thick and lemon colored then stir in milk and reserved rum.
- Pour custard over apples and bake at 350 for 50 minutes.
- Cool completely in pan before serving.

11. Apple Sour Cream Coffeecake Recipe

Serving: 12 | Prep: | Cook: 45mins | Ready in:

Ingredients

- Coffeecake
- ½ cup butter, softened
- 1 cup sugar
- 2 eggs
- 1 teaspoon vanilla extract
- 2 cups flour
- 1 teaspoon baking powder
- 1 teaspoon baking soda
- ½ teaspoon salt
- 1 cup sour cream
- 2 apples, pared and cored, sliced thinly
- Topping:
- ½ cup chopped pecans or walnuts
- 2 teaspoons cinnamon
- ½ cup sugar

Direction

- To make the coffeecake batter, cream together butter and sugar; add eggs and extract. Beat well.
- Add dry ingredients alternately with sour cream, blending together to a smooth batter.
- Mix topping ingredients together in a small bowl.
- Spread ½ of batter into greased and floured Bundt pan.
- Top batter with apple slices.

- Sprinkle ½ of topping mixture over apples.
- Cover apples and topping with remaining ½ of batter.
- Sprinkle batter with remaining topping.
- Bake at 375° for 40 to 45 minutes. Cool on rack for 30 minutes before removing from pan.
- NOTE: You can make this in a greased 9x13 pan, also, reducing the bake time to about 30 minutes.

12. Apple Streusel Coffeecake Recipe

Serving: 8 | Prep: | Cook: 25mins | Ready in:

Ingredients

- 2 cups all purpose baking mix
- 1 teaspoon ground cinnamon ground
- 2/3 cup sweetened applesauce
- 1 teaspoon vanilla
- 1/4 cup granulated sugar
- 1 egg
- 1/4 cup vegetable oil
- Topping:
- 1/4 cup all purpose baking mix
- 2 teaspoons firm butter
- 1/4 cups packed brown sugar
- 1/2 teaspoons ground cinnamon
- 2 teaspoons finely chopped nuts

Direction

- Grease a round baking pan well.
- Mix all ingredients except topping until moistened then spread in pan.
- Combine topping ingredients and sprinkle over top.
- Bake in a preheated 400 oven for 25 minutes then allow to cool 5 minutes and serve warm.

13. Apple Walnut Oatmel Coffee Cake Recipe

Serving: 12 | Prep: | Cook: 40mins | Ready in:

Ingredients

- 1 c old fashioned oats
- 1 1/4 c flour
- 3/4 c whole wheat flour
- 1 1/2 tsp baking powder
- 1 tsp baking soda
- 2 tsp ground cinnamon, divided
- 1/2 tsp ground allspice
- 1/2 tsp salt
- 3/4 c packed light brown sugar
- 2 eggs
- 1/2 c canola oil
- 1 1/4 c butter milk
- 3 tbs molasses
- 2 c diced peeled granny smith apples (about 2 med)
- 1 c chopped walnuts, toasted and divided
- 2/3 c golden rasins
- 2 tbs raw turbinado sugar or regular granulated sugar

Direction

- Heat over to 350f. Spray 9 inch square baking pan with cooking spray. Place oats on baking sheet and bake 8 to 10m or until lightly toasted, cool.
- Process oats in food processor until very finely ground. Whisk oats, flours, baking powder, soda, 1 tsp. cinnamon, allspice and salt in large bowl
- Beat brown sugar, eggs and oil in large bowl until blended. Beat in buttermilk and molasses until combined. Stir into dry ingredients just until blended. Stir in apples, 1/2 c walnuts, and raisins. Spoon batter into pan.
- Combine remaining 1/2 c walnuts, raw sugar and 1tsp cinnamon; sprinkle over batter.
- Bake 35-40 min or until golden brown and toothpick inserted in center comes out clean.

Cool on wire rack. Serve warm or at room temp.

14. Apple Cream Cheese Coffee Cake Recipe

Serving: 10 | Prep: | Cook: 13mins | Ready in:

Ingredients

- 1 package (8 oz) cream cheese
- 1/3 cup sugar
- 1 teaspoon grated lemon peel
- 2 teaspoons lemon juice
- 2 cups Original Bisquick® mix
- 1 package (3 oz) cream cheese
- 1/4 cup firm butter or margarine
- 1/3 cup milk
- 2 tablespoons sugar
- 1/2 teaspoon ground cinnamon
- 1 can (21 oz) apple pie filling
- 1/4 cup chopped walnuts
- .

Direction

- 1. Heat oven to 425°F. Lightly grease cookie sheet. In medium bowl, beat 8 ounces cream cheese, 1/3 cup sugar, the lemon peel and lemon juice with electric mixer on medium speed until smooth; reserve.
- 2. In large bowl, place Bisquick mix. Cut in 3 ounces cream cheese and the butter using pastry blender (or pulling 2 table knives through ingredients in opposite directions) until crumbly. Stir in milk. Place dough on surface well sprinkled with Bisquick mix; roll in Bisquick mix to coat. Knead 8 to 10 times.
- 3. Roll dough into 12x8-inch rectangle.
- Place on cookie sheet. Spread reserved cream cheese mixture down center of rectangle. Make cuts, 2 1/2-inches long, at 1 inch intervals on 12 inch sides of rectangle. Fold strips over filling, overlapping strips.
- In small bowl, mix 2 tablespoons sugar and the cinnamon; sprinkle over top.
- 4. Bake 12 to 15 minutes or until golden brown. Cool 10 minutes.
- Carefully place on cooling rack; cool completely. Spoon pie filling down center of coffee cake. Sprinkle with walnuts. Store in refrigerator.

15. Apple Nut Ring Recipe

Serving: 20 | Prep: | Cook: 30mins | Ready in:

Ingredients

- 2 8-ounce cans refrigerated buttermilk biscuits
- 3/4 cup sugar
- 1 Tbsp sugar
- 1/4 cup butter, melted
- 2 medium apples
- 1/3 cup chopped nuts
- 1/4 cup raisins (optional)

Direction

- Separate the biscuits into 20 pieces.
- Combine sugar and cinnamon.
- Dip biscuits into melted butter, then roll in sugar mixture.
- Arrange biscuits in a round deep dish baker or 9 x 11 baking dish starting at the outer edges first and then filling in the middle.
- Peel, core and slice apples into thin slices.
- Place an apple slice between each biscuit and place apple slices all around outer edge of the baking dish.
- Mix nuts and raising with remaining sugar mixture and pour all over the biscuits.
- Bake at 400 degrees for 25-30 minutes.
- Yield 20 rolls.

16. Apple Topped Cake Recipe

Serving: 10 | Prep: | Cook: 50mins | Ready in:

Ingredients

- 3 tablespoons butter, softened
- 3/4 cup sugar
- 1 egg
- 1 egg white
- 1 cup vanilla yogurt
- 1/3 cup unsweetened applesauce
- 2 tablespoons canola oil
- 2 teaspoons vanilla extract
- 2 cups all-purpose flour
- 1 teaspoon baking powder
- 1/2 teaspoon baking soda
- 1/2 teaspoon salt
- 1-1/2 cups chopped peeled apples
- 2 tablespoons chopped walnuts
- 1 tablespoon brown sugar
- 1/2 teaspoon ground cinnamon
- 1/8 teaspoon ground allspice

Direction

- In a large mixing bowl, beat butter and sugar until crumbly, about 2 minutes. Add the egg, egg white, yogurt, applesauce, oil and vanilla; beat until smooth. Combine the dry ingredients; add to butter mixture, beating just until moistened.
- Pour into a 9-in. springform pan coated with cooking spray. Sprinkle with apples and walnuts. Combine the brown sugar, cinnamon and allspice; sprinkle over top.
- Bake at 375° for 47-52 minutes or until a toothpick inserted near the center comes out clean. Cool on a wire rack. Run a knife around edge of pan to loosen. Remove sides of pan. Refrigerate leftovers.

17. Apricot Almond Coffee Cake Recipe

Serving: 10 | Prep: | Cook: 25mins | Ready in:

Ingredients

- 1 c flour
- 1/2 c white whole wheat flour or whole wheat flour
- 1 tsp baking powder
- 1/4 tsp salt
- 1/4 tsp ground cinnamon 1/8 tsp ground ginger
- 1 egg
- 1/2 c snipped dried apricots
- 1/2 c fat-free milk
- 1/2 c sugar
- 1/4 c unsweetened applesauce
- 1/4 c canola oil 2 Tbs reduced-sugar apricot preserves, melted
- 2 Tbs slice almonds, toasted

Direction

- Preheat oven to 350. Lightly coat an 8x1-1/2" round baking dish with non-stick cooking spray; set aside. In med. bowl, stir together flour, whole wheat flour, baking powder, salt, cinnamon and ginger.
- In med. bowl, lightly beat egg with fork; stir in dried apricots. Stir in milk, sugar, applesauce, and oil. Add apricot mixture all at once to flour mixture, stir till combined. Spread batter into prepared pan.
- Bake 25 to 30 mins or till toothpick comes out clean. Cool in pan on wire rack for 10 mins. Cut up ant large pieces of fruit in preserves; spoon over coffee cake. Sprinkle with toasted almonds. Serve warm or room temperature.

18. Apricot Lemon Coffeecake Recipe

Serving: 8 | Prep: | Cook: 45mins | Ready in:

Ingredients

- 15 ounce can apricot halves drained and juice reserved
- 1-1/4 cup all -purpose flour
- 1/2 cup granulated sugar
- 1/2 cup butter softened 1/2 cup sour cream
- 2 eggs
- 1 teaspoon baking powder
- 1 teaspoon grated lemon peel
- 1/3 cup granulated sugar
- 2 tablespoons butter
- 2 tablespoons all purpose flour
- 1 teaspoon grated lemon peel
- 1/2 cup powdered sugar
- 1 tablespoon reserved apricot juice

Direction

- Heat oven to 350.
- Pat apricots dry with paper towels then cut into slices and set aside.
- Combine flour, sugar, butter, sour cream, eggs, baking powder and lemon peel.
- Beat at low speed scraping bowl often until well mixed about 2 minutes.
- Spread into greased square baking pan.
- Stir together 1/3 cup sugar, butter, flour and lemon peel until crumbly.
- Arrange apricots over batter then spoon crumbly mixture over apricots.
- Bake 45 minutes.
- Stir together powdered sugar and enough reserved apricot juice for desired glazing consistency.
- Drizzle glaze over warm coffeecake.

19. Apricot Chocolate Ring Recipe

Serving: 12 | Prep: | Cook: 30mins | Ready in:

Ingredients

- 1/3 cup butter - diced
- 4 cups self-rising flour - sifted
- 4 Tblspns super-fine sugar
- 2 eggs - beaten
- 2/3 cup milk
- .
- Filling & Decoration:-
- 2 Tblspns butter - melted
- 2/3 cup dried aprocots - chopped
- 3 1/2 ozs semi-sweet chocolate chips
- 1 - 2 Tblspns milk - to glaze
- 1 oz dark or semi-sweet chocolate - melted

Direction

- Pre-heat oven to 350 degrees.
- Grease a 10" round cake pan & line with wax paper.
- Rub the butter into the flour until the mixture resembles fine bread crumbs.
- Stir in the sugar, eggs & milk to form a soft dough.
- Roll out the dough on a lightly floured surface to form a 14" square.
- Brush the melted butter over the surface of the dough.
- Mix together the apricots & the chocolate chips & spread them over the dough to within 1" of the top & bottom.
- Roll up the dough tightly, like a jelly roll & cut it into 1" slices.
- Lay the slices around the edge of the pan, overlapping slightly.
- Brush with a little milk.
- Bake for about 30 mins, or until cooked & lightly golden.
- Cool the cake in the pan for about 15 mins & then carefully transfer to a wire rack to cool.
- Drizzle the melted chocolate over the ring to decorate.

- NOTE: Best served the same day it is made. It is wonderful served warm.
- Golden raisins can be used instead of the chocolate chips.

20. Asian Pear And Ricotta Coffee Cake Recipe

Serving: 12 | Prep: | Cook: 45mins | Ready in:

Ingredients

- 2 tbsp ground flaxseed
- ¼ cup hot water
- ¼ cup melted butter
- 1 cup full-fat ricotta cheese (I used Richer Ricotta)
- ½ cup whole milk
- 1 tsp vanilla
- ¾ cup flour
- ½ cup spelt (or whole wheat) flour
- ½ cup sugar
- 2 ¼ tsp baking powder
- ½ tsp cinnamon
- ½ tsp cardamom
- ½ tsp salt
- 1 large Asian pear, peeled and chopped

Direction

- Preheat the oven to 400 F and grease an 8" pan.
- In a bowl, whisk together the flaxseed and hot water. Set aside for 10 minutes.
- Beat in the butter, ricotta, milk and vanilla until well combined.
- Stir in the flours, sugar, baking powder, cinnamon, cardamom and salt, then fold in the Asian pear.
- Bake for 25-30 minutes or until toothpick comes out clean.
- Cool completely in the pan.

21. Banana Coffee Cake Recipe

Serving: 10 | Prep: | Cook: 50mins | Ready in:

Ingredients

- 250g butter
- 200g castor sugar
- 1 tsp vanilla essence
- 1 tsp coffee essence
- 3 eggs
- 4 ripe bananas, mashed
- 240g self-raising flour
- 1/4 cup milk

Direction

- Preheat oven to 180C.
- Cream butter, sugar and vanilla essence until light and fluffy.
- Add eggs one at a time, beating well after each addition.
- Stir in mashed bananas.
- Fold in flour gently.
- Add milk gradually.
- Pour in mixture into cake tin.
- Bake for 40 to 50 minutes.

22. Banana Coffee Cake With Chocolate Chip Streusel Recipe

Serving: 12 | Prep: | Cook: 45mins | Ready in:

Ingredients

- 11/4c   semi sweet chocolate chips
- 2/3c   packed brown sugar
- 1/2c   chopped pecans or walnuts
- 1Tbsp   cinnamon
- 11/2c   all purpose flour
- 3/4tsp   baking soda
- 3/4tsp   baking powder
- 1/4tsp   salt
- 3/4c   granulated sugar
- 1/2c   soft butter, unsalted

- 1   egg
- 1 1/3c   mashed ripe bananas, about 3 large
- 3Tbsp   buttermilk

Direction

- Preheat oven to 350F.
- Butter and flour 8x8x2 metal baking pan
- Mix chocolate chips, nuts, brown sugar and cinnamon together in a small bowl. Set aside.
- Sift flour, baking soda, baking powder and salt into a medium bowl.
- Beat butter and sugar until fluffy, add egg. Beat until well mixed.
- Mix in flour mixture alternately with the bananas and buttermilk, starting with the dry ingredients.
- Spread half the batter evenly into prepared pan. Sprinkle evenly with chocolate mixture. Repeat with last of the batter and topping.
- Bake for about 45 minutes.

23. Banana Coffee Cake With Chocolate Chip Streusel Recipe

Serving: 12 | Prep: | Cook: 45mins | Ready in:

Ingredients

- 1 1/4 cups semisweet chocolate chips (about 8 ounce)
- 2/3 cup packed golden brown sugar
- 1/2 cup chopped walnuts
- 1 tablespoon ground cinnamon
- 1 1/2 cups all-purpose flour
- 3/4 teaspoon baking soda
- 3/4 teaspoon baking powder
- 1/4 teaspoon salt
- 3/4 cup granulated sugar
- 1/2 cup (1 stick) unsalted butter, room temperature
- 1 large egg
- 1 1/3 cups mashed very ripe bananas (about 3 large)
- 3 tablespoons buttermilk

Direction

- Preheat oven to 350 degrees F. Butter and flour an 8-inch square baking pan.
- Stir chocolate chips, brown sugar, walnuts and cinnamon in small bowl until well blended; set streusel aside.
- Sift flour, baking soda, baking powder and salt into medium bowl.
- Using electric mixer, beat sugar, room temperature butter and egg in large bowl until fluffy. Beat in mashed bananas and buttermilk. Add dry ingredients and blend well.
- Spread half of batter (about 2 cups) in prepared baking pan. Sprinkle with half of streusel. Repeat with remaining batter and streusel.
- Bake coffee cake until tester inserted into center comes out clean, about 45 minutes. Cool coffee cake in pan on rack.

24. Banana Coffeecake Recipe

Serving: 8 | Prep: | Cook: 50mins | Ready in:

Ingredients

- Batter
- 1 stick margarine at room temperature
- 3 large bananas mashed
- 1 egg white whipped
- 1 tablespoon lemon peel grated
- 1 teaspoon vanilla
- 1/2 cup skim milk at room temperature
- 2 cups unbleached flour
- 3/4 cup granulated sugar
- 1 /4 teaspoon salt
- 1 tablespoon baking powder topping
- 1/3 cup brown sugar packed
- 1 /3 cup unbleached flour
- 3/4 teaspoon cinnamon

Direction

- Preheat oven at 375 then spray a spring form pan with cooking spray and coat lightly with flour.
- Combine margarine, bananas, egg white, lemon peel, vanilla and milk.
- In another bowl combine flour, sugar, salt and baking powder.
- Mix wet ingredients with dry ingredients just until moistened then pour into prepared pan.
- To prepare topping combine brown sugar, flour and cinnamon then sprinkle over batter.
- Bake 45 minutes then allow to cool before serving.

- In medium bowl, place all topping ingredients.
- Cut together with a long tined fork until well blended.
- Pour 1/4 of batter into each pan, top with 1/4 crumb mixture.
- Pour remaining batter over and top with remaining crumb mixture.
- Bake for 45 minutes to an hour at 350.or tested done when toothpick inserted in center comes out clean.
- Cool completely.
- May be frozen.

25. Banana Crumb Coffee Cake Recipe

Serving: 16 | Prep: | Cook: 60mins | Ready in:

Ingredients

- 2C sugar
- 1 C milk
- 1 C chopped nuts (optional)
- 2 C self rising flour
- 1 stick margarine
- 2 eggs
- 3 bananas
- 1 tsp vanilla
- Crumb Topping
- 1 stick (1/2 c) margarine
- 1 Cup brown sugar (dark or light)
- 1 cup flour (self rising or plain, whatever you have on hand)

Direction

- Spray two loaf or 8×8 pans with cooking spray.
- Place peeled bananas in mixing bowl, add sugar.
- Mix until bananas are liquefied.
- Add margarine, mix until creamed together with banana mixture.
- Add all other ingredients and blend well.

26. Banana Walnut Coffee Cake Recipe

Serving: 8 | Prep: | Cook: 45mins | Ready in:

Ingredients

- 1-1/2 cups chopped walnuts
- 1/3 cup granulated sugar
- 1 tablespoon ground cinnamon
- 2 cups all purpose flour
- 1 tablespoon baking powder
- 1/4 teaspoon salt
- 1 cup unsalted butter softened
- 2 cups granulated sugar
- 2 eggs
- 1 cup sour cream
- 2 ripe bananas mashed
- 1 firm banana for slicing
- 1 tablespoon pure vanilla extract

Direction

- Preheat oven to 350.
- Butter a tube pan and dust with flour tapping out the excess and set aside.
- To make the walnut and sugar sprinkle combine walnuts, sugar and cinnamon in a small bowl and set aside.

- To make the banana batter sift together the flour, baking powder and salt onto a sheet of waxed paper and set aside.
- In a large bowl cream the butter with an electric mixer on high speed until it is light.
- Gradually beat in the sugar and continue beating until light and fluffy.
- Change the mixer speed to medium.
- Beat in the eggs one at a time beating well after each addition then beat in the sour cream, mashed bananas and vanilla.
- Change speed to low then beat in the flour mixture just until blended.
- Spoon half of the batter into the prepared pan.
- Scatter half of the walnut and sugar sprinkle over the batter.
- Thinly slice the third banana over the batter.
- Top with the remaining batter and scatter the remaining walnut and sugar sprinkle over the top.
- Bake for 15 minutes then let cool in the pan on a wire rack for 20 minutes.
- Carefully loosen the cake from the sides and tube of the pan, then invert onto a wire rack and turn right-side-up.
- Serve warm or cool sprinkled with sifted confectioners' sugar.

27. Banana Sour Cream Coffee Cake From The Bent Creek Lodge Recipe

Serving: 1 | Prep: | Cook: 45mins | Ready in:

Ingredients

- 1 1/4 cup sugar, divided into 1/4 cup & 1 cup
- ½ cup chopped pecans
- 1 tsp ground cinnamon
- 1/2 cup (4 oz) butter or margarine, softened
- 2 large eggs
- 1 cup mashed banana (2 bananas)
- ½ cup sour cream
- ½ tsp vanilla extract
- 2 cups AP flour
- 1 tsp baking powder
- 1 tsp baking soda
- 1/4 tsp salt

Direction

- Preheat oven to 350.
- Stir together 1/4 cup sugar, pecans, & cinnamon; sprinkle ½ mixture in a well-greased Bundt pan. Beat butter at medium speed until creamy. Gradually add remaining 1 cup sugar, beat 5 to 7 minutes till light & fluffy. Add eggs, 1 at a time, beating just until yellow disappears. Add banana, sour cream & vanilla. Beat at low speed just until blended. Combine flour, powder, soda & salt. Fold into butter mixture.
- Pour ½ batter into prepared pan. Sprinkle with remaining pecan mixture. Top with remaining batter.
- Bake for 45 minutes or until a wooden pick comes out clean.

28. Banana Nana Pecan Bread Recipe

Serving: 12 | Prep: | Cook: 55mins | Ready in:

Ingredients

- 1 cup oats (either quick or old-fashioned) uncooked
- 1 Tablespoon flaxseed
- 1/2 cup chopped pecans
- 3 Tablespoons butter, melted
- 2 Tablespoons firmly packed brown sugar
- 14 oz. package banana bread quick bread mix
- 1 cup water
- 1/2 cup mashed ripe banana (about 1 large or 2 small)
- 2 eggs, lightly beaten
- 3 Tablespoons vegetable oil (or a very light olive oil)

Direction

- Heat oven to 375 degrees. Lightly grease & flour bottom only of 9x5 loaf pan. Combine oats, flaxseed, pecans, butter and sugar; mix well. Reserve 1/2 cup oat mixture for topping, set aside. In large bowl, combine remaining oat mixture, quick bread mix, water, banana, eggs and oil. Mix just until dry ingredients are moistened. Pour into prepared pan. Sprinkle top of loaf with reserved oat mixture. Bake 50 to 55 minutes or until wooden toothpick inserted in center comes out clean. Cool 10 minutes in pan; remove to wire rack and cool completely.

29. Basic Coffee Cake Recipe

Serving: 9 | Prep: | Cook: 25mins | Ready in:

Ingredients

- Cake:
- 3/4 cup sugar
- 1/4 cup sweet butter, room temp
- 1 egg
- 1 cup milk -- OR -- sour cream
- 1 tsp vanilla extract
- 1 1/2 cup sifted all-purpose flour
- 2 tsp baking powder
- 1/2 tsp salt
- Streusel:
- 1/2 cup brown sugar
- 2 Tbsp all-purpose flour
- 2 Tbsp softened butter
- 2 tsp cinnamon
- 1/4 cup chopped nuts, or chocolate chips, and/or raisins
- 2 Tbsp shredded coconut - optional

Direction

- Grease a 9" cake pan and dust lightly with dried breadcrumbs
- Cream the butter and sugar. Add the egg. Alternately add the dry, sifted ingredients and the milk with the vanilla mixed into it.
- Pour half the batter into the prepared pan. Top with 1/2 the streusel and a bit of the coconut. Top with the remaining batter and then the streusel.
- Bake until tests done. I find it varies greatly by the oven it's baked in, ranging from 25 minutes to 45, so just test it to be sure. That is the only "fussiness" of this recipe, it is easy and reliable.

30. Best Of The West Blackberry Coffeecake Recipe

Serving: 8 | Prep: | Cook: 45mins | Ready in:

Ingredients

- 2 cups all purpose flour
- 1 cup granulated sugar
- 2 teaspoons baking powder
- 1/2 teaspoon salt
- 1/2 cup milk
- 1 stick butter melted
- 2 large eggs
- 1 teaspoon almond extract
- 2 cups fresh blackberries
- Topping:
- 1/2 cup all purpose flour
- 1/2 cup granulated sugar
- 4 tablespoons butter softened
- 1 teaspoon ground cinnamon

Direction

- Preheat oven to 350 then spray angel food cake pan with non-stick cooking spray.
- Lightly dust pan with flour.
- In medium mixing bowl sift together flour, sugar, baking powder and salt.
- In large bowl beat together milk, butter, eggs and extract.

- Beat in flour mixture a little at a time then gently fold in berries and pour into prepared pan.
- To prepare topping combine flour, sugar, butter and cinnamon in small bowl until a crumbly.
- Sprinkle topping over cake batter then bake 45 minutes.
- Remove from oven and let cool 5 minutes before inverting and placing on wire rack to cool.

31. Bisquick Coffee Cake Recipe

Serving: 8 | Prep: | Cook: 20mins | Ready in:

Ingredients

- For Streusel topping:
- 1/3 cup Bisquick
- 1/3 cup brown sugar, packed
- 1/2 tsp. cinnamon
- 2 Tbs. butter or margarine
- For the cake batter:
- 2 cups Bisquick
- 2 Tbs. sugar
- 2/3 cup milk
- 1 egg

Direction

- Preheat oven to 375F. Grease a 9" round cake pan.
- To make Streusel topping: mix the first three ingredients together in a small bowl. Cut in margarine or butter with a fork or pastry blender until the mixture is crumbly. Set aside.
- Mix all the batter ingredients together and spread into prepared pan. Sprinkle with the Streusel topping. Bake for 18 to 22 minutes until golden brown on top. Let cool for a few minutes before cutting. Serve warm.

32. Blackberry Crunch Coffeecake Recipe

Serving: 6 | Prep: | Cook: 30mins | Ready in:

Ingredients

- 1/4 cup butter
- 1/2 cup granulated sugar
- 1 large egg
- 1 cup all purpose flour
- 1 teaspoon baking powder
- 1/4 teaspoon salt
- 1/3 cup milk
- 1/2 teaspoon vanilla extract
- 2 cups fresh blackberries
- Topping:
- 1/4 cup butter
- 1/2 cup sugar
- 1/3 cup flour
- 1/2 teaspoon ground cinnamon

Direction

- Preheat oven to 350 then grease a square baking pan and set aside.
- Cream butter, sugar and egg together until light and fluffy.
- Combine dry ingredients and stir by hand into creamed mixture alternately with milk and vanilla.
- Spread batter in prepared baking pan and top with berries.
- Combine topping ingredients using pastry blender until mixture resembles coarse crumbs.
- Sprinkle over the berries then bake for 30 minutes then cool slightly before serving.

33. Blackberry Streusel Coffeecake Recipe

Serving: 8 | Prep: | Cook: 30mins | Ready in:

Ingredients

- 1/2 cup brown sugar packed
- 3 tablespoons flour
- 2 teaspoons cinnamon
- 2 tablespoons butter
- 3/4 cup chopped walnuts
- Batter:
- 2 cups all purpose flour
- 1 teaspoon baking powder
- 1 teaspoon soda
- 1/2 teaspoon salt
- 1/2 cup butter
- 1 cup sugar
- 2 teaspoons grated lemon rind
- 3 eggs
- 1 cup sour cream
- 2 cups fresh blackberries

Direction

- Preheat oven to 350 then grease rectangular pan and set aside.
- Combine brown sugar, flour, cinnamon, butter and walnuts until mixture resembles fine crumbs.
- Stir in nuts and reserve.
- Cream butter until fluffy then add sugar and lemon rind and beat well.
- Add eggs one at a time and beat well after each addition.
- Mix dry ingredients then add dry mixture alternately with sour cream to creamed mixture.
- Blend well after each addition then spread batter evenly in prepared baking pan.
- Sprinkle berries over batter then sprinkle reserved topping over berries.
- Bake for 30 minutes and serve warm.

34. Blueberry Applesauce Coffeecake Recipe

Serving: 8 | Prep: | Cook: 60mins | Ready in:

Ingredients

- 2 cups self raising flour
- 2 teaspoons baking powder
- 2 teaspoons ginger
- 2 teaspoons cinnamon
- 1/2 teaspoon allspice
- 1/2 teaspoon salt
- 1/2 teaspoon finely chopped fresh rosemary
- 1/4 cup olive oil
- 1 cup sugar
- 1 teaspoon vanilla
- 1-1/3 cups unsweetened applesauce
- 3/4 cup blueberries
- 3 large egg whites
- 1/4 cup brown sugar
- 1/4 cup grape nuts cereal
- 1 tablespoon cinnamon

Direction

- Preheat oven to 350.
- Sift together flour, baking powder, ginger, cinnamon, allspice and salt.
- Beat together olive oil, sugar, vanilla and unsweetened applesauce then add to flour mixture.
- Fold in blueberries then beat egg whites until peaked and fold into mix.
- Pour into greased square pan then bake 60 minutes.
- Mix together brown sugar, cereal and cinnamon then spread topping over cake.

35. Blueberry Buckle Coffee Cake Recipe

Serving: 6 | Prep: | Cook: 40mins | Ready in:

Ingredients

- Topping
- 1/3 cup (2 ounces) sugar
- 1/2 cup (2 ounces) King Arthur Unbleached all-purpose flour

- 1 teaspoon cinnamon
- 1/4 cup (1/2 stick) butter or margarine
- Batter
- 2 cups (8 1/2 ounces) King Arthur Unbleached all-purpose flour
- 2 teaspoons baking powder
- 1/2 teaspoon salt
- 3/4 cup (5 1/4 ounces) sugar
- 1/4 cup (1/2 stick, 2 ounces) butter or margarine
- 1 large egg
- 1 teaspoon vanilla
- 1/2 cup (4 ounces) milk
- 2 cups fresh or frozen blueberries, well drained

Direction

- First: Preheat your oven to 375°F.
- Making the Topping: Mix the sugar, flour and cinnamon in a small bowl. Cut or rub in the butter or margarine with the side of a fork, two knives or your fingertips until it reaches a crumbly state. Set aside.
- Making the Batter: Blend the flour, baking powder and salt together in a medium sized mixing bowl. In a large bowl cream together the sugar, butter or margarine, egg and vanilla. Alternately add the milk and the flour mixture to the creamed mixture, ending with flour. Stir only enough to blend. Fold in the blueberries.
- Assembling & Baking: Pour the batter into a well-greased and floured, 9-inch cake pan. Sprinkle the topping over the batter and bake for 40 to 45 minutes or until a cake tester or knife comes out clean.
- Let the buckle cool for 10 minutes. Loosen the sides with a knife or spatula. Holding the cake pan in your left hand, gently tip the cake out onto your right hand, remove the pan, and gently right the cake onto a serving dish.

36. Blueberry Buckle With Cream Cheese Whipped Cream Recipe

Serving: 8 | Prep: | Cook: 55mins | Ready in:

Ingredients

- Streusel:
- 1/2 c. all-purpose flour
- 1/2 c. packed light brown sugar
- 2 T. granulated sugar
- 1/4 t. ground cinnamon
- Pinch table salt
- 4 T. unsalted butter (1/2 stick), cut into 8 pieces, softened but still cool
- Cake:
- 1 1/2 c. all-purpose flour
- 1 1/2 t. baking powder
- 10 T. unsalted butter (1 1/4 sticks), softened but still cool
- 2/3 c. granulated sugar
- 1/2 t. table salt
- 1/2 t. grated lemon zest
- 1 1/2 t. vanilla extract
- 2 large eggs, room temperature
- 4 c. fresh blueberries
- cream cheese Whipped Cream:
- 4 ounces cream cheese, room temperature
- 1/3 c. confectioners' sugar
- pinch table salt
- 1/2 t. vanilla extract
- 1 c. heavy cream

Direction

- 1. For streusel: In standing mixer fitted with flat beater, combine flour, sugars, cinnamon, and salt on low speed until well combined and no large brown sugar lumps remain, about 45 seconds. Add butter and mix on low until mixture resembles wet sand and no large butter pieces remain, about 2 1/2 minutes. Transfer streusel to small bowl and set aside.
- 2. For the cake: Adjust oven rack to lower-middle position; heat oven to 350 degrees F. Spray 9-inch round cake pan with 2-inch sides with non-stick cooking spray, line bottom with

parchment or waxed paper round, and spray round; dust pan with flour and knockout excess.

- 3. Whisk flour and baking powder in small bowl to combine; set aside. In standing mixer fitted with flat beater, cream butter, sugar, salt, and lemon zest at medium-high speed until light and fluffy, about 3 minutes; using rubber spatula, scrape down bowl. Beat in vanilla until combined, about 30 seconds. With mixer running at medium speed, add eggs one at a time; beat until partially incorporated, then scrape down bowl and continue to beat until fully incorporated (mixture will appear broken). With mixer running on low speed, gradually add flour mixture; beat until flour is almost fully incorporated, about 20 seconds. Disengage bowl from mixer; stir batter with rubber spatula, scraping bottom and sides of bowl, until no flour pockets remain and batter is homogenous; batter will be very heavy and thick. Using rubber spatula, gently fold in blueberries until evenly distributed.
- 4. Transfer batter to prepared pan; with rubber spatula, using a pushing motion, spread batter evenly to pan edges and smooth surface. Squeeze handful of streusel in hand to form large cohesive clump; break up clump with fingers and sprinkle streusel evenly over batter. Repeat with remaining streusel. Bake until deep golden brown and toothpick or wooden skewer inserted into center of cake comes out clean, about 55 minutes. Cool on wire rack 15 to 20 minutes (cake will fall slightly as it cools).
- 5. Run paring knife around sides of cake to loosen, Place upside-down plate (do not use plate or platter on which you plan to serve the cake) on top of cake pan; invert cake to remove from pan, lift off cake pan, then peel off and discard parchment. Re-invert cake onto serving platter. Cool until just warm or to room temperature, at least 1 hour. Cut into wedges and serve with Cream Cheese Whipped Cream with directions stated below.
. .

- DIRECTIONS FOR CREAM CHEESE WHIPPED CREAM:
- In bowl of standing mixer fitted with whisk attachment, whisk cream cheese, confectioners' sugar, and salt at medium-high speed until light and fluffy, 1-2 minutes, scraping down bowl with rubber spatula as needed. Add vanilla and beat at medium speed until combined, about 30 seconds; scrape down bowl. With machine running at low speed, add heavy cream in slow steady stream; when almost fully combined, increase speed to medium-high and beat until mixture holds soft peaks when whisk is lifted, another 1-2 minutes, scraping down bowl as needed. Serve with blueberry buckle.

37. Blueberry Coffee Cake Recipe

Serving: 18 | Prep: | Cook: 40mins | Ready in:

Ingredients

- 1/2 cup shortening
- 1/2 cup buttter
- 1 3/4 cups sugar
- 4 eggs
- 1 teaspoon vanilla
- 3 cups flour
- 1 1/2 teaspoons baking powder
- pinch of salt
- 1 can blueberry (or other) pie filling
- powdered sugar for dusting

Direction

- Cream the shortening, butter and the sugar together in a large bowl. Add the eggs into the creamed mixture and beat well. Add in the vanilla and the dry ingredients and mix well.
- Pour 2/3 of the batter into a greased 10 x 15 inch pan. Spread the can of pie filling over the top of the batter. Add in the rest of the batter by dropping by teaspoons onto the top, leaving dots on top of the pie filling.

- Bake at 350 degrees for 35 to 40 minutes. Let it cool for a little while and then sprinkle powdered sugar over the top while it is still warm.

38. Blueberry Cream Cheese Brunch Buckle Recipe

Serving: 12 | Prep: | Cook: 40mins | Ready in:

Ingredients

- ½ cup butter, softened
- 1 (8 ounce) package cream cheese, softened
- 1 cup white sugar
- ¼ cup brown sugar
- 2 eggs
- 1 tablespoon vanilla extract
- 2 cups flour
- ½ teaspoon baking soda
- ½ teaspoon baking powder
- ¼ teaspoon salt
- ⅓ cup whole milk
- 1 pint washed and well drained fresh blueberries
- Topping
- ½ cup brown sugar
- ½ cup flour
- 4 tablespoons melted butter
- 1 teaspoon cinnamon

Direction

- Beat together butter, cream cheese and sugars.
- Add eggs and vanilla.
- Mix in dry ingredients alternately with milk; beat until smooth.
- Gently fold in blueberries.
- Mix dry topping ingredients together with a fork.
- Stir in melted butter until mixture is crumbly.
- Pour batter into a greased 9x13 pan.
- Sprinkle with topping.
- Bake at 350 degrees for 35 to 40 minutes.

- NOTE: If you prefer, you can put 1/2 the batter into the pan, sprinkle with 1/2 the topping, spread remaining batter over the topping, then sprinkle batter with remaining 1/2 of the topping.

39. Blueberry Crumb CoffeeCake Recipe

Serving: 15 | Prep: | Cook: 42mins | Ready in:

Ingredients

- Crumb cake batter:
- ¼ cup solid shortening (such as Crisco)
- ¼ cup butter, softened
- 2 cups white sugar
- 2 eggs
- 1 cup sour cream with 1 tablespoon vinegar stirred in
- 1 teaspoon vanilla extract
- ½ teaspoon almond extract
- 3 cups flour
- 1 teaspoon baking soda
- ½ teaspoon cream of tartar
- 2 cups washed and well drained fresh blueberries (I blot them dry with paper toweling)
- Topping:
- ½ cup flour
- ½ cup sugar
- 2 tablespoons melted butter
- 1 teaspoon cinnamon

Direction

- Mix together shortening, butter and sugar. Stir in eggs; add sour cream mixture and both extracts. Stir in flour, baking soda and cream of tartar. Gently fold in blueberries. Batter will be very thick. Pour batter into greased 9x13 baking dish. Mix together topping ingredients with fork until crumbly; sprinkle over batter. Bake at 350 degrees for 40 to 45 minutes.

- Note: If you like a streusel filling in the middle, double topping ingredients and pour ½ of batter into pan; cover with ½ of topping; pour remaining batter into pan and sprinkle with rest of topping.

40. Blueberry Monkey Pull Apart Bread Recipe

Serving: 8 | Prep: | Cook: 60mins | Ready in:

Ingredients

- 1 cup sugar
- 1 Tablespoon cinnamon
- 4 cans refrigerated biscuits(larger cans)
- 1 cup fresh or frozen blueberries
- 3/4 cup margarine
- ** **
- bundt cake pan
- ** **

Direction

- Preheat oven to 350 degrees F
- Grease & flour Bundt pan.
- Mix sugar & cinnamon.
- Cut biscuits into bite size pieces.
- Cover each piece with the cinnamon & sugar mixture.
- Start layering biscuits, blueberries and a sprinkle of cinnamon/sugar.
- Melt margarine with remaining cinnamon sugar mixture.
- Bake for 1 hour or when done.
- ** *****************
- The best things in life cannot be seen but are felt in the heart!
- ** *****************

41. Blueberry Ricotta Cheese Streusel Coffeecake Recipe

Serving: 8 | Prep: | Cook: 45mins | Ready in:

Ingredients

- Ingredients for Crumbs:
- 2-1/3 cups flour
- 1-1/2 cup white sugar
- 1 teaspoon salt
- 1/2 cup butter or vegetable oil
- Ingredients for Cake:
- 2 teaspoons baking powder
- 3/4 cup milk
- 3 eggs
- 1 teaspoon almond flavoring
- 1 cup blueberries, fresh or frozen
- Second Layer:
- 1 cup nonfat ricotta cheese
- 2 Tablespoons white sugar
- 1 Tablespoon lemon juice
- Ingredients for Topping:
- 1 cup reserved crumbs
- 1/2 cup ground pecans
- 1/2 cup brown sugar
- 1 teaspoon cinnamon

Direction

- Crumbs: Mix flour, white sugar, salt and butter until crumbly. Reserve 1 cup of crumbs for the topping.
- Cake: Take crumbs mixture minus the 1 cup and add baking powder, milk, 2 eggs, almond flavoring and blueberries. Mix until blended. Pour into a 9 X 13 inch sprayed or greased pan. Mix ricotta cheese, 1 egg, white sugar and lemon juice and drop over first layer of batter.
- Topping: Mix reserved crumbs, pecans, brown sugar and cinnamon together. Sprinkle over 2nd layer. Bake at 350 degrees for 45 to 60 minutes until the topping is golden brown and springs back from touch.

42. Blueberry N Cheese Coffee Cake Recipe

Serving: 8 | Prep: | Cook: 60mins | Ready in:

Ingredients

- Serves 8.
- 1 1/2 cups granulated sugar, divided
- 1/2 cup plus 2 tablespoons butter, divided
- 2 eggs
- 2 1/2 cups all-purpose flour
- 1 tablespoon baking powder
- 1 teaspoon salt
- 3/4 cup milk
- 1/4 cup water
- 2 cups fresh blueberries
- 8 ounces cream cheese, cubed
- 2 teaspoons lemon rind, grated, divided

Direction

- Cream together 1 1/4 cups sugar and 1/2 cup butter until light and fluffy; add eggs, one at a time, mixing well after each addition.
- Combine 2 cups flour, baking powder and salt. Add to creamed mixture alternately with milk and water.
- Toss blueberries in 1/4 cup flour; fold into batter with cream cheese and 1 teaspoon lemon rind. Pour into greased and floured 13 x 9-inch baking pan.
- Combine remaining sugar, flour and rind; cut in remaining butter until mixture resembles coarse crumbs. Sprinkle over batter.
- Bake in preheated 375 degree F oven for 1 hour.
- NOTE: two cups frozen, thawed, drained blueberries can be substituted for fresh blueberries.

43. Blueberry Streusel Bread Recipe

Serving: 8 | Prep: | Cook: 45mins | Ready in:

Ingredients

- 4 tbsp buttere or margarine, at room temp
- 3/4 cup sugar
- 1 egg, room temp
- 1/2 cup skim milk
- 2 cups flour
- 2 tsp baking powder
- 1/2 tsp salt
- 2 cups fresh blueberries
- TOPPING:
- 1/2 cup sugar
- 1/3 cup flour
- 1/2 tsp cinnamon
- 4 tbsp butter, cut into pieces

Direction

- Preheat oven to 375 degrees, grease a 9 inch baking dish.
- With mixer, cream the butter with sugar until light and fluffy. Add the egg, beat to combine, then mix in the milk.
- In separate bowl, mix flour, powder and salt.
- Mix with the creamed mixture. Add blueberries and stir.
- Transfer to baking dish.
- TOPPING:
- Place sugar, flour, cinnamon and butter in bowl. Using pastry blender, cut butter in.
- Sprinkle the topping over the batter.
- Bake about 45 minutes or until toothpick inserted comes out clean.

44. Blums Coffee Crunch Cake Recipe

Serving: 12 | Prep: | Cook: 10mins | Ready in:

Ingredients

- 1 1/2 cups sugar
- 1/4 cup strong coffee
- 1/4 cup light corn syrup
- 1 tablespoon baking soda
- 1 cup whipping cream, whipped
- 1 angel food cake (or sponge cake)

Direction

- Combine sugar, coffee and corn syrup in saucepan at least 5 inches deep.
- Bring mixture to boil and cook until it reaches 310F on candy thermometer or reaches hard-crack stage (when small amount dropped in cold water breaks with brittle snap).
- Press baking soda through sieve to remove lumps.
- Remove syrup from heat. Immediately add baking soda and stir vigorously just until mixture thickens and pulls away from sides of pan.
- (Mixture foams rapidly when soda is added. Do not destroy foam by beating excessively.) Immediately pour foamy mass into ungreased 9-inch square metal pan (do not spread or stir).
- Let stand without moving, until cool.
- When ready to garnish cake, knock topping mixture out of pan and crush between sheets of wax paper with rolling pin to form coarse crumbs.
- Frost cake with whipped cream.
- Cover frosted cake generously and thoroughly with crushed topping.
- Refrigerate until ready to serve.
- Makes 1 (9-inch) cake.

45. Brandied Coffee And Honey Cake Recipe

Serving: 8 | Prep: | Cook: 45mins | Ready in:

Ingredients

- TIME TO MATURE: 7 days
- ADD YOUR FAVORITE brandy OR rum FOR A LITTLE BAM!
- OR SERVE WITH brandiED whipped cream
- 1/2 cup of mocha coffee
- 1 6 oz jar of pure honey
- 1 pound bag of cake flour
- 1/2 cup of sugar
- 2 eggs
- 1 teaspoon of baking soda
- 1/2 cup olive oil
- lots of raisins and walnuts and a little cinnamon

Direction

- Preheat the oven at 325 degrees.
- Combine the flour, sugar and cinnamon in a bowl.
- Add the honey, oil and eggs and beat into a smooth batter with a whisk.
- Stir the baking soda and then the coffee into the batter.
- Gently fold in the raisins and walnuts.
- Pour the batter into a greased 4 x 8 meatloaf pan or double recipe as I do and use Bundt pan and baked for about 45 minutes, until the top of the cake is dark brown and a toothpick comes out dry.
- Allow the cake to cool completely, wrap in aluminum foil and place in a cool, dry place (not in the refrigerator) to mature for 7 days.

46. Butter Crumb Coffee Cake With Cranberries Recipe

Serving: 16 | Prep: | Cook: 60mins | Ready in:

Ingredients

- Crumb Topping:
- 1 1/3 cup flour
- 2/3 cup light brown sugar
- 1/2 tsp allspice
- 1/8 tsp salt
- 1/9 tsp nutmeg

- 1/2 cup cold, unsalted butter
- 1/2 cup walnuts, chopped
- Cake:
- 1/2 cup sweetened, dried cranberries
- 1 1/2 cup flour
- 1 1/2 tsp baking powder
- 1/4 tsp salt
- 6 tbsp butter
- 2/3 cup light brown sugar
- 1 tsp vanilla
- 2 eggs
- 6 oz low fat vanilla yogurt

Direction

- Heat oven to 350 degrees. Coat 9 inch springform or other pan with cooking spray.
- Crumb Topping: In bowl, mix flour, brown sugar, allspice, salt and nutmeg. Work in 1/2 cup cold unsalted butter with fingertips until mixture resembles coarse meal. Stir in walnuts.
- Cake: In bowl, soften cranberries in boiling water to cover, 10 min.
- Drain and finely chop. In 2nd bowl, whisk together flour, baking powder and salt.
- In 3rd bowl, beat butter until creamy. Beat in light brown sugar and vanilla until fluffy, 2 min. Add eggs. Beat in yogurt with flour mixture. Fold in chopped cranberries. Scrape batter into pan. Sprinkle with crumb topping. Bake until cake top is browned, 60 min. Let cool in pan 15 min. Remove side of pan. Cut into wedges.
- Serve slightly warm.

47. Buttercup Squash Coffeecake Recipe

Serving: 8 | Prep: | Cook: 50mins | Ready in:

Ingredients

- 1/4 cup packed brown sugar
- 1/4 cup sugar
- 1/4 cup all purpose flour
- 1/4 cup quick cooking oats
- 1-1/2 teaspoon ground cinnamon
- 3 tablespoons cold butter
- 1/2 cup butter flavored shortening
- 1 cup sugar
- 2 eggs
- 1 cup mashed cooked buttercup squash
- 1 teaspoon vanilla
- 2 cup all purpose flour
- 2 teaspoon baking powder
- 1-1/2 teaspoon ground cinnamon
- 1/2 teaspoon baking soda
- 1/2 teaspoon salt
- 1/4 teaspoon ground ginger
- 1/4 teaspoon ground nutmeg
- Pinch ground cloves
- 1/2 cup unsweetened applesauce
- Glaze:
- 1/2 cup confectioners sugar
- 1/4 teaspoon vanilla extract
- 1-1/2 teaspoon hot water

Direction

- Combine brown sugar, sugar, flour, oats and cinnamon then cut in butter and set aside.
- In mixing bowl cream shortening and sugar then beat in eggs one at a time.
- Beat in squash and vanilla.
- Combine dry ingredients then gradually add to creamed mixture.
- Spoon half into greased spring form pan and spread applesauce over batter.
- Sprinkle with half of the streusel then spoon remaining batter evenly over streusel.
- Top with remaining streusel and bake at 350 for 50 minutes.
- Cool 10 minutes then remove sides of pan.
- Combine glaze ingredients and drizzle over coffeecake.

48. Buttermilk Cinnamon Bread Recipe

Serving: 12 | Prep: | Cook: 55mins | Ready in:

Ingredients

- 4 cups flour
- 2 tsp. baking soda
- 1 tsp. salt
- 1/2 cup vegetable oil
- 2 1/2 cups sugar, divided
- 2 cups buttermilk
- 2 eggs
- 1 tbls. cinnamon
- 1-2 tbls. walnuts, finely chopped

Direction

- Preheat oven to 350.
- In large mixing bowl, combine flour, baking soda and salt.
- In small bowl, combine oil and 1 1/2 cups sugar.
- Add buttermilk and eggs and mix well.
- Stir into dry ingredients until just moistened.
- Fill two greased 8 x 4 inch loaf pans about a third full.
- Combine cinnamon and 1 cup sugar.
- Sprinkle half over batter.
- Top with remaining batter and cinnamon sugar.
- Swirl batter with a knife.
- Sprinkle with nuts.
- Bake 45-55 minutes or until a toothpick inserted near the center comes out clean.

49. Butternut Squash Coffeecake Recipe

Serving: 8 | Prep: | Cook: 50mins | Ready in:

Ingredients

- 1/4 cup packed brown sugar
- 1/4 cup sugar
- 1/4 cup all purpose flour
- 1/4 cup quick cooking oats
- 1-1/2 teaspoon ground cinnamon
- 3 tablespoons cold butter
- 1/2 cup butter flavored shortening
- 1 cup sugar
- 2 eggs
- 1 cup mashed cooked buttercup squash
- 1 teaspoon vanilla
- 2 cup all purpose flour
- 2 teaspoon baking powder
- 1-1/2 teaspoon ground cinnamon
- 1/2 teaspoon baking soda
- 1/2 teaspoon salt
- 1/4 teaspoon ground ginger
- 1/4 teaspoon ground nutmeg
- Pinch ground cloves
- 1/2 cup unsweetened applesauce
- Glaze:
- 1/2 cup confectioners sugar
- 1/4 teaspoon vanilla extract
- 1-1/2 teaspoon hot water

Direction

- Combine brown sugar, sugar, flour, oats and cinnamon then cut in butter and set aside.
- In mixing bowl cream shortening and sugar then beat in eggs one at a time.
- Beat in squash and vanilla.
- Combine dry ingredients then gradually add to creamed mixture.
- Spoon half into a greased spring form pan then spread applesauce over batter.
- Sprinkle with half of the streusel then spoon remaining batter evenly over streusel.
- Top with remaining streusel and bake at 350 for 50 minutes.
- Cool for 10 minutes then remove sides of pan.
- Combine glaze ingredients and drizzle over coffeecake.

50. CHRISTMAS BREAD Recipe

Serving: 30 | Prep: | Cook: 45mins | Ready in:

Ingredients

- (for two large loaves)
- 2 kg flour
- 130 gr yeast
- 1 cup tepid water
- 800 gr sugar
- 2 wine glasses of olive oil
- 2 cups warm red wine
- pinch of salt
- 2 tsp mastic grounded
- 2 cups of walnuts, roughly chopped
- 2 cups of gr raisins
- 1 cup of coarsely chopped almonds
- 1 cup of stoned and cut dates
- 1 glass of dried spoon sweets (or fruits glaces)
- 2 tsp cinnamon and ground cloves
- Peel of two oranges, finely chopped
- 1 small glass of orange juice
- 1 small glass of brandy
- For the decoration (optional)
- olive oil
- sesame seeds
- chopped walnuts

Direction

- Prepare yeast mixture the previous night, mixing 350 gr of flour with the yeast and some tepid water. In the morning, add 25 gr of sugar, half of the olive oil and some flour.
- Knead dough well and leave it to rise in a warm place.
- Then add remaining ingredients and knead dough very well so it is smooth and not sticky.
- Cover dough and leave it to rise in a warm place for about 90 minutes.
- Separate into two loaves and place on two large, oiled baking pans.
- Let the loaves rise then brush them with oil and sprinkle with sesame seeds and walnuts.
- Bake in the oven at 200C for 15 minutes then at 150C for 35 to 40 minutes.

51. COCONUT CHOCOLATE CHIP COFFEE CAKE Recipe

Serving: 10 | Prep: | Cook: 55mins | Ready in:

Ingredients

- 1 tablespoon dry bread crumbs
- 2 cups unbleached all-purpose flour
- 1 1/2 cups packed light brown sugar, plus 2 tablespoons, (divided)
- 1 teaspoon table salt
- 10 tablespoons unsalted butter (1 1/4 sticks), softened
- 1 teaspoon baking powder
- 1/2 teaspoon baking soda
- 3/4 cup buttermilk (or low-fat plain yogurt)
- 1 large egg, at room temperature
- 1 teaspoon vanilla extract
- 1 cup chocolate chips (preferably miniature)
- 1 cup sweetened shredded coconut
- 1/2 cup walnuts (or pecans), finely chopped

Direction

- Note: This cake is best eaten on the day it is baked, though it may be made a day ahead. The batter is quite heavy, so you may prefer to beat it with an electric mixer at medium-high speed for a minute or so, rather than whisk it by hand. Do not insert a skewer into this cake to test for doneness until the center appears firm when the pan is shaken. If you do, the topping may squeeze air out, and the middle of the cake may sink.
- 1. Adjust oven rack to center position and heat oven to 350 degrees. Generously grease bottom and lightly grease sides of 10-inch springform pan. Sprinkle bottom of pan with dry bread crumbs, then shake lightly to coat. Tap out excess crumbs.
- 2. Whisk flour, all but 1/2 cup of the brown sugar, and salt in large mixing bowl until blended. Add butter and cut with whisk until

mixture resembles coarse crumbs. Remove 1 cup of crumbs to separate bowl.

- 3. Whisk baking powder and soda into mixture remaining in large mixing bowl. Add buttermilk or yogurt, egg, and vanilla; whisk vigorously until batter is thick, smooth, fluffy, and frosting like, 1 1/2 to 2 minutes. Using a rubber spatula, stir in chocolate chips, then scrape batter into prepared pan and smooth top.
- 4. Add coconut, nuts, and remaining 1/2 cup brown sugar to reserved crumbs; toss with a fork or your hands until blended. Sprinkle crumbs over batter, pressing lightly so that mixture adheres. Bake cake until center is firm and cake tester comes out clean, 50 to 55 minutes. Transfer cake to rack; remove pan sides. Let cake cool completely, about 2 hours, before serving. When completely cooled, cake can be slid off pan bottom onto serving plate.

52. CREAM CHEESE COFFEE CAKE DIABETIC FRIENDLY Recipe

Serving: 24 | Prep: | Cook: 20mins | Ready in:

Ingredients

- Ingredients:
- 1 cup (8-oz) fat-free sour cream
- ½ cup sugar substitute (Equal or Equivalent)
- ½ cup margarine or butter
- 1 tsp. salt (low sodium)
- 2 packages (¼ -oz each) active dry yeast
- ½ cup warm water Temp. (110 to 115)
- 2 eggs, beaten
- 4 cups all-purpose flour
- Filling:
- 2 packages (8-oz each) 1/3 less fat cream cheese, softened
- ¾ cup sugar substitute
- 1 egg, beaten
- 2 tsp. vanilla extract
- 1/8 tsp. salt (low sodium)
- Glaze:
- 2 ½ cups confectioners' sugar
- ¼ cup 1% milk
- 1 tsp. vanilla extract
- toasted sliced almonds, optional

Direction

- Preheat oven at 375.
- 1) In a saucepan, combine sour cream, sugar substitute, margarine and salt. Cook over medium-low heat, stirring constantly, for 5 – 10 minutes or until well blended. Cool to room temperature.
- 2) In a mixing bowl, dissolve yeast in warm water. Add sour cream mixture and egg; mix well. Gradually stir in flour. (Dough will be very soft.) Cover and refrigerate overnight.
- 3) Next day, combine filling ingredients in a mixing bowl until well blended. Turn dough onto a floured board; knead 5 – 6 times. Divide into four equal portions.
- 4) Roll each portion into a 12-inch x 8-inch rectangle. Spread ¼ of the filling on each to within 1-inch of edges. Roll up jelly-roll style from long side; pinch seams and ends to seal. Place seam side down, on greased baking sheet. Cut six X's on the top of loaves. Cover and let rise until nearly doubled, about 1 hour.
- 5) Bake at 375 for 20 – 25 minutes or until golden brown. Cool on wire racks. Combine the first three glaze ingredients; drizzle over loves. Sprinkle with almonds if desired. Store in the refrigerator.
- Diabetic Friendly
- Serving size: 1 piece
- Calories per serving: 264, Fat: 4g, Cholesterol: 54mg, Sodium: 165mg, Carbohydrate: 38g
- Note: I modified the recipe for a diabetic friendly one by cutting the sugar, fat, and the sodium.

53. Cafe Au Lait Breakfast Cake Recipe

Serving: 14 | Prep: | Cook: 80mins | Ready in:

Ingredients

- Filling:
- 1/2 tbsp cinnamon
- 1/2 cup old-fashioned oats (not instant)
- 3 tbsp hot chocolate beverage mix
- 1/2 tbsp instant coffee granules
- 3 tbsp canola oil
- ---
- Cake:
- 4 oz butter, softened
- 3/4 cup brown sugar
- 1/2 block (6 oz) silken firm tofu (I use Mori-Nu lite), pureed
- 1 cup sour cream
- 1 tsp vanilla
- 2 tablespoons instant espresso powder
- 2 tablespoons hot water
- 2 cups flour
- 3/4 cup whole wheat flour
- 1 tablespoon baking powder
- 1/2 teaspoon baking soda
- 1/4 tsp nutmeg
- 1/4 teaspoon salt
- 1 cup (1%) milk

Direction

- Preheat the oven to 350 degrees F. Grease and line a 9" springform pan (trust me, you want to line it!).
- Combine the dry "filling" ingredients in a small bowl until crumbly, adding a little water if necessary. Set aside.
- For cake, cream butter and sugar until light.
- Beat in tofu puree, sour cream and vanilla.
- Combine the instant espresso powder and hot water, stirring well. Add to the creamed mixture and beat thoroughly.
- In another bowl, whisk together flours, baking powder, baking soda, nutmeg and salt.
- In alternate additions with the milk, begin adding the dry ingredients to the creamed mixture, blending well after each.
- Pour 1/2 the batter in the prepared springform pan, then sprinkle with 3/4 of the filling mixture.
- Top with remaining batter and crumble.
- Cover with foil and bake 80 minutes, or until tests done.
- Cool completely in the pan before releasing from the springform - it is very moist.

54. Canadian Banana Coffee Cake Recipe

Serving: 4 | Prep: | Cook: 20mins | Ready in:

Ingredients

- 2 tbsp flour
- 2 tbsp rolled oats
- 1/4 tsp baking soda
- 1/4 tsp baking powder
- 1 medium overripe banana
- 1 1/2 tbsp brown sugar
- 1 tbsp canola oil
- 1 tbsp water
- 1 tsp vanilla
- 1 tbsp chopped pecans
- 2 "fun size" coffee Crisp bars (16g each), chopped

Direction

- Preheat the oven to 350F. Grease a 4" pan with baking spray and set aside.
- Combine flour, oats, baking soda and baking powder in a small bowl.
- Separately, mash the banana with the brown sugar, oil, water and vanilla.
- Gently stir the banana mixture into the dry ingredients and fold in the pecans and chocolate pieces.
- Bake for 20 minutes and cool completely on a wire rack.

minutes; remove from pan. Serve warm or cool.
- Serves: 12

55. Captains Raspberry Almond Coffee Cake Recipe

Serving: 12 | Prep: | Cook: 35mins | Ready in:

Ingredients

- Ingredients for Topping
- 6 Tablespoons all purpose flour
- 6 Tablespoons sugar
- 2 to 3 Tablespoons coarsely ground, roasted almonds
- 4 Tablespoons butter
- ....
- Ingredients for coffee cake
- 2 cups all-purpose flour
- 1 cup sugar
- 1 Tablespoon baking powder
- 1/2 teaspoon baking soda
- 1/2 teaspoon salt
- 2 cups fresh or frozen raspberries
- 1/2 cup chopped roasted almonds
- 2 eggs
- 1/3 cup orange juice
- 4 Tablespoons butter, melted
- 3/4 cup buttermilk

Direction

- In a small bowl, combine flour, sugar, and almonds. Cut in butter until mixture resembles coarse crumbs. Set aside.
- Heat oven to 375 degrees. Grease and flour a 9-inch tube pan. Set aside. In a large bowl, combine the dry ingredients. Mix well. Beat eggs in a medium bowl. Stir in juice, cooled along with melted butter and buttermilk. Add dry ingredients along with raspberries and almonds. Stir just until dry ingredients are moistened -- do not overmix. Spoon batter into prepared pan; sprinkle with topping.
- Bake for 35 to 40 minutes or until top springs back when gently touched. Cool 10 to 15

56. Caramel Nut Twisted Sweet Potato Coffee Cake Recipe

Serving: 12 | Prep: | Cook: 35mins | Ready in:

Ingredients

- *****CARAMEL TOPPING***********
- 1/3 cup butter or margarine
- 1/2 cup packed brown sugar
- 1/4 cup corn syrup
- 1/2 cup chopped pecans
- **********DOUGH*******************
- 2 1/2 cups baking mix
- 2/3 cup mashed cooked fresh or canned sweet potatoes
- 1/3 cup milk
- 2 tablespoons butter or margarine - softened
- 3 tablespoons brown sugar

Direction

- Heat oven to 400 degrees F.
- **TO MAKE TOPPING**
- Melt butter in an ungreased 9 inch square baking pan in oven.
- Stir in brown sugar and corn syrup.
- Sprinkle with pecans.
- ***TO MAKE DOUGH***
- In a bowl, stir baking mix, sweet potatoes and milk until dough forms.
- Place dough on surface dusted with baking mix.
- Knead lightly 10 times.
- Roll or pat into 12" square.
- Spread butter over dough.
- Sprinkle with brown sugar.
- Fold dough into thirds; press edges together to seal.
- Cut crosswise into 1 inch strips.

- Twist edges of strips into opposite directions.
- Arrange twists on pecans in pan.
- Bake at 400 degrees F for 25-30 minutes or until golden brown.
- Immediately turn pan upside down onto heat proof serving plate.
- Leave pan over cake for 1 minute.
- Remove pan and serve warm.
- Enjoy this with some ice cream!
- **
- -Some pursue happiness - others create it - Anonymous
- **

- To use, roll out the dough on a lightly floured surface into a large rectangle about 12 x 16 inches. Then, cut into two 6 x 16 pieces. Fill as desired with the long side facing you, and roll up. Wrap the dough in wrap again and chill for 30 minutes. Or, if you want, you can freeze the log to use later in the week.
- To cook, slice the log into 1-inch cross sections, and place each little round about 1 inch apart on a parchment lined baking sheet. Bake at 350F for about 15 minutes, or until the dough is a light golden brown. Allow the pinwheels to cool for about 15 minutes before serving. They will keep up to 4 days, depending on your filling.

57. Cheaters Puff Pastry Pinwheels Recipe

Serving: 6 | Prep: | Cook: 15mins | Ready in:

Ingredients

- 4 oz butter, at room temperature
- 4 oz cream cheese or quark, at room temperature
- 1 cup flour
- 1/4 t salt
- 1/2 t sugar
- Any kind of filling that you like!

Direction

- Sift together the flour, salt and sugar. Set aside.
- Cream the butter and soft cheese together on medium until it is light and fluffy. Reduce the speed to low and slowly add the dry ingredients, beating until well combined. Increase the speed to medium, and beat for about 15 seconds.
- Scrape the dough onto plastic wrap and press into a flat disk. Then, double rap the dough and refrigerate overnight.

58. Cheesecake Coffee Cake Recipe

Serving: 6 | Prep: | Cook: 30mins | Ready in:

Ingredients

- cake part
- 3 cups of Bisquick
- 1/4 cup sugar
- 1/4 cup margarine or butter
- 1/2 cup milk
- cheesecake filling
- 1/2 cup sugar
- 1 teaspoon vanilla
- 2 eggs
- 8 oz. cream cheese
- Topping strawberry preserves

Direction

- Heat oven to 375 degrees.
- Mix Bisquick, sugar, butter, and milk beat vigorously 30 seconds. Turn dough onto surface well dusted with baking mix. Knead 30 times. Pat dough evenly in bottom and the sides of the ungreased 9" pan.
- Prepare cheese filling and beat all ingredients with beater till smooth. Pour over dough.

- Bake till edge is golden brown and filling is set. About 30 min.
- Cool 10 min. Spread with preserves. Serve warm.

59. Cherry Sourdough Coffee Cake Recipe

Serving: 9 | Prep: | Cook: 40mins | Ready in:

Ingredients

- 1 1/2 cups unbleached flour
- 1/2 cup sugar
- 1/2 tsp baking powder
- 1/2 tsp baking soda
- 3/4 cup butter
- 1/2 cup sourdough starter (see recipe below)
- 1 egg
- 1 tsp vanilla
- Cherry Filling (canned pie filling used also)
- 1/3 cup quick-cooking rolled oats
- 1/4 cup packed brown sugar
- 1/4 cup chopped nuts
- 3 tbsp unbleached flour

Direction

- Mix the 1 1/2 cups flour, sugar, baking powder, baking soda, and 1/4 teaspoon salt. Cut in 1/2 cup butter till mixture resembles fine crumbs. Mix Sourdough Starter, egg, and vanilla; add flour mixture. Stir just till moistened. Spread half of the batter in a greased 9x9x2-inch baking pan. Spread Cherry Filling atop. Drop remaining batter in small mounds over filling. Mix oats, brown sugar, nuts, and 3 tablespoons flour. Cut in 1/4 cup butter till mixture resembles coarse crumbs; sprinkle over batter. Bake in a 350 degrees F oven for 35 - 40 minutes or till golden. Serves 9.
- Cherry Filling:
- Bring 1 1/2 cups fresh or frozen unsweetened pitted tart red cherries to boiling; reduce heat. Cover and simmer for 5 minutes. Stir in 1 tablespoon lemon juice. Combine 1/2 cup sugar and 2 tablespoons cornstarch; add to cherry mixture. Cook and stir till bubbly. Cook and stir 2 minutes more. Cool completely.
- Sourdough Starter:
- When using starter; don't use quick-rising yeast.
- In a large bowl dissolve 1 package active dry yeast in 1/2 cup warm water. Stir in 2 cups warm water, 2 cups unbleached flour, and 1 tablespoon sugar or honey. Beat till smooth. Cover bowl with cheesecloth. Let stand at room temperature for 5 to 10 days or till mixture has a fermented aroma, stirring 2 or 3 times a day. (Fermentation time depends on room temperature; a warmer room hastens fermentation.)
- To store, transfer Sourdough Starter to a jar. Cover with cheesecloth and refrigerate. Do not cover jar tightly with a metal lid.
- To use starter, bring desired amount to room temperature. Replenish starter after each use by stirring 3/4 cup unbleached flour, 3/4 cup water, and 1 teaspoon honey or sugar into remaining starter. Cover; let stand at room temperature at least 1 day or till bubbly. Refrigerate for later use.
- If starter isn't used within 10 days, stir in 1 teaspoon sugar or honey. Repeat every 10 days unless replenished.

60. Cherry Cashew Coffeecakes Recipe

Serving: 8 | Prep: | Cook: 30mins | Ready in:

Ingredients

- 3/4 cup warm water
- 1 package active dry yeast
- 3/4 cup warm milk
- 2 tablespoons honey
- 2 tablespoons vegetable oil

- 1 teaspoon salt
- 2-1/2 cups all purpose flour
- 2 cups whole wheat flour
- Filling:
- 2 tablespoons butter melted
- 1/2 cup packed light brown sugar
- 1 teaspoon ground cinnamon
- 1 cup chopped dried cherries
- 1 cup chopped cashews
- Glaze:
- 1/4 cup honey
- 1 tablespoon butter

Direction

- Place 1/4 cup warm water in large warm bowl then sprinkle in yeast and stir until dissolved.
- Add remaining water, warm milk, honey, vegetable oil, salt and 1-1/2 cups all-purpose flour.
- Blend well then stir in whole wheat flour and enough remaining flour to make soft dough.
- Knead on lightly floured surface until smooth and elastic about 8 minutes.
- Place in greased bowl turning to grease top then cover and let rise in warm place 45 minutes.
- Punch dough down then remove to lightly floured surface and divide in half.
- Roll each to rectangle and transfer to two greased baking sheets and brush with melted butter.
- In small bowl combine brown sugar, cinnamon, cherries and cashews then stir well.
- Sprinkle half of the brown sugar mixture over center third of each rectangle.
- Along each side of coffeecake cut 1" wide strips from edge of filling to edge of dough.
- Starting at one end alternately fold six strips from each side across filling toward opposite end.
- Repeat from other end using six strips from each side.
- Loosely tie together remaining two center strips on top of loaf.
- Repeat with second coffeecake.
- Cover and let rise in warm draft free place until almost doubled in size about 40 minutes.
- Bake at 375 for 25 minutes and switch positions of sheets halfway through baking.
- Remove from sheets and cool on wire racks then brush with glaze.
- To make glaze stir 1/4 cup honey and 1 tablespoon butter over medium heat until butter melts.

61. Cherry Coffee Cake Recipe

Serving: 8 | Prep: | Cook: 45mins | Ready in:

Ingredients

- 3/4 cups sugar
- 1/4 cup each butter and solid vegetable shortening
- 2 eggs
- 3/4 teaspoon baking powder
- 1/8 salt
- 1/2 teaspoon each vanilla and almond extract
- 1 1/2 cups all-purpose flour
- 1/2 to 3/4 of a can of a 21oz. can of cherry pie filling

Direction

- Preheat oven to 350 F.
- In a mixing bowl, combine sugar, butter, shortening, eggs, baking powder, salt and flavorings.
- Beat, scraping sides of bowl occasionally, for 3 minutes or until well blended.
- Stir in flour, mixing well.
- Spoon 2/3 of the batter into a 9-inch greased square pan. Evenly spread the pie filling over the batter.
- Using a tablespoon, drop the remaining batter over the top (pie filling will not be completely covered).
- Bake at 350.F for 40 to 45 minutes or until done.
- TIP:

- You can use apple or blueberry pie filling, if you wish. Eliminate the almond extract and increase the vanilla to 1 teaspoon. While warm, drizzle with a glaze made by mixing together 1/2 cup powder sugar and 2 to 4 teaspoons milk (optional).

62. Cherry Cream Coffeecake Recipe

Serving: 8 | Prep: | Cook: 45mins | Ready in:

Ingredients

- 1-3/4 cups all purpose flour
- 1/2 cup granulated sugar
- 3/4 cup butter softened
- 2 eggs
- 1/2 teaspoon baking powder
- 1/2 teaspoon baking soda
- 1/4 teaspoon salt
- 1 teaspoon vanilla
- 1/4 cup granulated sugar
- 8 ounces cream cheese softened
- 1 egg
- 1 teaspoon grated lemon peel
- 10 ounce jar cherry preserves
- 1/3 cup powdered sugar
- 3 teaspoons lemon juice

Direction

- Preheat oven to 350.
- Grease and flour bottom and sides of a spring form pan.
- Combine flour, sugar, butter, eggs, baking powder, baking soda, salt and vanilla.
- Beat at medium speed scraping bowl often until well mixed about 2 minutes.
- Spread batter on bottom and 2" up sides of prepared pan.
- Combine 1/4 cup sugar, cream cheese, egg and lemon peel in large mixer bowl.
- Beat at medium speed scraping bowl often until smooth about 3 minutes.
- Pour over batter in pan then spoon preserves evenly over filling.
- Bake 45 minutes then cool for 20 minutes.
- Loosen sides of cake from pan by running knife around inside of pan then remove side of pan.
- Stir together powdered sugar and lemon juice until smooth then drizzle over warm coffeecake.
- Serve warm or cold.

63. Cherry Rhubarb Coffee Cake Recipe

Serving: 10 | Prep: | Cook: 50mins | Ready in:

Ingredients

- 4 cups fresh or frozen rhubarb
- 2 tablespoons lemon juice
- 1 cup sugar
- 1/3 cup cornstarch
- 1 can cherry pie filling
- 3 cups flour
- 1 cup sugar
- 1 teaspoon baking powder
- 1 teaspoon baking soda
- 1/2 teaspoon salt
- 1 cup butter
- 1 cup buttermilk
- 2 eggs slightly beaten
- 1 teaspoon vanilla
- 1 cup sugar
- 1 cup flour
- 1/2 cup butter
- If using frozen rhubarb thaw.

Direction

- In saucepan cook rhubarb and lemon juice over medium low heat for 5 minutes stirring often.
- Combine sugar and cornstarch then add to rhubarb mixture.

- Cook and stir 5 minutes more until thickened and bubbly then stir in pie filling and set aside.
- Combine sugar and flour then cut in butter until mixture forms coarse crumbs.
- Combine flour, sugar, baking powder, baking soda and salt in a large bowl.
- Cut in butter until mixture resembles fine crumbs.
- In a mixing bowl beat buttermilk, eggs and vanilla then add to flour mixture and stir to moisten.
- Spread a little more than half of the batter into a greased rectangular pan.
- Spread cooled filling over batter then drop remaining batter by teaspoonfuls onto filling.
- Sprinkle crumb topping over batter and bake at 350 for 45 minutes.

64. Childhood Cinnamon Cake Recipe

Serving: 12 | Prep: | Cook: 50mins | Ready in:

Ingredients

- 2 cups brown sugar
- 1/2 tsp cinnamon
- 2 cups flour
- 1 tsp baking soda
- 1/2 cup (salted) butter
- 1 cup plain yogurt
- 1 tsp vanilla

Direction

- Preheat oven to 350F. Grease a loaf pan.
- Combine all the dry ingredients (sugar, cinnamon, flour and baking soda) with the butter and blend with your fingers until the mixture resembles breadcrumbs.
- Take 1/2 of the crumbs for cake topping.
- To remaining mixture, add the yogurt and vanilla.
- Blend until just combined.
- Pour mixture into greased loaf pan and sprinkle crumbs on top.
- Bake 50 minutes.
- Cool 10 minutes in pan before turning out.

65. Choc Chip Pound Cake Recipe

Serving: 6 | Prep: | Cook: 112mins | Ready in:

Ingredients

- 2 1/2 cup all purpose flour
- 1 tea spoon baking powder
- 1/2 tea spoon salt
- 1 1/2 cups butter
- 2 1/4 cup sugar
- 2 tea spoon vanilla extract
- 5 large eggs
- 3/4 cup butter milk
- 1 cup semisweet chocolate chip

Direction

- Hit oven 350 F.
- Beat butter, sugar & vanilla fast speed with electric mixer.
- After creamy add the eggs at once until combine in medium speed.
- In slow speed add all dry ingredients.
- With spoon stir chocolate chip in and butter milk until combined.
- Spoon the batter into the prepared pan and bake for 75-85 minutes.
- Cool it 15 mins and pour chocolate for topping.
- Let's eat.

66. Chocolate Chip Pumpkin Spice Bread Recipe

Serving: 10 | Prep: | Cook: 45mins | Ready in:

Ingredients

- (dry)
- 1 ¾ cup flour
- ½ tsp salt
- ¼ ginger
- ¼ ground cloves
- ½ tsp cinnamon
- ½ tsp nutmeg
- 1 tsp baking soda
- (wet)
- 1 cup sugar
- 2 eggs
- 1 tsp. vanilla
- ½ cup butter
- ¾ cup pumpkin
- ¾ cup choc chips
- glaze
- ½ cup powdered sugar
- ¼ tsp allspice
- ¼ tsp cinnamon
- 1-2 tbls. heavy cream

Direction

- In medium bowl mix dry ingredients. Set aside.
- In large bowl, mix butter with sugar well, add vanilla and eggs and remix until creamy.
- Now add a ¼ of dry ingredients to the large wet ingredient's bowl and mix. Then add some pumpkin and mix. Repeat alternating dry and pumpkin ending with dry.
- Add chips.
- Pour into 9 inch, well-greased loaf pan and bake at 350 for 45 min. (Double the recipe to fill a Bundt pan.) Cover loaf with tin foil for first 30 minutes. Remove foil for last 15-20 minutes. Check at 40 minutes and then every 5 minutes with a knife into the center for dryness. Let cool in pan until warm.
- Glaze-
- Add a little cream and mix well. Add more cream until you get a thick syrup consistency.
- Drizzle glaze over warm loaf so it melts down the sides.

67. Chocolate Chunk Coffee Cake Recipe

Serving: 9 | Prep: | Cook: 35mins | Ready in:

Ingredients

- nut Layer:
- 4 ounces German sweet chocolate, chopped
- 1/2 cup nuts
- 1/4 cup sugar
- 1 tsp cinnamon
- Cake:
- 1 3/4 cup flour
- 1/2 tsp baking powder
- 1/4 tsp salt
- 1 cup sour cream
- 1 tsp baking soda
- 1/2 cup butter or margarine
- 1 cup sugar
- 2 eggs
- 1/2 tsp vanilla

Direction

- Heat oven to 350 degrees.
- Mix chocolate, nuts, 1/4 cup sugar and cinnamon; set aside.
- Mix flour, powder and salt; set aside. Combine sour cream and baking soda; set aside.
- Beat margarine and 1 cup sugar until light and fluffy. Add eggs, one at a time, beating well after each addition. Add vanilla. Add flour mixture alternately with sour cream mixture, beginning and ending with flour mixture. Spoon 1/2 the batter into greased 9 inch square pan. Top with 1/2 the chocolate nut mixture, spreading carefully with spatula. Repeat layers.
- Bake for 30 to 35 minutes or until cake begins to pull away from sides of pan. Cool in pan; cut into squares.

68. Chocolate Chunk Ricotta Cake Recipe

Serving: 16 | Prep: | Cook: 50mins | Ready in:

Ingredients

- 6 oz dry ricotta cheese
- 1/4 cup buttermilk
- 1 egg
- 1 tbsp vanilla
- 2.5 oz salted butter
- 3/4 cup granulated sugar
- 3/4 cup flour
- pinch salt
- 1/2 tbsp baking powder
- 3 oz dark bar chocolate, broken into chunks

Direction

- Preheat oven to 350F, line a 9" pan with parchment or greased foil.
- Puree ricotta, buttermilk, egg, and vanilla.
- Cream butter and sugar, add ricotta mixture and beat well.
- Stir in flour, salt and baking powder.
- Pour the batter into the pan and sprinkle with chocolate chunks.
- Bake 30 minutes. Chill before cutting.

69. Chocolate Coffee Fudge Cake Recipe

Serving: 6 | Prep: | Cook: 50mins | Ready in:

Ingredients

- 150 gm Soft cheese Light
- 1/2 tsp vanilla extract
- 1 c caster sugar
- 200g self raising flour
- 3 heaped tsp Van Houten pure cocoa pwd
- 2 eggs
- 1/2 c demerara sugar .
- 1/2 cup grape seed oil or olive oil
- 2 tsp Nescafe Blend 37 instant coffee pwd
- 3 tbsp Evaporated low fat milk
- icing
- 1 tsp Nescafe Blend 37 instant coffee pwd
- 2 tsp heaped tsp Van Houten pure cocoa pwd
- 100g icing sugar
- 1 tbsp grape seed oil or olive margarine
- 1/2 cup water .
- 1 tbsp Evaporated low fat milk
- 1/4 C beaten cream cheese and condensed milk

Direction

- Whip the Cheese, Vanilla and Caster sugar. Keep inside fridge.
- Preheat oven 180 deg.
- Sift the flour and the Cocoa powder.
- Beat the eggs. Add the demerara sugar. Add the oil, coffee powder and the milk.
- Pour half the batter into greased pan. Pour the cheese mixture. Level it. Pour the remaining batter.
- Bake for 45 to 50 mins.
- Meanwhile gently heat the coffee powder, cocoa powder, and icing sugar.
- Once caramelized, add the oil, water. Let it boil in low flame. Add the milk. Cool it.
- Pour it on top of the cake.
- Drizzle some condensed milk and cream cheese mixture on top with a spoon.

70. Chocolate Hazelnut Nutella Coffee Ring Recipe

Serving: 22 | Prep: | Cook: 30mins | Ready in:

Ingredients

- 3/4 cup milk
- 1 egg
- 1/4 cup margarine or butter, cut up
- 3 tablespoons water
- 4 cups bread flour

- 1/3 cup sugar
- 1 teaspoon salt
- 1-1/2 teaspoons active dry yeast or bread machine yeast
- 1/2 cup chocolate hazelnut spread*
- 1/2 cup chopped hazelnuts
- 1/4 cup chocolate hazelnut spread

Direction

- 1. Add first 8 ingredients to the bread machine pan according to the manufacturer's directions. Select dough cycle. When cycle is complete, remove dough from machine. Punch down. Cover; let rest for 10 minutes.
- 2. On a lightly floured surface, roll the dough into an 18x10-inch rectangle. Spread with the 1/2 cup chocolate hazelnut spread and sprinkle with hazelnuts.
- 3. Starting from a long side, roll up into a spiral; seal edge. Place, seam side down, on a greased large baking sheet. Bring ends together to form a ring. Moisten ends; pinch together to seal ring. Using kitchen scissors or a sharp knife, cut from the outside edge toward center, leaving about 1 inch attached. Repeat around the edge at 1-inch intervals. Gently turn each slice slightly so the same side of all slices faces upward.
- 4. Cover and let rise in a warm place for 45 to 60 minutes or until nearly double. Bake in a 350 degree F oven for 30 to 35 minutes or until bread sounds hollow when lightly tapped (the center may be lighter in color). If necessary, loosely cover with foil last 10 minutes to prevent overbrowning. Remove from baking sheet; cool on a wire rack.
- 5. In a microwave-safe container heat the 1/4 cup chocolate hazelnut spread on 100 percent power (high) for 30 to 60 seconds or until of drizzling consistency. Drizzle over bread. Makes 22 servings.

71. Chocolate Macadamia Sock It To Me Cake Recipe

Serving: 12 | Prep: | Cook: 85mins | Ready in:

Ingredients

- 1 box of white or yellow cake mix
- 1 1/4 cup fresh sour cream
- 1/2 cup of veg. oil
- 4 eggs
- 3/4 cup of chopped macadamia nuts *see note below
- 1 cup of premium chocolate chips
- 1/4 cup of granulated sugar
- 2 tsp. cinnamon
- *Other nuts can be used but Macs are great in this recipe. If you can't find raw macadamia nuts, you can use dry roasted and salted nuts. Just roll the salted nuts out on a dish towel until some of the salt is removed and then chop them.

Direction

- Preheat oven to 325 degrees.
- Use a Baker's Spray in the bottom of an angel or tube pan OR oil and lightly flour the bottom of the pan.
- In a large bowl, combine the eggs, oil, sour cream and cake mix.
- Combine thoroughly.
- Mix the sugar, nuts and cinnamon in a separate bowl.
- Place half of the cake batter into your pan.
- Sprinkle all but about 2TBs of the nut and cinnamon mixture over this layer.
- Pour the chocolate chips over the nut and cinnamon layer.
- Cover with the rest of the cake batter.
- Sprinkle the top of the cake with the remaining nuts and cinnamon mix.
- Bake for 1 hour and 10 minutes and check using a stick, knife or toothpick to see if cake is done. If not, bake for 10 more minutes.
- Let cake cool completely before removing from pan and serve.

72. Chocolate Nut Bread Recipe

Serving: 36 | Prep: | Cook: 55mins | Ready in:

Ingredients

- 2 cups all-purpose flour
- ½ cup granulated sugar
- ½ teaspoon baking powder
- /2 tablespoon baking soda
- 1 teaspoon salt
- 1 large eggs
- ¾ cups milk
- 1/3 cup vegetable oil
- 1 teaspoon vanilla
- 6 ounces semi-sweet chocolate morsels divided
- 1/2 cups chopped walnuts

Direction

- PREHEAT oven to 350° F. Grease one 9x5-inch loaf pan.
- COMBINE flour, sugar, baking powder, baking soda and salt in large bowl.
- COMBINE eggs, milk and vegetable oil in medium bowl. Add to flour mixture; mix just until moistened. Stir in 1 1/2 cups morsels and nuts. Spoon into prepared loaf pans.
- BAKE for 55 to 60 minutes or until wooden pick inserted in center comes out clean. Cool in pans for 10 minutes; remove from pans. Cool on wire racks.
- MICROWAVE remaining morsels in heavy-duty plastic bag on HIGH (100%) power for 45 seconds; knead bag to mix. Microwave at additional 10- to 20-second intervals, kneading until smooth. Cut a small hole in corner of bag; squeeze to drizzle over bread. Sprinkle with additional nuts.

73. Chocolate Peanut Butter Coffee Cake Muffins Recipe

Serving: 16 | Prep: | Cook: 30mins | Ready in:

Ingredients

- Topping:
- 1/2 cup packed brown sugar
- 1/4 cup all-purpose flour
- 1/4c. oats
- 1/4 cup peanut butter crunchy
- 3 tablespoons margarine or butter
- 1/4 cup miniature semisweet chocolate pieces
- cake
- 2 cups all-purpose flour
- 1 cup packed brown sugar
- 2 teaspoons baking powder
- 1/2 teaspoon baking soda
- 1/4 teaspoon salt
- 1 cup milk
- 1/2 cup peanut butter
- 2 eggs
- 1/4 cup margarine or butter
- 1/2 cup miniature semisweet chocolate pieces

Direction

- For topping, in a bowl stir together 1/2 cup brown sugar and 1/2 cup all-purpose flour; cut in 1/4 cup peanut butter and 3 tablespoons margarine or butter till crumbly, add 1/4 cup miniature semisweet chocolate pieces and stir--set aside.
- In a bowl stir together 2 cups flour, 1 cup brown sugar, the baking powder, baking soda, and salt. Add milk, 1/2 cup peanut butter, the eggs, and 1/4 cup margarine or butter. Beat with an electric mixer on low speed till blended. Beat at high speed for 3 minutes, scraping the sides of the bowl frequently. Stir 1/2 cup miniature semi-sweet chocolate pieces into the batter after beating.
- Pour batter into a greased muffin tins. . Sprinkle with topping mixture. Bake in a 375 oven about 30 minutes or till a toothpick

inserted near the center comes out clean. Serve warm or cool (serves 16).

74. Chocolate Peanut Butter Cup Bread Recipe

Serving: 0 | Prep: | Cook: 30mins | Ready in:

Ingredients

- Dough:
- 3/4 cup warm water (105 degrees F to 115 degrees F)
- 2 teaspoons plus 1/3 cup sugar
- 2 envelopes active dry yeast
- 2 tablespoons butter, at room temperature
- 1/4 cup smooth peanut butter
- 1 egg
- 3 cups bread flour
- 1 teaspoon salt
- Filling:
- 18 mini chocolate-peanut butter cups
- Glaze:
- 8 mini chocolate-peanut butter cups
- 1 tablespoon milk

Direction

- 1. Dough: Mix together warm water and the 2 teaspoons sugar in small bowl to dissolve sugar. Sprinkle with yeast. Let stand until foamy, 5 to 10 minutes.
- 2. Mix together butter, peanut butter, egg, 2 cups bread flour, the salt and remaining sugar in large bowl. Add yeast mixture. Beat with mixer on medium speed for 3 minutes or until well combined. Stir in 1 cup of the flour or more as needed for dough to come together.
- 3. Transfer dough to work surface. Knead until smooth and elastic, about 8 minutes, adding more flour as needed to prevent the dough from sticking. Transfer dough to greased bowl, turning to coat. Cover with clean kitchen towel or plastic wrap. Let rise in warm place until doubled in volume, about 1-3/4 hours.
- 4. Punch dough down. Let rest for 5 minutes. Gently pat, or roll dough into 9-inch square. With sharp knife or pizza cutter, cut square into 36 equal squares (6 pieces across each side).
- 5. Filling: Unwrap and cut chocolate-peanut butter cups in half. Taking 1 piece of dough, wrap around a peanut-butter cup half. Pinch together, forming ball that covers cup. Repeat with remaining dough and cup halves. Place balls, smooth side down, in bottom of greased 6-cup Bundt pan or 9-inch round layer-cake pan. Continue lining pan with balls of dough until all pieces are used up and the pan is full.
- 6. Place pan in COLD oven. Turn oven on to 375 degrees F. Bake for 30 to 35 minutes or until top is golden and puffed. Immediately remove bread from pan to wire rack to cool.
- 7. Glaze: Meanwhile, melt 8 mini peanut butter cups in small saucepan over very low heat. Stir in milk until smooth. Drizzle over the bread. To serve, either cut into slices or pull the pieces apart.

75. Chocolate Raspberry Quick Bread Recipe

Serving: 8 | Prep: | Cook: 50mins | Ready in:

Ingredients

- • 1 cup semisweet chocolate chips
- • 1/4 cup butter
- • 2 cups all-purpose flour
- • 1/2 cup sugar
- • 1 teaspoon baking soda
- • 1/2 teaspoon baking powder
- • 1/4 teaspoon salt
- • 1 cup finely chopped walnuts or pecans
- • 2 eggs, lighly beaten
- • 3/4 cup milk
- • 1/2 cup seedless raspberry jam
- • 1 teaspoon vanilla

Direction

- Lightly grease a 9- by 5-inch loaf pan; set aside. Preheat oven to 350°. Melt chocolate chips and butter in a small saucepan; set aside.
- In a large bowl combine flour, sugar, baking soda, baking powder and salt. Add nuts; stir well. In a separate bowl combine eggs, milk, raspberry jam, and vanilla. Beat until blended. Add melted chocolate mixture and milk mixture to the flour mixture; stir just until moistened. Pour into prepared pan.
- Bake for 50 to 60 minutes, or until a toothpick inserted in the center of the loaf comes out clean. Place the pan on a wire rack for 10 minutes, then remove the loaf to cool completely.

76. Chocolate Sticky Buns Recipe

Serving: 14 | Prep: | Cook: 25mins | Ready in:

Ingredients

- 1/4 c butter
- 1/2 c light corn syrup
- 3/4 c fimrly packed bown sugar
- 2 1/2 T and 3/4 t unsweetened Dutch-processed cocoa powder - separated
- 1/4 c chopped pecans
- 1/3 package (48 oz size) frozen bread dough, thawed
- 1 T butter, meldted
- 1 1/2 t sugar
- 1/4 t ground cinnamon

Direction

- Melt 1/4 c butter in a medium saucepan over med-low heat.
- Add corn syrup, brown sugar, and 2 1/2 T cocoa.
- Bring to boil, stiffing constantly.
- Boil for 1 minute.
- Remove from heat.
- Pour into greased 9 inch cake pan.
- Sprinkle with pecans and set aside.
- On a lightly floured surface, roll dough into a 10x14 inch rectangle.
- Brush with the 1 T melted butter.
- In a small bowl, combine sugar, remaining cocoa, and cinnamon.
- Sprinkle over melted butter.
- Roll up, jelly roll fashion, starting at long edge.
- Cut into 1-inch thick slices.
- Arrange slices over chocolate sauce in pan.
- Cover and let rise 45 minutes in warm place, or until doubled in size.
- Preheat oven to 350.
- Remove from oven and immediately invert onto serving platter.

77. Chocolate Tea Bread Recipe

Serving: 1 | Prep: | Cook: 60mins | Ready in:

Ingredients

- 1/2 cup applesauce
- 1/3 cup shortening
- 2 large eggs
- 1/3 cup water
- 1-1/2 cups all-purpose flour
- 1/3 cup baking cocoa
- 1 teaspoon baking soda
- 3/4 teaspoon salt
- 1/4 teaspoon baking powder
- 1 cup semi-sweet chocolate chips
- 1/3 cup chopped nuts, optional and of choice
- Glaze:
- 1/2 cup confectioners' sugar
- 1-2 tablespoons milk
- 1/4 teaspoon vanilla
- pinch of salt

Direction

- In a mixing bowl, combine applesauce, shortening, eggs, water and sugar.
- Beat on low speed for 30 seconds.

- In a separate bowl, combine dry ingredients.
- Gradually add to applesauce mixture.
- Beat on low for 30 seconds to 1 minute.
- Switch to high and beat for 2-1/2 minutes, scraping bowl occasionally.
- Fold in the chocolate chips and nuts.
- Pour into a greased and floured 9x5x3-inch loaf pan.
- Bake at 350° for 60-70 minutes or until cake test comes out done.
- Cool in pan 10 minutes before removing to a wire rack to cool completely.
- In a bowl, combine glaze ingredients until mixed well.
- Drizzle over warm bread.

78. Chocolate Chip Coffee Cake Recipe

Serving: 12 | Prep: | Cook: 40mins | Ready in:

Ingredients

- 1 cup sugar
- 1/2 cup butter
- 2 eggs
- 1 (8 ounce) light sour cream
- 1 tsp vanilla
- 2 cups flour
- 1 tsp baking powder
- 1/2 tsp baking soda
- 1/4 tsp salt
- 1 cup chopped nuts
- 1/2 cup sugar
- 1/2 cup packed brown sugar
- 1 (6 ounce) pkg chocolate chips
- 1 tsp cinnamon

Direction

- Combine 1 cup sugar and butter with mixer until fluffy. Add eggs and beat till combined, beat in sour cream and vanilla.
- Combine flour, powder, soda and salt. Add to beaten mixture, beating till smooth.
- In another mixing bowl, stir together the remaining ingredients.
- Evenly spread half of the batter in a greased 9 x 13 pan. Sprinkle with half the chocolate mixture. Top with remaining batter, then rest of the chocolate.
- Bake in 350 degree oven for about 40 minutes or till a toothpick inserted in the center comes out clean.
- Serve warm.

79. Chocolate Coffee Bean Ice Cream Cake

Serving: 1 | Prep: | Cook: 25mins | Ready in:

Ingredients

- 1-3/4 cups chocolate wafer crumbs (about 28 wafers)
- 1/4 cup butter, melted
- 2 quarts coffee ice cream, softened
- 1/3 cup chocolate-covered coffee beans, finely chopped
- 2-1/4 cups heavy whipping cream
- 1 cup plus 2 tablespoons confectioners' sugar
- 1/2 cup plus 1 tablespoon baking cocoa
- 1/2 teaspoon vanilla extract
- Chocolate curls and additional chocolate-covered coffee beans

Direction

- In a small bowl, combine wafer crumbs and butter; press onto the bottom and up the sides of a greased 9-in. springform pan. Freeze for 10 minutes.
- In a large bowl, combine ice cream and coffee beans; spoon over crust. Cover and freeze for 2 hours or until firm.
- In a large bowl, beat cream until it begins to thicken. Add confectioners' sugar, cocoa and

vanilla; beat until stiff peaks form. Spread over ice cream. (Pan will be full.)
- Cover and freeze for 4 hours or overnight. Remove from the freezer 10 minutes before serving. Garnish with chocolate curls and coffee beans.
- Nutrition Facts
- 1 slice (calculated without chocolate curls): 512 calories, 36g fat (20g saturated fat), 105mg cholesterol, 185mg sodium, 46g carbohydrate (34g sugars, 1g fiber), 7g protein.

80. Cinnamon Walnut Coffee Cake Recipe

Serving: 16 | Prep: | Cook: 1hours | Ready in:

Ingredients

- 1 cup flour
- 1 cup spelt flour
- 1 tsp baking soda
- 1 tsp baking powder
- pinch sea salt
- 2 tsp cinnamon
- 3/4 cup sugar
- 4 oz salted butter, room temperature
- 2 eggs
- 1 cup low-fat (not fat free) sour cream
- 1 tsp vanilla
- 1/4 cup whole milk
- 1/2 cup chopped walnuts
- 1/2 cup cinnamon chips (I used cinnamon-baking-chips.html">cinnamon Baking chips)

Direction

- Preheat the oven to 350F and grease a 9" square pan.
- In a bowl, whisk together the flours, baking soda, baking powder, salt, cinnamon and sugar. Set aside.
- In a large bowl, cream together the butter, eggs, sour cream and vanilla until well blended.

- Add half the dry ingredients, beating well, then add the milk and mix in.
- By hand, mix in the remaining dry ingredients, then fold in the walnuts and cinnamon chips.
- Spread in the pan (batter will be thick) and bake 30 minutes. Do not overbake!
- Cool in the pan before turning out and slicing.

81. Cinnamon Bread Recipe

Serving: 12 | Prep: | Cook: 50mins | Ready in:

Ingredients

- 11/2c sugar,divided
- 2tsp ground cinnamon
- 2c flour
- 11/2tsp. baking powder
- 1/2tsp salt 1 egg,beaten
- 1c milk
- 1c cooking oil

Direction

- Preheat oven to 350.
- Grease and flour a 9x5x3" loaf pan. Mix 1/2c sugar with the cinnamon; set aside in a large mixing bowl, combine the flour, baking powder, salt and remaining sugar. In a separate bowl combine the egg, milk and oil; add to the flour mixture. Stir until just moistened.
- Pour half the batter in the prepared pan. Sprinkle with half the cinnamon/sugar mixture. Repeat with remaining batter and cinnamon mixture. Draw a knife thru the batter to marble the bread.
- Bake at 350 for 45-50 mins or till toothpick inserted in center comes out clean. Cool in pan for 10 mins. Remove from pan. Cool. Wrap and store bread overnight before slicing.

82. Cinnamon Chip Pumpkin Bread Recipe

Serving: 8 | Prep: | Cook: 70mins | Ready in:

Ingredients

- 4 eggs
- 1 3/4 cups sugar
- 1 1/2 cups canned unsweetened pumpkin
- 1 cup vegetable or canola oil
- 3 cups all purpose flour
- 2 tsp baking powder
- 1 tsp baking soda
- 1 tsp ground ginger
- 1 tsp salt
- 1/4 tsp ground nutmeg
- 2 cups chopped walnuts or pecans (optional)
- 1 1/2 cups cinnamon chips

Direction

- Heat the oven to 350 degrees.
- Whisk the eggs, sugar, pumpkin, and oil in a large bowl until thoroughly blended.
- Sift the flour, baking powder, baking soda, ginger, salt, and nutmeg into the pumpkin mixture.
- Fold in the nuts, if using, and cinnamon chips.
- Divide the batter between 2 greased 8 x 4 x 2 inch pans.
- Bake for 70 minutes or until a knife inserted in the center comes out clean.
- Cool on a rack for at least 10 minutes before removing from pan.
- Cool completely before slicing.
- These can be double wrapped in plastic wrap and stored in the freezer for up to 3 months.

83. Cinnamon Cream Cheese Spirals Recipe

Serving: 32 | Prep: | Cook: 12mins | Ready in:

Ingredients

- NOTE: This is best prepared the night before, at the very minimum four hours before baking.
- 1 two lb. loaf of sliced white bread
- 1 lb. package of cream cheese at room temperature
- 2 egg yolks
- 1/2 cup of sugar
- 1/2 tsp of vanilla
- a pinch of salt
- 1 1/2 cups of light brown sugar
- 1 1/2 tsp of cinnamon
- 3 sticks of unsalted butter, melted

Direction

- Again, the night before prep is best for these little tasty toasties.
- Cut the crusts off each slice of bread and use a rolling pin to roll the bread as thin as possible.
- Beat the cream cheese, the egg yolks, the sugar, vanilla and salt until light and fluffy.
- Spread this mixture on one third of each slice of bread.
- Do not worry if the proportions don't equal out. Sometimes I have more bread left and other times there is extra cream cheese. No worries.
- Roll up the slices as tightly as you can, pressing down on the edges to seal them tight.
- Line a cookie sheet with parchment paper.
- Combine the brown sugar and cinnamon in a shallow pie plate.
- Dip each rolled up piece of bread and cream cheese into the melted butter, coating it on all sides.
- Then immediately coat it with the brown-sugar mixture.
- Put the rolls on the cookie sheet seam side down and FREEZE them for at least four hours.
- You can make them ahead and freeze them tightly wrapped for 2 months.
- When you are ready to have a delicious treat.
- Preheat the oven to 375 degrees.

- Use a sharp knife to slice each frozen roll into 3 or 4 sections.
- Return the slices to the greased or parchment-covered cookie sheet, sliced side down.
- Bake for five minutes, turn them over, and bake them for five minutes more on the other side, until lightly browned.
- Serve immediately.

84. Cinnamon Streusel Coffeecake Recipe

Serving: 24 | Prep: | Cook: 50mins | Ready in:

Ingredients

- Streusel topping
- 1 1/4 cups granulated sugar
- ¼ teaspoon salt (if you use unsalted butter)
- 1 1/2 cups King Arthur Unbleached all-purpose flour
- 1 tablespoon ground cinnamon
- 6 tablespoons butter, melted
- Filling
- 1 cup brown sugar, light or dark
- 1 1/2 tablespoons ground cinnamon
- 1 teaspoon unsweetened cocoa powder, Dutch-process or natural
- cake
- 3/4 cup butter
- 1 teaspoon salt (1 ¼ teaspoons if you use unsalted butter)
- 1 1/2 cups granulated sugar
- 1/3 cup brown sugar
- 2 1/2 teaspoons baking powder
- 2 teaspoons vanilla extract
- 3 large eggs
- 3/4 cup sour cream or plain yogurt
- 1 1/4 cups milk (anything from skim to whole)
- 3 3/4 cups King Arthur Unbleached all-purpose flour

Direction

- 1) Preheat the oven to 350°F. Lightly grease a 9" x 13" pan, or two 9" round cake pans.
- 2) Make the topping by whisking together the sugar, salt, flour, and cinnamon. Add the melted butter, stirring till well combined. Set the topping aside.
- 3) Make the filling by mixing together the brown sugar, cinnamon, and cocoa powder. Note that the cocoa powder is used strictly for color, not flavor; leave it out if you like. Set it aside.
- 4) To make the cake: In a large bowl, beat together the butter, salt, sugars, baking powder, and vanilla until well combined and smooth.
- 5) Add the eggs one at a time, beating well after each addition.
- 6) In a separate bowl, whisk together the sour cream or yogurt and milk till well combined. You don't need to whisk out all the lumps.
- 7) Add the flour to the butter mixture alternately with the milk/sour cream mixture, beating gently to combine
- 8) Pour/spread half the batter (a scant 3 cups) into the prepared pan(s), spreading all the way to the edges. If you're using two 9" round pans, spread 1 1/3 cups batter in each pan.
- 9) Sprinkle the filling evenly atop the batter
- 10) Spread the remaining batter atop the filling. Use a table knife to gently swirl the filling into the batter, as though you were making a marble cake. Don't combine filling and batter thoroughly; just swirl the filling through the batter.
- 11) Sprinkle the topping over the batter in the pan.
- 12) Bake the cake until it's a dark golden brown around the edges; medium-golden with no light patches showing on top, and a toothpick or cake tester inserted into the center comes out clean, about 55 to 60 minutes for the 9" x 13" pan, 50 to 55 minutes for the 9" round pans. When pressed gently in the middle, the cake should spring back.
- 13) Remove the cake from the oven and allow it to cool for 20 minutes before cutting and serving. Serve cake right from the pan

85. Cinnamon And Raisins Swirl Recipe

Serving: 10 | Prep: | Cook: 30mins | Ready in:

Ingredients

- 250 ml warm water
- 10 g fresh yeast
- 150 g all-purpose flour
- 200 g of strong flour
- 1 tablespoon sugar
- 4 tablespoons melted butter
- 150 g raisins
- 70 g cane sugar + 1 teaspoon
- 4 teaspoons cinnamon
- 1/2 teaspoon grated nutmeg
- 1 egg beaten

Direction

- Crumble the yeast in the kneader bowl (normal large bowl, if kneading by hand), add a pinch of sugar, and then dissolve everything with the warm water. Let it rest for 10-15 minute, until it foams.
- Add flours, sugar, and half the butter. Knead for 10 minutes on medium speed. Add raisins and knead for another 5 minutes. Form a ball and place it in an oiled bowl. Cover with plastic and let it rest until it doubles, for 1-2 hours.
- Roll out the dough in a 30x25 centimetres square. Mix cane sugar with cinnamon, nutmeg and the remaining melted butter. Brush the rolled dough with some of the beaten egg, sprinkle with the sugar-cinnamon-butter mixture and rub everything together with the back of a spoon. Roll up the dough tightly, beginning from the short side. Close the ends and lay the sausage in a buttered plum-cake pan, 22x12 centimetres. Let it rise for 30 minutes in a warm environment.
- Preheat the oven at 220° C.
- When the dough is well risen, brush it with the remaining beaten egg and a teaspoon of cane sugar. Bake for 15 minutes, then lower the temperature at 180° C and bake for another 15 minutes.
- Let it cool before to slice it.
- Warning: gives addiction.

86. Cinnamon Coffee Pecan Cake Recipe

Serving: 10 | Prep: | Cook: 60mins | Ready in:

Ingredients

- Cake:
- 1 tbsp baking powder
- 2 cups plain flour
- 1 tsp salt
- ¾ cup butter, softened
- 1 cup caster sugar
- 2 eggs
- 2 tsp instant espresso coffee, dissolved in 3 tbsp warm water
- 1 cup fresh milk
- 1 ½ cups pecans, chopped
- Topping:
- ½ cup plain flour
- 3 tbsp butter
- 1 tsp cinnamon
- ½ cup pecans, coarsely ground
- powder sugar for dusting

Direction

- Cake:
- Preheat oven to 340F and grease a 22cm cake pan.
- Sift together the baking powder, flour and salt. Set aside.
- Cream butter and sugar until light and fluffy. Add eggs and instant coffee. Alternately beat in the sifted ingredients and milk. Add Pecans, stir and pour in the pan.

- Topping:
- Combine flour and cinnamon, rub in butter and add Pecans. Mix well and sprinkle over the top. Bake for about 60 minutes. Cool before cutting. Dust with powder sugar.

87. Coconut Coffee Liqueur Cake Recipe

Serving: 12 | Prep: | Cook: 60mins | Ready in:

Ingredients

- 1   pkg. French vanilla cake mix
- 2 1/2 tsp. instant coffee granules
- 1/2   cup coffee liqueur
- 1 3/4 cups milk
- 1   large pkg. instant vanilla pudding mix
- 1 1/2 cups heavy whipping cream
- 3   Tbsp. sugar
- 3   cups flaked coconut

Direction

- In a medium bowl, add instant coffee to cake mix and prepare cake according to directions on package.
- Pour batter into 2 greased and floured 9" round cake pans.
- Bake according to instructions on package.
- Cool completely on wire racks.
- With dental floss or a large serrated knife, split each layer horizontally to make 4 layers.
- With a brush, using 1/4 cup coffee liqueur, brush it onto each of the 4 layers.
- Make the pudding accord to package directions, but use 1 3/4 cup of milk and add the remaining coffee liqueur.
- Spread 1/3 of pudding between each layer of cake as you assemble.
- Whip cream with sugar until stiff peaks form.
- Spread on top and sides of cake.
- Sprinkle with coconut.

88. Coffee Almond Cake Recipe

Serving: 20 | Prep: | Cook: 55mins | Ready in:

Ingredients

- 200 ml lo fat evaporated milk
- 3 tbsp fresh lemon juice
- 3 tbsp Nescafe Blend 37 mixed in sme hot water
- 250 g flour
- 250 caster sugar
- 1tsp bi carbonate of soda
- 1 tsp baking pwd
- 1 tsp salt
- 1/2 cup olive oil
- 1 tsp vanilla
- 2 L eggs
- handful of chopped almonds
- syrup
- 2 tbsp olive margarine
- 2 tbsp coffe pwd mixed in hot water
- 2 tbsp icing sugar
- 1 tsp vanilla essence
- 1 tbsp lo fat evaporated milk

Direction

- Preheat oven to 180 degrees.
- Mix the milk and the lemon to curdle.
- Sift the flour, salt, soda, and baking powder.
- Beat the eggs. Add the oil.
- Add the flour in 3 stages and curdled milk in 2 stages alternatively.
- Fold in 3/4 of the chopped nuts.
- Grease the cake pan and line it.
- Sprinkle the remaining 1/4 of the nuts.
- Pour the batter.
- Bake for 50 mins.
- Cool it.
- Beat the margarine, instant coffee, caster sugar and the vanilla essence and the milk.
- Pour the syrup on top which will be absorbed by the cake.

89. Coffee Cake Muffins Recipe

Serving: 12 | Prep: | Cook: 20mins | Ready in:

Ingredients

- FILLING:
- 3/4 cup brown sugar, packed
- 4 tablespoons flour
- 4 tablespoons cinnamon
- 1/2 cup nuts, finely chopped
- 4 tablespoons melted butter (no substitues please)
- Mix filling in a medium bowl, using a fork, and set aside.
- MUFFINS:
- 1 1/2 cups all-purpose flour
- 2 tablespoons baking powder
- 1/2 cup sugar
- 1/2 teaspoon salt
- 1/4 cup shortening
- 1/2 cup milk
- 1 beaten egg
- .

Direction

- Preheat oven to 350.
- For muffins, stir together dry ingredients well, using either a fork or a whisk to combine and break up any lumps.
- Cut in the shortening as you would for a pie crust.
- Mix together the beaten egg and milk.
- Pour liquid over the other ingredients and stir just until well moistened.
- Fill each muffin liner about 1/2 way with batter.
- Sprinkle some topping mixture (about a spoonful) over each.
- Fill remainders of muffins to 3/4 full.
- Top each with rest of topping, divided evenly.
- Bake at 350 for about 20 minutes, or until pick inserted comes out clean.
- (You can choose to top these with a little bit of powdered sugar icing if you wish!)

90. Coffee Cake Recipe

Serving: 4 | Prep: | Cook: 25mins | Ready in:

Ingredients

- 100 gm plain flour
- 1 1/2 tbsp instant coffee powder
- 1/2 tsp baking powder
- 40 gm dark brown sugar
- 90 ml full cream boiled milk
- 1/2 cup cream
- 5 tsp sugar
- 1 tsp cinnamon powder
- a drop vanilla essence
- 1 well beaten egg
- 75 gm butter and 1 tbsp butter to grease the tray
- 75 gm castor sugar

Direction

- Blend the instant coffee powder, vanilla essence and the boiled milk in a mixer and keep it aside.
- Sift together plain flour, baking powder and cinnamon powder. Keep it aside.
- Beat together butter, castor sugar and the dark brown sugar and then add the beaten egg and whisk the mixture.
- Then add the plain flour mixture and coffee powder mixture to it and mix them well for 3 mins at least.
- Grease the baking tray and bake in a microwave oven for 20-25 mins. (Check with a skewer, inserting to the cake mixture, till it comes out clean).
- Meanwhile blend the cream and sugar together in a mixer for a min and keep that aside.

- After the cake is made cut that into 2 halves and sandwich the sweetened cream mixture in between the cake pieces.
- Serve them with cardamom tea (since it's made of coffee powder).

91. Coffee Crisp Coffee Cake Recipe

Serving: 12 | Prep: | Cook: 2hours | Ready in:

Ingredients

- ¼ cup unsalted butter
- ½ cup granulated sugar
- 6 packets Truvia (or 1 ½ tbsp Spoonable formula)
- 1 tbsp vanilla
- 1 cup flour
- 1 cup whole wheat flour
- ¼ cup psyllium husk fibre
- 2 tsp instant espresso
- ½ tsp nutmeg
- 2 tbsp ground flax seed
- 1 tbsp baking powder
- ¾ tsp salt
- 1 ½ cups whole milk
- 12 miniature coffee Crisp bars, chopped (about 2 cups / 144g)

Direction

- Heat oven to 375°F and grease a 9-inch springform pan. Line the bottom with parchment.
- Cream the butter, sugar and Truvia until fluffy. Add the vanilla and beat well.
- Whisk together the flours, psyllium, espresso, nutmeg, flaxseed, baking powder and salt.
- Stir half the dry ingredients into the butter mixture, followed by the milk.
- Stir in the remaining dry mixture until just mixed. Fold in Coffee Crisp pieces.
- Bake 45 to 50 minutes or until tests done.
- Cool in the pan 10 minutes, then remove pan sides and cool completely on a rack.

92. Coffee Lover's Coffee Cake

Serving: 10 | Prep: | Cook: 50mins | Ready in:

Ingredients

- 1/3 cup sugar
- 4 teaspoons instant coffee granules
- 1-1/2 teaspoons ground cinnamon
- BATTER:
- 3 tablespoons butter, softened
- 1/2 cup sugar
- 1 large egg, room temperature
- 1 teaspoon vanilla extract
- 1-1/2 cups all-purpose flour
- 1 teaspoon baking powder
- 1/2 teaspoon baking soda
- 1/8 teaspoon salt
- 1 cup plain yogurt
- 2 tablespoons chopped walnuts or pecans

Direction

- Preheat oven to 350°. Mix sugar, coffee granules and cinnamon. In a large bowl, beat butter and sugar until crumbly, about 2 minutes. Beat in egg and vanilla. In another bowl, whisk together flour, baking powder, baking soda and salt; add to butter mixture alternately with yogurt, beating just until blended. (Batter will be thick.)
- Spread half of the batter evenly into a 8-in. square baking pan coated with cooking spray; sprinkle with half of the coffee mixture. Top with remaining batter; sprinkle with remaining coffee mixture. Cut through batter with a knife to swirl. Sprinkle with nuts.
- Bake until a toothpick inserted in center comes out clean, 25-30 minutes. Cool 5 minutes before serving.
- Nutrition Facts
- 1 piece: 220 calories, 6g fat (3g saturated fat), 34mg cholesterol, 207mg sodium, 37g carbohydrate (20g sugars, 1g fiber), 4g protein.

93. Coffee Marshmallow Icebox Cake Recipe

Serving: 8 | Prep: | Cook: 5mins | Ready in:

Ingredients

- 2 Tb. instant coffee granules or flakes
- 1 cup hot water
- 1/2 pound of mini marshmallows or cut large marshmallows
- 1 cup heavy cream or manufacturer's cream, whipped
- 1/2 cup heavy cream, whipped
- 18-20 lady fingers
- Topping options: chocolate curls or mini chocolate chips, coconut, chopped toasted almonds or chopped walnuts, cocoa powder, cookie or cake crumbs, toffee bits, etc!

Direction

- The Day before Serving!
- In a saucepan, dissolve 2 TB instant coffee in 1 cup of hot water.
- Add the marshmallows to the coffee mixture and stir until melted.
- Refrigerate until slightly thickened.
- Fold in 1 cup of heavy cream.
- Line the lady fingers in the bottom of a 10x8x2 or 9 inch round pan.
- Cover with half of the coffee mixture and repeat cookie and coffee layer.
- Refrigerate at least 8 hours!
- To serve:
- Top with 1/2 cup heavy whipped cream and choice of toppings and serve.
- I'm sorry that I can't provide a photograph! So if you make one in the next few days, please post it here? Thanks!

94. Coffee N Cream Strusel Cake Recipe

Serving: 8 | Prep: | Cook: 220mins | Ready in:

Ingredients

- butter flavor Cooking Spray
- parchment paper
- 1 box (16 oz.) pound cake mix (I use Betty Crocker)
- 2 large eggs
- 3/4 cup water
- 1/4 cup plus 2 tablespoons Viennese-style coffee drink mix
- 1/4 cup packed brown sugar
- Nut topping (I use walnuts)
- 1 tablespoon all-purpose flour

Direction

- Lightly coat a 6 cup soufflé dish with cooking spray. Cut parchment paper to fit the bottom of the soufflé dish. Place in soufflé dish. Coat parchment paper with cooking spray; set aside.
- In a large mixing bowl, combine cake mix, eggs water, and 1/4 cup of the coffee drink mix. Using a hand held electric mixer, beat on low speed for 3 minutes, scraping down the sides of the bowl. Pour into prepared soufflé dish.
- In a small bowl, combine the remaining 2 tablespoons of coffee drink mix, brown sugar, 1/2 cup of the nut topping, and flour. Sprinkle over top of cake batter; set aside.
- Crumple aluminum foil to create a "ring base" about 5 inches in diameter and 1 inch think. Place ring in a 5-quart slow cooker. Place soufflé dish on top of ring. Stack 8 paper towels; place on top of slow cooker to absorb moisture. Secure with lid.
- Cook on LOW heat setting for 3 to 4 hours. (Do not lift lid for the first 2 hours of cooking.)
- Transfer soufflé dish to a wire rack; cool completely. Using a thin-bladed knife, loosen edge of cake from dish. Invert onto a serving

plate. Sprinkle with additional nut topping (optional).

- 1 piece: 859 calories, 36g fat (13g saturated fat), 80mg cholesterol, 621mg sodium, 133g carbohydrate (109g sugars, 2g fiber), 5g protein.

95. Coffee Chocolate Cake

Serving: 3 | Prep: | Cook: 3mins | Ready in:

Ingredients

- 2 cups sugar
- 1 cup canola oil
- 1 cup whole milk
- 1 cup brewed coffee, room temperature
- 2 large eggs, room temperature
- 1 teaspoon vanilla extract
- 2 cups all-purpose flour
- 3/4 cup baking cocoa
- 2 teaspoons baking soda
- 1 teaspoon baking powder
- 1 teaspoon salt
- BUTTERCREAM FROSTING:
- 1 cup butter, softened
- 8 cups confectioners' sugar
- 2 teaspoons vanilla extract
- 1/2 to 3/4 cup whole milk

Direction

- In a large bowl, beat the sugar, oil, milk, coffee, eggs and vanilla until well blended. Combine the flour, cocoa, baking soda, baking powder and salt; gradually beat into sugar mixture until blended.
- Pour into 2 greased and floured 9-in. round baking pans. Bake at 325° for 25-30 minutes or until a toothpick inserted in the center comes out clean. Cool in pans for 10 minutes before removing to wire racks to cool completely.
- For frosting, in a large bowl, beat butter until fluffy. Beat in confectioners' sugar and vanilla. Add milk until frosting reaches desired consistency. Spread frosting between layers and over top and sides of cake.
- Nutrition Facts

96. Coffee Chocolate Layer Cake With Mocha Mascarpone Frosting Recipe

Serving: 12 | Prep: | Cook: 40mins | Ready in:

Ingredients

- 2 cups cake flour
- 3/4 cup natural unsweetened cocoa powder
- 1 1/2 teaspoons baking soda
- 3/4 teaspoon salt
- 3/4 cup (1 1/2 sticks) unsalted butter, room temperature
- 2 cups (packed) golden brown sugar
- 3 large eggs
- 1 1/2 teaspoons vanilla extract
- 1 cup buttermilk
- 4 teaspoons instant espresso powder dissolved in 3/4 cup hot water
- Frosting:
- 1/3 cup natural unsweetened cocoa powder
- 1 tablespoon instant espresso powder
- 1 1/2 cups chilled heavy whipping cream, divided
- 1 1/3 cups sugar
- 2 8-ounce containers chilled mascarpone cheese*
- bittersweet chocolate curls (optional)

Direction

- For cake:
- Position rack in center of oven; preheat to 325°F. Generously butter two 9-inch cake pans with 2-inch-high sides; dust with flour, tapping out any excess. Line bottom of pans with parchment paper.

- Sift 2 cups cake flour, cocoa, baking soda, and salt into medium bowl. Using electric mixer, beat butter in large bowl until smooth. Add brown sugar and beat until well blended, about 2 minutes. Add eggs 1 at a time, beating well after each addition. Mix in vanilla. Add flour mixture in 3 additions alternately with buttermilk in 2 additions, beating just until blended after each addition. Gradually add hot espresso-water mixture, beating just until smooth.
- Divide batter between pans; smooth tops. Bake cakes until tester inserted into center comes out clean, about 40 minutes. Cool cakes in pans on rack 15 minutes. Run small knife around sides of pans to loosen cakes. Invert cakes onto racks; lift pans off cakes and remove parchment. Place wire rack atop each cake; invert again so top side is up. Cool completely. DO AHEAD: Can be made 1 day ahead. Wrap each cake in plastic and store at room temperature.
- For frosting:
- Sift cocoa powder into large bowl; add espresso powder. Bring 1 cup cream to boil in small saucepan. Slowly pour cream over cocoa mixture, whisking until cocoa is completely dissolved, about 1 minute. Add 1/2 cup cream and sugar; stir until sugar dissolves. Chill until cold, at least 2 hours.
- DO AHEAD: Can be made 1 day ahead. Cover; keep chilled.
- Add mascarpone to chilled cocoa mixture. Using electric mixer, beat on low speed until blended and smooth. Increase speed to medium-high; beat until mixture is thick and medium-firm peaks form when beaters are lifted, about 2 minutes (do not overbeat or mixture will curdle).
- Using pastry brush, brush off crumbs from cakes. Place 1 cake layer, top side up, on platter. Spoon 13/4 cups frosting in dollops over top of cake. Using offset spatula, spread frosting to edges. Top with second cake layer, top side up, pressing to adhere. Spread thin layer of frosting over top and sides of cake. Chill 10 minutes. Using offset spatula, spread remaining frosting over top and sides of cake, swirling decoratively.
- Top with chocolate curls, if desired.
- DO AHEAD: Can be made 1 day ahead. Cover with cake dome; chill. Let stand at room temperature 20 minutes before serving.
- *An Italian cream cheese; sold at many supermarkets and at Italian markets.

97. Coffee Orange Fudge Cake Recipe

Serving: 10 | Prep: | Cook: 55mins | Ready in:

Ingredients

- 1 Devil's Food OR German chocolate cake mix. (18 1/4 oz)
- 1 250g container sour cream
- 1/2 cup vegetable oil
- 1/2 cup water
- 4 eggs
- 1 pkg instant chocolate fudge pudding mix (4 serving size)
- 1/4 cup coffee liqueur
- 2 tablespns fresh finely grated orange peel
- 1 teaspn ground cinnamon
- 2 cups semisweet chocolate pieces
- Confectioners sugar

Direction

- Pre-heat oven to 350. Grease & flour a 10-inch fluted tube pan & set aside
- In large mixing bowl, combine cake mix, sour cream, oil, water, eggs, pudding mix, liqueur, orange peel & cinnamon.
- Scraping sides of bowl constantly, beat with an electric mixer on low speed until blended.
- Beat on medium speed for 4 mins.
- Stir in chocolate pieces.
- Pour into prepared pan & bake in preheated oven until a toothpick inserted near the center comes out clean. 50 -60 mins

- Cool in pan on wire rack for 10 mins. Invert on wire rack to cool completely. Sprinkle with confectioners' sugar.

98. Country Blueberry Coffee Cake Recipe

Serving: 4 | Prep: | Cook: 60mins | Ready in:

Ingredients

- 1/4 cup firmly packed brown sugar
- 1 teaspoon cinnamon
- 4 Pillsbury Home Baked Classics frozen biscuits
- 2 Tablespoons butter, melted
- 1/2 cup quick cooking oats
- 3/4 cup blueberries
- 2 Tablespoons granulated white sugar
- 1 teaspoon butter, softened

Direction

- Preheat oven to 375 degrees F.
- Generously grease and 8x4 inch loaf pan (I use Pam spray).
- In small bowl, stir together brown sugar and cinnamon with fork.
- Microwave biscuits uncovered on DEFROST about 45 seconds.
- Cut each biscuit into fourths.
- Dip each piece into melted butter; coat with brown sugar mixture.
- Arrange in single layer pan.
- Top with any remaining butter and brown sugar mixture.
- Sprinkle with 1/4 cup of the oats.
- Top with blueberries.
- In medium bowl, stir together granulated sugar, remaining oats and softened butter.
- Sprinkle over blueberries
- Bake 30 - 35 minutes or until golden brown and center is done.
- Cool for 15 minutes.

- Serve warm
- Makes 4 servings, but sounds like 1 to me!!
- ***Look for the extraordinary in the ordinary
- **

99. Cowboy Coffee Cake Recipe

Serving: 12 | Prep: | Cook: 45mins | Ready in:

Ingredients

- 2 1/2 cups flour
- 2 cups brown sugar
- 1/2 tsp salt
- 2/3 cup shortening
- 2 tsp baking powder
- 1/2 tsp baking soda
- 1/2 tsp cinnamon
- 1/2 tsp nutmeg
- 1 cup sour milk
- 2 eggs

Direction

- Mix flour, sugar, salt and shortening until crumbly.
- Add powder, soda, and spices.
- Mix well.
- Add milk and eggs.
- Pour into greased, floured 9 x 13 pan.
- Bake 375 degree bake 35-45 min.

100. Cranberry Pecan Coffeecakes Recipe

Serving: 8 | Prep: | Cook: 30mins | Ready in:

Ingredients

- 3/4 cup warm water
- 1 package active dry yeast
- 3/4 cup warm milk
- 2 tablespoons honey
- 2 tablespoons vegetable oil
- 1 teaspoon salt
- 2-1/2 cups all purpose flour
- 2 cups whole wheat flour
- Filling:
- 2 tablespoons butter melted
- 1/2 cup packed light brown sugar
- 1 teaspoon ground cinnamon
- 1 cup chopped dried cranberries
- 1 cup chopped pecans toasted
- Glaze:
- 1/4 cup honey
- 1 tablespoon butter

Direction

- Place 1/4 cup warm water in large warm bowl then sprinkle in yeast and stir until dissolved.
- Add remaining water, warm milk, honey, vegetable oil, salt and 1-1/2 cups all-purpose flour.
- Blend well then stir in whole wheat flour and enough remaining flour to make soft dough.
- Knead on lightly floured surface until smooth and elastic about 8 minutes.
- Place in greased bowl turning to grease top then cover and let rise in warm place 45 minutes.
- Punch dough down then remove to lightly floured surface and divide in half.
- Roll each to rectangle and transfer to two greased baking sheets and brush with melted butter.
- In small bowl combine brown sugar, cinnamon, cranberries and pecans then stir well.
- Sprinkle half of the brown sugar mixture over center third of each rectangle.
- Along each side of coffeecake cut 1" wide strips from edge of filling to edge of dough.
- Starting at one end alternately fold six strips from each side across filling toward opposite end.
- Repeat from other end using six strips from each side.
- Loosely tie together remaining two center strips on top of loaf.
- Repeat with second coffeecake.
- Cover and let rise in warm draft free place until almost doubled in size about 40 minutes.
- Bake at 375 for 25 minutes and switch positions of sheets halfway through baking.
- Remove from sheets and cool on wire racks then brush with glaze.
- To make glaze stir 1/4 cup honey and 1 tablespoon butter over medium heat until butter melts.

101. Cranberry Sauce Coffee Cake Recipe

Serving: 12 | Prep: | Cook: 25mins | Ready in:

Ingredients

- 2 cups biscuit/baking mix (Bisquick, for example)
- 2 tbsp. sugar
- 2/3 cup milk
- 1 egg, lightly beaten
- 2/3 cup jellied cranberry sauce
- Topping:
- 1/2 cup chopped walnuts
- 1/2 cup packed brown sugar
- 1/2 tsp. ground cinnamon
- Glaze:
- 1 cup confectioners' sugar
- 2 tbsp. milk
- 1/4 tsp. vanilla extract

Direction

- Preheat oven to 400 F.
- In a large bowl, combine the biscuit mix, sugar, milk and egg. Pour into a greased 8 " square baking dish. Drop cranberry sauce by teaspoonfuls over batter.

- Combine topping ingredients; sprinkle over cranberry sauce. Bake at 400 for 18 to 23 minutes or until a toothpick inserted near the centre comes out clean. Cool on a wire rack.
- In a small bowl, combine the glaze ingredients; drizzle over the cake.

102. Cranberry Vanilla Coffee Cake Recipe

Serving: 10 | Prep: | Cook: 47mins | Ready in:

Ingredients

- 1/2 vanilla bean, split lengthwise
- 1 3/4 cups sugar
- 2 cups fresh OR thawed frozen cranberries
- 2 cups plus 1 tablespoon all purpose flour, divided
- 2 teaspoons baking powder
- 3/4 teaspoon salt
- 1 stick plus 1 tablespoon unsalted butter, softened and divided
- 2 large eggs
- 1/2 cup whole milk
- confectioners' sugar for dusting

Direction

- Preheat oven to 375 degrees F. with rack in middle.
- Generously butter a 9x2" round cake pan and line with parchment, then butter parchment.
- Scrape seeds from vanilla bean into a food processor.
- Add sugar and pulse to combine.
- Transfer mixture to a bowl.
- Pulse cranberries with 1/2 cup vanilla sugar in processor until finely chopped NOT pureed.
- Whisk together 2 cups flour, baking powder and salt.
- Beat together 1 stick butter and 1 cup vanilla sugar in bowl with electric mixer at medium-high speed until pale and fluffy.
- Add eggs one at a time, beating well after each addition.
- Scrape down sides of bowl.
- Reduce speed to low and mix in flour mixture and milk alternately in batches, beginning and ending with flour, until just combined.
- Spread half of batter in pan.
- Spoon cranberries over batter, leaving 1/2" border at edges.
- Spoon small bits of remaining batter over the cranberries.
- Smooth gently.
- Using your fingertips, blend remaining 1/4 cup vanilla sugar with remaining tablespoon butter and flour.
- Crumble over the top of the cake.
- Bake 45 to 50 minutes OR until cake tests done with toothpick into CAKE part of cake OR until cake begins to pull away from the pan.
- Remove from oven.
- Cool in pan for 30 minutes.
- Remove cake from pan and cool completely, crumb side up.

103. Cream Cheese Braids Recipe

Serving: 20 | Prep: | Cook: 15mins | Ready in:

Ingredients

- DOUGH:
- 1 cup sour cream
- 1/2 cup sugar
- 1 tsp. salt
- 1/2 c. melted butter
- 2 pkgs. dry yeast
- 1/2 c. warm water
- 2 beaten eggs
- 4 c. flour
- FILLING:
- 2 (8oz.) pkgs. cream cheese
- 3/4 c. sugar
- 1 beaten egg

- 1/8 tsp. salt
- 2 tsps. vanilla
- GLAZE:
- 2 c. powdered sugar
- 4 Tbsp. evaporated milk
- 2 tsp. vanilla

Direction

- Heat sour cream over low heat, stir in sugar, salt and butter; cool to lukewarm.
- Sprinkle yeast over warm water in large bowl, stirring until yeast is dissolved.
- Add sour cream mixture, eggs, and flour, mix well.
- Cover tightly and refrigerate overnight.
- Next day, divide dough into 4 parts, roll out each on floured surface into a 12" x 8" rectangle.
- Make filling, creaming the cheese and sugar together, then adding the egg, salt, and vanilla.
- Spread 1/4 of filling on each rectangle, roll up in jelly roll fashion, beginning at long end. Pinch edges and fold ends under. Place rolls seam side down on greased baking sheets.
- Using a sharp knife, make about 4 X shaped cuts on top of each roll. Cuts should be about 2/3 the way into the roll.
- Cover and let rise in a warm place about an hour until doubled.
- Bake at 375 for about 15 min. - just until light golden brown.
- Combine all glaze ingredients, and spread over warm braids.
- A bit of almond flavoring in the filling and glaze really spiffs up the flavor!

104. Cream Cheese Coffee Cake Recipe

Serving: 12 | Prep: | Cook: 25mins | Ready in:

Ingredients

- 1 cup sour cream
- 1/2 cup sugar
- 1/2 cup butter or margarine
- 1 teaspoon salt
- 2 packages active dry yeast
- 1/2 cup warm water
- 2 eggs, beaten
- 4 cups flour
- Filling:
- 2 packages cream cheese - softened, (8 ounces)
- 3/4 cup splenda
- 1 egg - beaten
- 2 teaspoons vanilla
- 1/8 teaspoon salt
- Glaze:
- 2 1/2 cups confectioner's sugar
- 1/4 cup milk
- 1 teaspoon vanilla
- sliced almonds, toasted

Direction

- In a saucepan, combine sour cream, sugar, butter and salt.
- Cook over medium-low heat, stirring constantly for 5 to 10 minutes or until well blended. Cool to room temperature. In a mixing bowl, dissolve yeast in water. Add sour cream mixture and eggs, mix well.
- Gradually stir in flour. (Dough will be very soft.) Cover and refrigerate overnight.
- Next day, combine filling ingredients in a mixing bowl until well blended. Turn dough onto a floured board, knead 5 to 6 times. Divide into four equal portions. Roll each portion into a 12 x 8- inch rectangle.
- Spread 1/4 of the filling on each to within 1 inch of edges. Roll up jelly-roll style from long side; pinch seams and ends to seal. Place, seam side down, on greased baking sheet. Cut six 'x's on top of loaves.
- Cover and let rise until nearly doubled, about 1 hour. Bake at 375 degrees Fahrenheit for 20 to 25 minutes or until golden brown. Cool on wire racks. Combine the first three glaze ingredients, drizzle over loaves. Sprinkle with almonds if desired. Store in refrigerator.

105. Creamy Blueberry Coffeecake Recipe

Serving: 8 | Prep: | Cook: 60mins | Ready in:

Ingredients

- 1 cup plus 2 teaspoons butter softened divided
- 1-3/4 cup granulated sugar divided
- 3 eggs
- 3-1/4 cup all-purpose flour divided
- 2 teaspoons baking powder
- 1 teaspoon vanilla extract
- 1 can blueberry pie filling
- 1 teaspoon ground cinnamon

Direction

- Preheat the oven to 350.
- Coat a rectangular baking dish with non-stick cooking spray.
- In a large bowl cream together 1 cup of the butter and 1-1/2 cups of the sugar.
- Add eggs one at a time.
- Add 3 cups of the flour, baking powder and vanilla and mix well.
- Spread half the batter in the baking dish then using a wet knife spread the pie filling even over batter then dollop remaining batter over pie filling and spread with a wet knife almost covering the pie filling.
- In a small bowl mix together with a fork the remaining flour, sugar and butter then stir in cinnamon until crumbly.
- Sprinkle over the batter and bake 1 hour.
- Cool in the baking dish on a wire cooling rack then cut and serve.

106. Creamy Mascarpone And Raspberry Coffee Cake Recipe

Serving: 12 | Prep: | Cook: 50mins | Ready in:

Ingredients

- 1 8-ounce package mascarpone or cream cheese, softened
- ½ cup margarine or butter
- 1 ¾ cups all-purpose flour (I used spelt flour), divided
- 1 cup sugar
- 2 eggs
- ¼ cup milk
- 1 tsp baking powder
- ½ tsp baking soda
- ½ tsp vanilla
- ½ cup seedless red raspberry OR strawberry preserves
- powdered sugar OR more preserves for garnishing (optional)

Direction

- Grease a 13x9x2 inch baking pan; set aside.
- In a large mixing bowl beat Mascarpone or cream cheese and margarine or butter with an electric mixer on medium to high speed about 30 seconds or till combined.
- Add about HALF of the flour to the cream cheese mixture. Then add the sugar, eggs, milk, baking powder, baking soda and vanilla. Beat on low speed till thoroughly combined, scrapping the sides of the bowl. Beat on medium speed for 2 minutes. Then beat in remaining flour on low speed JUST TILL COMBINED.
- Spread batter evenly in the prepared pan. Dollop preserves in small spoonfuls on top of the batter. Using a small narrow spatula or knife, gently swirl preserves into the batter to create a marbled effect.
- Bake in a 350°F oven for 30 to 35 minutes or till a wooden toothpick inserted near the center comes out clean. Cool in the pan on a wire rack for 15 minutes.
- Sift powdered sugar or preserves over the top. Cut into squares and serve warm or cooled.
- CREAM CHEESE AND RASPBERRY RING (my option as seen above):

- Prepare cake as directed, except spread HALF of the batter in a greased and floured 6-cup fluted tube pan. Dollop with HALF of the preserves. Repeat with remaining batter and preserves. Swirl as directed.
- Bake in a 350°F oven about 50 minutes or till a wooden toothpick inserted near the center comes out clean.
- Cool in the pan on a wire rack for 10 minutes. Loosen and invert the coffee cake onto the wire rack; cool completely.
- Sift powdered sugar or preserves over the top. Serve warm or cooled.

107. Creamy Peach Kuchen Recipe

Serving: 8 | Prep: | Cook: 35mins | Ready in:

Ingredients

- 2 cups sifted flour
- 1/4 cup granulated sugar
- 1/2 teaspoon salt
- 1/4 teaspoon baking powder
- 16 peach halves
- 4 egg yolks
- 2 cup heavy cream or sour cream
- 1/2 cup butter
- 1-1/2 cup sugar
- 1-1/2 teaspoon cinnamon

Direction

- Sift flour, sugar, salt and baking powder into bowl. Cut in butter using pastry blender until consistency of cornmeal. Pack into an ungreased rectangular pan pressing against bottom and up sides about 1". Arrange peach halves cut side up in rows. Into a small bowl combine the 1-1/4 cup sugar with the cinnamon. Sprinkle sugar evenly over the fruit and bake at 400 for 15 minutes. In small bowl beat egg yolks then stir in the cream. Remove kuchen from oven and pour cream mixture evenly over fruit and return to oven for 30 minutes. Remove from oven and cool in pan.

108. Crescent Carmel Swirl Recipe

Serving: 8 | Prep: | Cook: 55mins | Ready in:

Ingredients

- 1/2 cup butter (do not use margarine)
- 1/2 cup chopped nuts
- 3/4 cup firmly packed brown sugar
- 1 tablespoon water
- 2 (8-oz.) cans Pillsbury® Refrigerated Crescent Dinner Rolls

Direction

- Heat oven to 350°F. Melt butter in small saucepan. Coat bottom and sides of 12-cup fluted tube cake pan with 2 tablespoons of the melted butter; sprinkle pan with 3 tablespoons of the nuts. Add remaining nuts, brown sugar and water to remaining melted butter. Bring to a boil, stirring occasionally. Boil 1 minute, stirring constantly.
- Remove dough from cans; do not unroll. Cut each long roll into 8 slices. Arrange 8 slices, cut side down, in nut-lined pan; separate layers of each pinwheel slightly. Spoon half of brown sugar mixture over dough. Place remaining 8 dough slices alternately over bottom layer. Spoon remaining brown sugar mixture over slices.
- Bake at 350°F. for 23 to 33 minutes or until deep golden brown. Cool 3 minutes. Invert onto serving platter or waxed paper. Serve warm.

109. Crunch Topped Spice Cake Recipe

Serving: 9 | Prep: | Cook: 45mins | Ready in:

Ingredients

- 1/4 cup softened butter
- 1/4 cup low-fat cream cheese, softened
- 1/3 cup brown sugar
- 1 egg
- 1 tbsp vanilla
- 1 cup whole wheat flour
- 1/2 cup all purpose flour
- 1/4 tsp salt
- 1/2 tbsp baking powder
- 1 tsp baking soda
- 1 tbsp cinnamon
- 1 tsp allspice
- 1/4 tsp black pepper
- 2 tbsp ground flaxseed
- 1 cup buttermilk
- 2 tbsp crunchy granola

Direction

- Preheat oven to 350F, grease a 9" square pan.
- In a bowl, cream together butter, cheese, sugar, egg and vanilla.
- Stir in the dry ingredients, followed by the buttermilk, until a thick, smooth batter is formed.
- Spread in the prepared pan and top with granola.
- Bake 40-45 minutes, until tests done. Cool completely in the pan.

110. Danish Pastry Dough Recipe

Serving: 36 | Prep: | Cook: 20mins | Ready in:

Ingredients

- active dry yeast ½ oz (15 g)
- AP flour 1 lb 4 oz (600 g)
- Granulated sugar 4 oz (120 g)
- water, warm 4 fl oz (120 ml)
- milk, warm 4 fl oz (120 ml)
- eggs, room temperature 2 (2)
- salt 1 t (5 ml)
- vanilla extract 1 t (5 ml)
- cinnamon, ground ½ t (2 ml)
- unsalted butter, melted 1 ½ oz (45 g)
- unsalted butter, cold 1 lb (450 g)
- egg wash   as needed

Direction

- In a large bowl, stir together the yeast and 12 ounces of the flour (340 g). Add the sugar, water, milk eggs, salt, vanilla, cinnamon and melted butter. Stir until well combined.
- Add the remaining flour gradually, kneading the dough by hand or with a mixer fitted with a dough hook. Knead until the dough is smooth and only slightly tacky to the touch, approximately 2-3 minutes.
- Place the dough in a bowl that has been lightly dusted with flour. Cover and refrigerate for 1 to 1 ½ hours.
- Prepare the remaining butter while the dough is chilling. Start by sprinkling flour over the work surface and placing the cold butter on the flour (I do this on a marble slab). Then pound the butter with a rolling pin until the butter softens. Using a pastry scraper or the heel of your hand, knead the butter and flour until the mixture is spreadable. The butter should still be cold. If it begins to melt refrigerate it until firm. Keep the butter chilled until the dough is ready.
- On a lightly flour surface roll out the dough into a large rectangle. About ½ inch (1.2 centimeters) thick. Brush away excess flour.
- Spread the butter evenly over two thirds of the dough. Fold the unbuttered third over the center. Then fold the buttered third over the top. Press the edges together to seal in the butter.
- Roll the dough into a rectangle about 12 inches by 18 inches (30 centimeters by 45

centimeters). Fold the dough into thirds as before. This rolling and folding is called a turn and must be done a total of 6 times. Chill the dough between turns as necessary. After the final turn wrap the dough well and refrigerate for at least 4 hours or overnight.

- This recipe makes approximately 2 lbs. of dough. Use for Danish or anything else your heart desires. Makes about 36 Danish. If making Danish brush with egg wash before baking.

111. Delicious N Healthy Amish Rolled Oats Cake Recipe

Serving: 6 | Prep: | Cook: 40mins | Ready in:

Ingredients

- AMISH rolled oats cake
- 1 c. oats
- 1 1/4 c. boiling water
- 1/2 c. shortening
- 1 c. white sugar
- 1 c. brown sugar
- 2 eggs
- 1 tsp. vanilla
- 1 1/2 c. flour
- 1 tsp. soda
- 1/2 tsp. baking powder
- 1 tsp. cinnamon
- 1/2 tsp. nutmeg
- ~~~~~~~~~~~~~~~~~~~~~~~~~~~~~~~~
- TOPPING
- Mix well! (and use on warm cake)
- 4 tbsp. butter
- 1/2 c. brown sugar
- 1/2 c. milk
- Boil 7 minutes.
- Add 1/2 cup coconut and 1/2 cup nuts.

Direction

- Mix oats and boiling water; let stand 20 minutes.
- Cream together shortening, sugar, eggs, vanilla and add cooled oats with dry ingredients.
- Bake at 350 degrees for 35 minutes.
- 8 x 8" pan
- ~~~~~~~~~~~~~~~~~~~~~~~~~~~~~~~~
- TOPPING
- (SEE ABOVE PLEASE)

112. Easy Caramel Pecan Coffee Cake Recipe

Serving: 8 | Prep: | Cook: 25mins | Ready in:

Ingredients

- cooking spray
- 1 3/4 cup flour
- 2 envelopes rapid rise yeast
- 1 tbsp sugar
- 3/4 cup very warm water.
- 2 tbsp butter, melted
- Topping:
- 1/4 cup sugar
- 1 tsp cinnamon
- caramel pecan Topping:
- 1/3 cup light corn syrup
- 1/3 cup brown sugar
- 2 tbsp butter, melted
- 1/2 cup chopped pecans

Direction

- Mix batter ingredients in a pre-sprayed 9 1/2 inch deep dish pie plate. Stir together corn syrup, brown sugar and butter in a small bowl. Combine cinnamon and sugar topping in a small bowl.
- Top batter evenly with cinnamon sugar topping. Spoon caramel pecan topping evenly over the batter.

- Bake by placing in a COLD oven, set temp to 350 degrees. Bake 25 minutes, until lightly browned and firm in center.
- Serve warm.

113. Easy Delicious Apple Coffee Cake Recipe

Serving: 8 | Prep: | Cook: 40mins | Ready in:

Ingredients

- 1 box yellow cake mix
- 1 can apple pie filling
- 2 tablespoons oil
- 2 eggs
- 1 cup coarsely chopped toastED pecans
- brown sugar to sprinkle top

Direction

- In large bowl, mix all ingredients, (except pecans and brown sugar), by hand (a wooden spoon is perfect).
- Pour into a greased casserole dish.
- May use an 8 X 12 OR a 9 X 13, a thicker coffee cake with the 8 X 12 and a thinner one with the 9 X 13.
- Sprinkle top with the toasted pecans.
- Sprinkle brown sugar over top of toasted pecans.
- Bake at 350 degrees for 40-45 minutes.
- This is delicious, and I have already made it.
- Please read the alterations, thanks.

114. Easy Raspberry Cheese Danish Recipe

Serving: 6 | Prep: | Cook: 25mins | Ready in:

Ingredients

- 2 rolls of crescent roll dough
- 2 packages of room temperature cream cheese
- 1/2 cup of sugar
- 1/2 tsp of vanilla extract
- 1/2 tsp of fresh grated orange rind
- 1/2 cup of seedless raspberry jam, nuked 20 percent power/3 minutes
- 1 egg beaten
- 1 cup of confectioner's sugar
- 2 tsp of milk
- 1/2 tsp of fresh grated orange rind

Direction

- Preheat oven to 360 degrees (my oven needs to be calibrated).
- Line a 13 x 9 pan with one can of crescent rolls.
- Pinch seams to seal.
- Whip the cream cheese with the sugar, vanilla and the first part of the orange rind.
- Spread over the crescents leaving a small border.
- Melt jam, cool slightly, spread over the cream cheese mixture.
- Top with the other tube of crescent dough (I rolled it out on my cutting board to seal the edges, measure 13 x 9 approx. and rolled it over the rolling pin to transfer over the filing.)
- Beat egg, brush top of dough.
- Bake for 25 minutes until lightly golden.
- Allow to cool 15 minutes.
- While it cools, sift confectioner's sugar, add orange rind and milk to glazing consistency. Drizzle over cooled cheese crescents.
- Cut in squares and serve.

115. Emilys Half In And Half Out Coffee Cake Recipe

Serving: 6 | Prep: | Cook: 20mins | Ready in:

Ingredients

- Ingredients Cake:

- 1 cup milk
- 1 egg, beaten
- 1/4 cup butter, melted
- 2 cups flour
- 3 teaspoons baking powder
- 1 teaspoon salt
- 3 Tablespoons sugar
- Topping:
- 1/4 cup butter, melted
- 1 cup brown sugar
- 1/2 cup walnuts or pecans
- 1/2 teaspoon cinnamon
- 1/2 teaspoon cloves

Direction

- Preheat oven to 350 degrees (375 if your altitude is 5,000 feet or more) and grease and flour an 8- or 9-inch cake-type pan. (I use a pretty ceramic dish.)
- Measure dry cake ingredients into sifter. In a mixing bowl, mix wet cake ingredients (milk, egg, and butter). Sift the dry ingredients into the wet, and just mix until blended. In a separate bowl, mix the topping ingredients.
- Spread the cake mixture into the baking dish. Swirl 1/2 of the topping into the cake (as you would a marble cake). Spread the remaining 1/2 of the topping over the top of the cake. Bake until lightly browned, about 20 to 25 minutes.
- Serves: 6 to 8

116. Filled Coffee Ring Recipe

Serving: 10 | Prep: | Cook: 22mins | Ready in:

Ingredients

- 1 package dry yeast
- 1 cup warm water (105 to 115 degrees)
- 4 tablespoons sugar
- 2 tablespoons shortening
- 1 egg
- 3/4 teaspoon salt
- 3 to 3 1/2 cup bread flour, divided

Direction

- Dissolve yeast in warm water in a large bowl.
- Add sugar, shortening, egg, salt, and half the flour; beat at low speed of electric mixer until smooth.
- Stir in enough of remaining flour to make soft dough.
- Place dough in a greased bowl, turning to grease top.
- Cover and let rise in a warm place, free of drafts, 1 hour or until double in bulk, or cover and refrigerate up to 5 days.
- Punch dough down; turn out onto lightly floured surface, and knead 4 or 5 times. Shape and bake as directed
- Filled Coffee Ring
- 1 recipe Basic Roll Dough
- 2 tablespoons butter or margarine, melted
- 1/2 cup raisins
- 1/2 cup chopped pecans
- 1/3 cup sugar
- 1 teaspoon ground cinnamon
- 1 cup sifted powdered sugar
- 1 1/2 tablespoons milk
- Roll dough into a 21 x 7-inch rectangle on a lightly floured surface.
- Brush with butter evenly over dough, leaving a 1-inch margin.
- Roll up dough, jellyroll fashion, beginning at long side; pinch edges to seal. Place roll on a large, greased baking sheet, seam side down; shape into a ring, and pinch ends together to seal.
- Using kitchen shears, make cuts in dough every inch around ring, cutting two-thirds of the way through roll at each cut. Gently turn each piece of dough on its side, slightly overlapping slices. Cover, let rise in warm place, free from drafts for 45 minutes or doubled.
- Bake at 375 for 20 to 25 minutes or until golden brown. Transfer to a wire rack. Combine powdered sugar and milk; drizzle over bread while warm.

- Yield: 1 Coffee Cake

117. Four Seaons Chocolate Cake With Coffee Cream Frosting Recipe

Serving: 10 | Prep: | Cook: 25mins | Ready in:

Ingredients

- 1/2 - cup unsweetened cocoa powder
- 1 - tablespoon instant coffee powder
- 1/2 - cup hot water
- 1/2 - milk
- 13/4 - cups cake flour
- 1/2 - teaspoon baking powder
- 1 - teaspoon baking soda
- 1/2 - cup butter
- 11/4 - cups sugar
- 2 - eggs
- 1/2 teaspoon vanilla
- coffee Cream Frosting:
- 1 - tablespoon instant coffee powder
- 1 - tablespoon Creme de Cacao
- 1 - cup chilled all-purpose cream
- 1/4 - cup confectioners' or powdered sugar
- Topping:
- sliced fresh kiwi, stawberries, orange, or any fruit in season.

Direction

- Preheat oven to 350F, Grease and line two 9-inch round layer pans. Set aside.
- Dissolve cocoa powder and coffee in hot water. Add milk then set aside. In another bowl, combine cake flour, baking powder and baking soda. Set aside.
- Cream butter and sugar until light and fluffy. Add eggs, one at a time, beating well after each addition. Stir in vanilla. Add the flour mixture alternately with the liquid ingredients into the creamed mixture. Pour into prepared pans and bake for 20-25 minutes or until toothpick inserted in the center of the cake comes out clean. Coll. Prepare frosting.
- In a bowl, combine instant coffee, crème de cacao and all-purpose cream. Whip until stiff and double in volume. Fold in the confectioners' sugar.
- To Assemble: Put the first layer of cake on a platter. Spread come of the coffee cream frosting over the cake then top with half of the fresh fruits. Put second cake layer. Top with remaining coffee cream and fruits. Chill before serving.

118. French Roast Coffee Cake Recipe

Serving: 10 | Prep: | Cook: 40mins | Ready in:

Ingredients

- ¼ cup dark brown sugar
- 2 tbsp sugar
- 2 tsp cinnamon
- 2 tsp instant French vanilla flavoured coffee
- ½ tsp water
- ½ cup cultured unsalted butter, softened (no substitutes)
- 2/3 cup dark brown sugar
- 2 large eggs
- 1 tbsp vanilla
- ¼ cup brewed French roast coffee
- 2/3 cup light sour cream
- 1/3 cup non-fat vanilla yogurt
- 1 cup all-purpose flour
- 1 cup cake flour
- 1 tsp baking soda
- 1 tsp baking powder

Direction

- Preheat oven to 350F. Grease and flour a 9" spring-form pan.
- Mix brown sugar, sugar, cinnamon, coffee and water, set aside.

- In large bowl cream butter and sugar until fluffy.
- Beat in eggs, vanilla, coffee, sour cream, and yogurt.
- In a separate bowl, combine all dry ingredients then add to cream mixture.
- Pour half of batter followed by half the cinnamon-sugar mixture.
- Pour remainder of batter then top with remaining cinnamon-sugar.
- Rest cake for 10 minutes.
- Bake 40 minutes.

119. Fruit Filled Coffee Cake Recipe

Serving: 15 | Prep: | Cook: 50mins | Ready in:

Ingredients

- __Preheat oven 350*
- 4 cups apples, apricots, peaches, chopped pineapple or whole berries
- 1 c. water
- 2 tablespoons lemon juice
- 1 1/4 cups sugar
- 1/3 cups cornstarch
- _____
- 3 cups all-purpose flour
- 1 cup sugar
- 1 tablespoon baking powder
- 1 teaspoon salt
- 1 teaspoon ground cinnamon
- 1 cup butter (softened)
- 2 eggs, slightly beaten
- 1 cup milk
- 1 teaspoon vanilla
- _____
- 1/2 cups sugar
- 1/2 cups all-purpose flour
- 1/4 cups butter or marg.(softened)

Direction

- In a saucepan, combine choice of fruit and the water.
- Simmer, covered, about 5 minutes or until fruit is tender.
- Stir in lemon juice.
- Mix the 1-1/4 cups sugar and cornstarch; stir into fruit mixture.
- Cook and stir until thickened and bubbly.
- Cool.
- _____
- In a mixing bowl, stir together the flour, sugar, baking powder, salt, and cinnamon.
- Cut in the 1 cup butter or margarine until mixture resembles fine crumbs. Combine eggs, milk, and vanilla.
- Add to flour mixture, mixing until blended.
- Spread half of the batter into a greased 9x13 baking pan or two 8x8 baking pans.
- _____
- Spread the cooled fruit mixture over the batter.
- Spoon the remaining batter in small mounds over the fruit mixture, spreading out as much as possible.
- _____
- Combine the 1/2 cup sugar and 1/2 cup flour.
- Cut in the 1/4 cup butter until mixture resembles coarse crumbs. Sprinkle mixture over batter in pan.
- Bake 45-50 minutes for a 9x13 pan or 40-45 minutes for the two 8x8 pans, or until cake tests done.
- Cool (or not).

120. Fruity Coffee Cake Recipe

Serving: 18 | Prep: | Cook: 25mins | Ready in:

Ingredients

- 3 1/3 cups reduced-fat buttermilk baking mix
- 1/2 cup sugar
- 3 tablespoons unsalted butter or margarine

- 2/3 cup fat-free egg substitute
- 1/2 cup skim milk
- 1 teaspoon vanilla extract
- 1/2 teaspoon almond extract
- 1 cup spreadable fruit (strawberry, raspberry, blueberry, etc)
- 1/2 cup confectioners sugar

Direction

- Preheat the oven to 350 degrees F. Spray a 15×10 inch jelly-roll pan with non-stick cooking spray.
- In a large bowl, combine the baking mix and sugar. With a pastry blender, cut in the margarine until the mixture resembles coarse crumbs. Add the egg substitute, milk, and the extracts; with a wooden spoon, stir until just combined.
- Spread two-thirds of the batter into the pan and smooth the top. Spoon the spreadable fruit evenly over the batter. Drop the remaining batter by tablespoonfuls evenly over the fruit. Bake until light brown and a toothpick inserted in the center comes out clean, about 25 minutes. Cool in the pan on a rack for 10 minutes.
- Meanwhile, whisk the confectioners' sugar with 1 tablespoon of water until smooth. Drizzle evenly over the top of the cake while it is still warm.

121. GORILLA BREAD Recipe

Serving: 8 | Prep: | Cook: 30mins | Ready in:

Ingredients

- Ingredients
- 1/2 cup granulated sugar
- 3 tsp cinnamon or more depending on your taste
- 1/2 cup butter (1 stick)
- 1 cup packed brown sugar
- 1 package 8 oz cream cheese
- 2 cans 12 oz 10 count refrigerated biscuit
- 1 1/2 cup coarsely chopped walnuts or pecans

Direction

- Preheat oven to 350 degrees.
- Spray a Bundt pan with non-stick cooking spray.
- Mix the granulated sugar and cinnamon.
- In a saucepan, melt the butter and brown sugar over low heat, stirring well; set aside.
- Cut the cream cheese into 20 equal cubes. Press the biscuits out with your fingers and sprinkle each with 1/2 teaspoon of cinnamon sugar. Place a cube of cream cheese in the center of each biscuit, wrapping and sealing the dough around the cream cheese.
- Sprinkle 1/2 cup of the nuts into the bottom of the Bundt pan. Place half of the prepared biscuits in the pan. Sprinkle with cinnamon sugar, pour half of the melted butter mixture over the biscuits, and sprinkle on 1/2 cup of nuts.
- Layer the remaining biscuits on top, sprinkle with the remaining cinnamon sugar, pour the remaining butter mixture over the biscuits, and sprinkle with the remaining 1/2 cup of nuts.
- Bake for 30 minutes. Remove from the oven and cool for 5 minutes.
- Place a plate on top and invert. Make a pot of drip some coffee and share.

122. Ginger Ale Pumpkin Bread Recipe

Serving: 10 | Prep: | Cook: 55mins | Ready in:

Ingredients

- 2 cups all-purpose flour
- 1 cup whole wheat flour
- 2 teaspoons baking powder
- 1/4 teaspoon salt

- 1 tsp pumpkin pie spice
- 3 tablespoons vegetable oil
- 1/4 cup brown sugar
- 1/2 cup pumpkin puree
- 1/2 tsp fresh grated ginger
- 1 1/2 cups ginger ale (not diet)

Direction

- Preheat oven to 350F, grease a 9×5" loaf pan.
- Whisk together flours, baking powder, salt, and pumpkin pie spice.
- In a large bowl, beat together oil, brown sugar, pumpkin and fresh ginger.
- Add the flour mixture and stir briefly, then pour in the ginger ale and mix until just combined.
- Bake 55-60 minutes, until tests done. Cool 10 minutes in pan before unmoulding onto a rack and cooling completely.

123. Ginger Strawberry Raspberry Coffee Cake Recipe

Serving: 12 | Prep: | Cook: 30mins | Ready in:

Ingredients

- 1 cup butter, softened
- 2 cups sugar
- 2 eggs
- 1 cup sour cream
- 1 teaspoon vanilla extract
- 1 1/2 cup flour + 2 tablespoons, divided
- 1 teaspoon baking powder
- 1/4 teaspoon kosher salt
- 1/2 cup Fresh or frozen raspberries
- 1 cup Fresh or frozen strawberries, cut in to chunks
- 2 tablespoons Crystalized ginger chunks
- 1/2 cup brown sugar (For Streusel)
- 1 cup chopped pecans (For Streusel)
- 4 tbls butter, softened (For Streusel)
- 2 tbls flour (For Streusel)
- 2 tbls Crystalized ginger chunks (For Streusel)

Direction

- Preheat oven to 350°.
- Line 9x13 inch cake pan with Parchment paper. (Alternatively can grease and flour pan)
- Mix streusel ingredients together in a small bowl, set aside.
- Stir together the 1 1/2 cups of flour, baking powder and salt in a small bowl. Set aside.
- Cream Butter and Sugar together until fluffy.
- Add eggs one at a time to Butter mixture.
- Mix Sour Cream and Vanilla in to butter mixture.
- Stir flour mixture in to Butter mixture, until just combined
- Toss fruit in remaining 2 tbsp. flour, and stir in to batter.
- Pour batter in to parchment lined pan.
- Top with Streusel.
- Bake for 30 minutes, or until golden.
- Cool on wire rack.

124. Gooey Butter Coffee Cake Recipe

Serving: 10 | Prep: | Cook: 40mins | Ready in:

Ingredients

- 1 (16 oz) box pound cake mix
- 4 eggs, divided
- 1/2 cup butter, melted
- 1 (16 oz) box powdered sugar
- 1 (8 oz) package cream cheese softened
- 1 1/2 Tbsp vanilla

Direction

- Preheat oven to 300*.
- Combine cake mix, 2 eggs, and the butter.
- Pour into a well-greased 8 x 12 baking pan.
- Reserve 2 Tbsps. of sugar.

- Combine cream cheese, vanilla remaining eggs and sugar; mix well.
- Spread over batter.
- Bake 15 minutes.
- Remove from oven; Sprinkle removed sugar on top. Return to oven.
- Continue to bake for 25 minutes.
- Serve warm or cool on rack.

125. Grandma Janes Buttery Cinnamon Rolls Made With A Cake Mix Recipe

Serving: 24 | Prep: | Cook: 30mins | Ready in:

Ingredients

- Rolls:
- 1 package of a yellow cake mix (no pudding in the mix)
- 5 C. all-purpose flour
- 2 packages (1/4 ounce each) active dry yeast
- 2 1/2 C. hot water
- Grated orange peel to taste *optional but recommended
- butter softened about 2 sticks
- ground cinnamon to taste
- Granulated sugar about ½ C.
- brown sugar about 1 C.
- **The secret to a GREAT tasting cinnamon roll is to not skimp on the butter or cinnamon!**

Direction

- Combine cake mix, flour and yeast in large bowl. Stir until well blended. Stir in hot water. Mix well with an electric mixer. You may need to add more flour to the dough if sticky. Add flour a little at a time to for better dough consistency. Cover and let rise until doubled in bulk. (About 1 hour)
- Cut dough in half. (Each half of dough should weigh about 2 1/4 - 2 1/2 lbs.) Roll first half of dough into a large rectangle on a lightly floured surface. Spread with softened butter on entire dough. Grate orange peel about 1-2 t. and put on top of butter. Put both the brown sugar and granulated sugar on top of butter. Then cover entire roll with cinnamon on top of sugars. (I like a lot of cinnamon....)
- Roll up jelly-roll fashion, try to roll tight and cut into 12 slices (2"). Place rolls in a greased 13 x 9 x 2 inch pan. Repeat with the second half of dough. Let rise in pans until doubled. (About 1 hour)
- Preheat oven to 375 degrees.
- Topping:
- In saucepan combine 1/2 C. butter
- 1/4 C. firmly packed brown sugar
- 1/4 C. light corn syrup
- 2 t. vanilla
- 1 C. of chopped pecan or walnuts
- Heat all ingredients together until butter and sugar is melted. Then pour evenly over rolls.
- **I double the topping recipe for my family's tastes. Just depending on your tastes.
- Bake for 25-30 minutes or until lightly golden brown.
- Makes 24 rolls. ENJOY!!
- My kids love icing, so when rolls are cool, I put on top a powdered sugar icing which is powdered sugar, vanilla and a little milk (all to taste) mix until drizzle consistency. This is your option. What's a little more calories at this point!!

126. Grandmothers Coffee Buns Or Coffee Cake Recipe

Serving: 6 | Prep: | Cook: 30mins | Ready in:

Ingredients

- 500 g Mehl- flour   (about 4 1/2 cups flour)
- 125 ml Milch- milk
- 1 Pkg Trockenhefe- dry yeast
- 1 Stk Ei- 1 egg
- 1 Pr Salz- pinch salt

- 100 g Zucker- sugar (about 1/2 cup sugar)
- 50 g butter (geschmolzen) butter, melted (about 1/2 stick)
- geschmolzene butter für die Füllung- melted butter for the filling
- Zucker für die Füllung- sugar for the filling
- evtl. Zimt für die Füllung- some cinnamon for the filling

Direction

- Procedure:
- Prepare a soft pliable dough from the flour, milk, yeast, salt, sugar and butter by hand mixing and kneading (or mix ingredients in the bread machine instead.)
- When the dough is mixed be sure to let the dough rise double.
- The punch down lightly and form into one large log piece and cut out into 6 equal pieces.
- Roll out each piece into a circle and spread with butter and sprinkle heavily with some sugar and cinnamon.
- Roll each jelly roll style and fold in half by bringing one end over the other.
- Cut or slice into each piece vertically almost 2/3 through dough and expose and open the layers and then forming the dough into a roll.
- Tuck under and close the ends to seal.
- Place rolls on baking rack, middle oven and bake 200C (try 375F to 390F) until golden and done, about 20 to 40 minutes.
- Recipe may be made as one large coffee cake by above method and baked accordingly.
- Note: there were no instructions to let the formed rolls rise double so these are then baked after they are formed and will rise more in the oven during baking
- The baked rolls have a pretty fluted look.
- Powdered sugar may be sprinkled over the warm rolls
- Best eaten warm when freshly made.

---

127. Great Grandma Bailey's Coffee Cake Recipe

Serving: 0 | Prep: | Cook: 42mins | Ready in:

Ingredients

- 1 teaspoon salt
- 1 cup granulated sugar
- 1 egg
- 1 cup sour milk-(add 1 Tablespoon of vinegar to 1 cup of milk and let sit 5 min.)
- 1 Tablespoon of ginger
- 1 teaspoon baking powder
- 1 teaspoon baking soda
- ½ cup of butter softened
- flour (enough to make batter stiff)
- Topping:
- sugar and cinnamon
- Pot of hot coffee to pour over top

Direction

- Grease a 9X13 baking pan. Pre-heat oven to 350 degrees. Make sour milk by adding 1 Tablespoon of white vinegar to milk and let rest 5 min. Stir butter and sugar together until creamy. Add in the egg and stir.
- Putt baking soda into the cup of milk to dissolve, then add the milk to the batter mixture. Add in the all the other ingredients to the batter and enough flour to make batter stiff.
- Spread batter evenly into the 9X13 pan with a spatula. Sprinkle generous with sugar and cinnamon, repeat three to four times. Bake in oven for 35-40 minutes. Let cool on wire rack for 10 min. Cut into square pieces and serve in bowl with coffee poured over the top.

128. Hills And Valleys Coffee Cake Recipe

Serving: 12 | Prep: | Cook: 30mins | Ready in:

Ingredients

- (NOTE: since I can no longer find applesauce cake mixes, I would suggest you try a yellow, butter or banana cake mix and add ½ teaspoon cinnamon and use applesauce instead of water when preparing the batter…I tried using spice cake mix, but it was too spicy for me)
- 1 box applesauce cake mix
- ¾ cup water (or applesauce if you are using something other than applesauce cake mix)
- ⅓ cup vegetable oil
- ½ teaspoon vanilla extract
- 2 tablespoons butter, melted
- ¼ cup brown sugar
- ½ teaspoon cinnamon
- ⅓ cup chopped pecans
- ½ cup coconut
- glaze (optional):
- ½ cup powdered sugar
- ¼ teaspoon vanilla extract
- 3 to 4 tablespoons milk

Direction

- Mix cake mix, water, oil and vanilla together; reserve 1/3 cup for topping. Pour remaining batter into a greased 9x13 pan.
- Mix reserved cake batter with butter, brown sugar, and cinnamon until crumbly.
- Add nuts and coconut; the topping is quite moist, so it's difficult to sprinkle it over the batter. I just drop it by spoonfuls and then gently spread it a bit with fork tines - works best for me.
- Bake at 350 degrees for 35 to 40 minutes.
- While it's baking, prepare the glaze by beating ingredients together, adding milk to thin it enough to drizzle over coffeecake.
- Remove coffeecake from oven and drizzle with glaze immediately - the heat from the coffeecake will melt the glaze and allow it to soak into it, creating a deliciously gooey topping.
- NOTE: the glaze is optional - the coffeecake is good with OR without it, so just go with your preference.

129. Holiday Coffee Cake Recipe

Serving: 8 | Prep: | Cook: 60mins | Ready in:

Ingredients

- 2 cups sugar
- ½ cup softened butter
- 4 extra-large eggs
- 4 c. flour
- 1 tbsp. baking powder
- ½ tsp. baking soda
- ½ tsp. salt
- 1 ½ cups sour cream
- 1 tsp. vanilla extract
- 1 ½ tsp. rum flavoring or 2 tbsp. rum
- 1 - 1 ½ cups candied fruits
- 1 cup chopped pecans
- 1 cup golden raisins
- Marble:
- 1 tbsp. butter
- ¼ Cup brown sugar
- ½ cup chopped pecans (more if desired)

Direction

- Cream the sugar and butter. Beat eggs, add sour cream and add to sugar and butter. Sift the dry ingredients and blend with the sour cream mixture. Add the remaining ingredients.
- Add a tablespoon of milk to mixture, if it's too thick.
- Pour into a well-greased Bundt pan.
- Mix marble ingredients together and sprinkle on top of batter, use knife to marble into the batter, and bake in a 350°F oven for 1 hour.

130. Holy Mole Granola Crunch Bread Recipe

Serving: 10 | Prep: | Cook: 2hours | Ready in:

Ingredients

- ½ cup finely chopped walnuts
- ¼ cup crunchy granola cereal
- 2 tsp ground cinnamon
- 1 tsp chili powder
- 1 tbsp cocoa powder
- 1 tbsp turbinado sugar
- ¾ cup sugar
- 1 cup flour
- 1 cup 12-grain flour
- 1 tsp instant espresso powder
- ½ tbsp baking powder
- 1 tsp baking soda
- ½ tsp salt
- 2 tbsp ground flaxseed
- 3 tbsp hot water
- 1 cup buttermilk
- 1 tsp coffee extract
- 1 tsp vanilla extract
- 1/3 cup oil

Direction

- Preheat oven to 350F, grease a loaf pan.
- Mix together walnuts, granola, cinnamon, chili powder and cocoa powder in a small bowl. Set aside.
- Combine sugar, flours, espresso powder, baking powder, baking soda and salt in a medium bowl.
- In a large bowl, beat flaxseed with hot water. Let stand 10 minutes.
- Beat in the buttermilk, coffee extract, vanilla and oil.
- Add flour mixture and stir just until mixed. Do not overmix.
- Pour half of the batter into loaf pan.
- Sprinkle with the nut mixture (aim for a central "core" of filling) and top with remaining batter.
- Swirl mixtures together with a chopstick or knife.
- Bake for 40 to 50 minutes, cool in pan for about 20 minutes before turning out and cooling completely on a wire rack.

131. Honey Lemon Coffee Cake Recipe

Serving: 8 | Prep: | Cook: 25mins | Ready in:

Ingredients

- 1/4 c honey
- 3 Tbsp. butter, melted
- 1 Tbsp. light corn syrup
- 2 tsp. grated lemon peel
- 1 Tbsp. lemon juice
- 2 Cups biscuit mix
- 2 Tbsp. sugar
- 1 egg, beaten
- 1/2 Cup milk

Direction

- Mix honey, butter, corn syrup, one tsp. lemon peel and lemon juice. Pour into well-greased 8x8x2" baking pan.
- Combine biscuit mix, sugar and remaining lemon peel. Mix egg and milk; stir into dry ingredients only till moistened. Drop by spoonfuls over honey mixture.
- Bake 375° 20-25 minutes.
- Invert on serving plate.
- Serves 8.

132. Honey Glazed Buttermilk Oatmeal Coffee Cake Recipe

Serving: 9 | Prep: | Cook: 25mins | Ready in:

Ingredients

- 1/2 cup honey
- 1/3 cup butter, melted
- 2 Tbsp. light-colored corn syrup
- 2 tsp. finely shredded lemon peel
- 4 tsp. lemon juice
- 1/2 cup chopped pecans
- 1-1/2 cups rolled oats
- 1 cup all-purpose flour
- 3/4 cup packed brown sugar
- 1/2 cup chopped pecans
- 1 tsp. baking powder
- 1/2 tsp. baking soda
- 1/2 tsp. salt
- 2/3 cup buttermilk or sour milk (see note)
- 2 eggs, lightly beaten
- 1/4 cup butter, melted
- 1-1/2 tsp. vanilla
- honey (optional)

Direction

- 1. Generously grease a 9x9x2-inch baking pan. In a small bowl, combine 1/2 cup honey, 1/3 cup melted butter, corn syrup, lemon peel and lemon juice. Stir in 1/2 cup chopped pecans. Pour into prepared pan; set aside.
- 2. For cake: In a blender or food processor, blend or process oats until finely ground. Transfer to a large bowl. Stir in flour, brown sugar, 1/2 cup pecans, baking powder, baking soda, and salt. Make a well in the center of the dry ingredients. In a medium bowl, combine buttermilk, eggs, 1/4 cup melted butter, and vanilla. Add the milk mixture all at once to the flour mixture. Stir just until moistened (batter should be lumpy).
- 3. Spoon batter evenly over honey mixture. Bake in a 375 degree F oven about 25 minutes or until a wooden toothpick inserted in center comes out clean. Remove from oven and immediately invert cake onto a serving plate. Cool about 10 minutes. Serve warm drizzled with additional honey, if you like.
- Makes 9 servings.
- Note: Sour Milk
- To make 2/3 cup sour milk, place 2 teaspoons lemon juice or vinegar in a glass measuring cup. Add enough milk to equal 2/3 cup; stir. Let the mixture stand for 5 minutes before using.

133. Hungarian Coffee Cake Recipe

Serving: 812 | Prep: | Cook: 45mins | Ready in:

Ingredients

- 1 tsp. yeast
- 1 cup scalded milk
- 1/2 cup Crisco shortening
- 1/2 cup sugar
- 2 eggs, beaten
- 3 1/2 to 4 cups of flour
- mixture
- 2 tsp. cinnamon
- 3/4 cup sugar
- 1/2 cup melted butter
- 3/4 cup ground nuts
- 1 cup raisons
- Karyo syrup

Direction

- Put yeast in large bowl, put 1/2 cup sugar over that.
- Put 1/2 cup Crisco and 1 cup milk in saucepan, scald, do not boil.
- Be sure to let milk cool to barley warm.
- Add salt to yeast.
- Add beaten eggs.
- Pour cool milk and shortening in, stir.
- Add flour, beat with back of spoon, beat long and well (remember this is my grandmas recipe)!
- Cover let rise until doubled in bulk.
- Punch down and let rise again.
- Mix cinnamon, sugar and nuts in small bowl.
- Melt butter.
- Form balls of dough (size of a walnut).
- Dip ball in butter, roll in cinnamon mixture.

- Place each ball in greased Angel food pan.
- Sprinkle raisons over then another layer of balls and more raisons.
- Dribble a little white Karo syrup over the top.
- Let rise.
- Bake 45 minutes at 350*.

134. Irenes Famous Carrot Coffee Cake Recipe

Serving: 12 | Prep: | Cook: 75mins | Ready in:

Ingredients

- 1 (14.5 oz.) can carrots, drained and mashed
- 3 cups flour
- 2 tsp baking powder
- 2 tsp. cinnamon
- 2 cups sugar
- 2 tsp. baking soda
- 1 1/4 cup vegetable oil
- 4 eggs, unbeaten
- 3/4 cup chopped walnuts (optional)

Direction

- Mix carrots, flour, baking powder, baking soda, sugar, and cinnamon. Add oil, eggs, and 3/4 cup chopped nuts...mix well. Pour into tube or Bundt pan. Top with additional chopped nuts if desired. Bake at 350 degrees for 75 minutes or until cake tester comes out dry.

135. Java Calypso Loaves Recipe

Serving: 16 | Prep: | Cook: 50mins | Ready in:

Ingredients

- 3 cups of "biscuit mix"
- 3/4 cup of brown sugar
- 1/4 cup of a.p. flour
- 1 tbsp. of instant espresso powder
- 1/2 cup of milk
- 2 mashed bananas
- 1/4 teaspoon of ginger
- 1/2 teaspoon of cinnamon
- fresh nutmeg on rasp, six passes should do
- 1 egg, beaten
- 1 cup of snipped dates
- 1/2 cup of chopped pecans or black walnuts

Direction

- In a large bowl, combine biscuit mix, brown sugar and flour. Dissolve the espresso powder in the milk and add to the dry ingredients, along with the beaten egg, bananas and spices.
- Beat until well blended. Fold in dates and nuts.
- Pour into two prepared loaf pans (greased and floured) equally.
- Bake in preheated 350 degree oven for 40 to 50 minutes. (Smell is a great indicator of doneness, but I prefer to use the cake tester a few minutes before I think it is done. Cool in pans for 10 minutes and then cool on wire rack for another 20. Double wrap or zip lock for freshness.
- It is not so much our friends' help that helps us, as the confidence of their help.
- Epicurus

136. Jetts Cinnamon Swirl Tube Coffee Cake Recipe

Serving: 10 | Prep: | Cook: 65mins | Ready in:

Ingredients

- 1 cup butter
- 3 cups flour - All purpose
- 2 cups sugar
- 4 eggs
- 1 pint sour cream

- 1/2 teaspoon baking soda
- 1 tablespoon baking powder
- * Streusel filling mixture
- see below

Direction

- Preheat oven to 325 degrees.
- Cream butter and sugar thoroughly.
- Add eggs one at a time, beating well after each addition.
- Sift dry ingredients together.
- Add half of flour and beat well.
- Add half of sour cream & beat well
- Repeat
- Pour into large tube pan making 3 layers of batter alternating batter with cinnamon mixture (Streusel Mixture).
- Mix:
- 1 cup brown sugar
- 2 tablespoons cinnamon (or less if desired)
- 1 cup chopped nuts

137. Jetts Party Coffee Cake Recipe

Serving: 10 | Prep: | Cook: 35mins | Ready in:

Ingredients

- Cream - 1/2 lb(2 sticks) of butter and 1 Cup sugar
- Mix well
- Add - 3 eggs - 1 at a time; beating well after each addition
- Beat in 1 cup sour cream
- Add 2 1/2 cups all-purpose flour*
- 2 teaspoons baking powder*
- 1 teaspoon baking soda*
- *Sift the dry ingredients 3 times*
- Blend in 1 teaspoon fresh lemon juice with 1 teaspoon vanilla and 1 teaspoon almond flavoring.
- While cake is beating; prepare the filling**

- *Filling*
- 1 1/2 cups chopped toasted pecans
- 2/3 cup sugar
- 1 1/2 teaspoons cinnamon
- ....
- Grease 8 x 12 inch pan and spread half of the batter(Moisten hand with water and spread evenly)
- Sprinkle half of nut mixture filling then spoon on remaining batter and top with nut mixture.

Direction

- Bake at 350 degrees for 30 - 35 minutes
- ***
- --Many candles can be kindled from one candle without diminishing it--
- ***
- Let your light shine!

138. Jewish Coffee Cake Recipe

Serving: 16 | Prep: | Cook: 40mins | Ready in:

Ingredients

- 1 stick butter
- 1 cup white sugar
- 3 eggs
- 2 cups flour
- 1 tsp baking powder
- 1 tsp baking soda
- 1/8 tsp salt
- 1 tsp vanilla
- 1 cup sour cream
- 1 cup semi sweet chocolate chips (Put this into the batter after it is mixed but coat with flour first)
- TOPPING
- 1/2 cup chopped nuts
- 3/4 cup light brown sugar
- 2 Tbls softened butter

Direction

- Cream butter.
- Add sugar and eggs and beat well.
- Add sour cream and vanilla, mix well.
- Sift dry ingredients, add to wet mixture and mix just till blended.
- Pour half the batter into a greased tube pan.
- Put half of the topping over the batter, then top with remaining batter. Put the remaining topping on the top of the cake.
- Bake 40 minutes at 350 degrees.
- Let cool and remove from pan.

139. Joys Easy Apple Raisin Cake Recipe

Serving: 88 | Prep: | Cook: 30mins | Ready in:

Ingredients

- Preheat oven 350F for metal pan or 325 for glass pan
- Grease generously and flour the baking pan.
- 1 c. sugar
- 1/4 c oatmeal
- 1 c. flour
- 1/4 c. water
- 1 egg or 1/4 c. egg replacement
- 3/4 c. applesauce
- 1/2 c chopped raisins or currants(left whole) or dried cranberries, etc. etc.
- 1/4 c. chopped nuts
- 3/4 t. baking soda
- 3/4 t salt
- 1/4 t. baking powder
- 1/2 t. connamon
- 1/2 t. ground nutmeg
- 1/4 t. ground cloves

Direction

- 8" X 8" pan. Pam inside of pan. Dump all ingredients into a large bowl.
- Using electric handheld eggbeater, blend on low speed for 1 min.
- Scrape down bowl and blend 1/2 minute longer.
- Beat 2 1/2 minutes at highest speed, scraping bowl 3 times more.
- Pour into prepared pan.
- Bake until center springs back when pressed lightly.
- Cool cake in pan on rack 10 minutes.
- Turn out onto rack. When cool, you might sprinkle with confectioners' sugar or frost with cream cheese.
- The cake stands alone without any topping. A very nice cake.

140. LEMON COCONUT BREAD With Cheese Filling Recipe

Serving: 16 | Prep: | Cook: 50mins | Ready in:

Ingredients

- 1 cup sugar
- 1/2 cup LAND O LAKES® butter, softened
- 2 eggs
- 1/2 cup milk
- 3 tablespoons lemon juice
- 1 tablespoon freshly grated lemon peel
- 1 3/4 cups all-purpose flour
- 1 teaspoon baking powder
- 1/4 teaspoon salt
- Filling Ingredients
- 3/4 cup sweetened flaked coconut, toasted
- 1 (3-ounce) package cream cheese, softened
- 3 tablespoons powdered sugar
- glaze Ingredients
- 1/2 cup powdered sugar
- 2 - 3 teaspoons LAND O LAKES™ Traditional or Fat Free Half & Half

Direction

- Heat oven to 350°F. Grease and flour 8x4-inch loaf pan; set aside.

- Combine sugar, butter and eggs in large bowl. Beat at medium speed, scraping bowl often, until creamy. Add 1/2 cup milk, lemon juice and lemon peel; continue beating until well mixed. Stir in flour, baking powder and salt until well mixed.
- Reserve 2 tablespoons coconut; set aside. Combine cream cheese and 3 tablespoons powdered sugar in small bowl until well mixed. Stir in remaining coconut.
- Spoon half of batter into prepared pan. Drop teaspoonfuls of filling mixture evenly over batter. Spoon remaining batter over filling; smooth top with back of spoon.
- Bake for 50 to 55 minutes or until top is deep golden brown. Cool in pan 10 minutes. Remove from pan to cooling rack; cool completely.
- Combine 1/2 cup powdered sugar and enough half & half in small bowl for desired glazing consistency. Spoon over bread; sprinkle with reserved coconut.
- Recipe Tip
- To toast coconut, spread coconut into single layer on ungreased baking sheet. Bake at 350°F. for 5 to 10 minutes, stirring occasionally, until light golden brown. Remove from baking sheet. Cool completely.

141. Land Of Nod Recipe

Serving: 8 | Prep: | Cook: 25mins | Ready in:

Ingredients

- Land of Nod
- 20 frozen balls of dough (Like, bag of Rhodes frozen rolls)
- 1 cup brown sugar
- 1/4 pkg. vanilla instant pudding (small package)
- 2 Tablespoons cinnamon
- 1 cup chopped nuts
- 1 stick melted oleo

- glaze :
- 2 teaspoons oleo
- 1 teaspoon vanilla
- 1 1/2 Tablespoons milk
- Dash of salt
- 1 cup powdered sugar

Direction

- Grease a Bundt pan.
- Put frozen dough balls in bottom of prepared pan.
- Mix brown sugar, pudding, and cinnamon together. Sprinkle on top of rolls.
- Put nuts on top of that.
- Drizzle with melted oleo.
- Cover with a damp cloth and leave sitting on counter or in the refrigerator overnight.
- In the morning bake in preheated oven at 350* for 25 min.
- Leave in pan about 5 min.
- Dump out on plate, and pour warm glaze over them immediately.
- Glaze:
- Mix all glaze ingredients and heat on top of stove, DO NOT BOIL.
- Pour warm glaze over top of rolls straight from the oven (after they've been removed from pan).

142. Lemon Coffee Cake Recipe

Serving: 1 | Prep: | Cook: 30mins | Ready in:

Ingredients

- 1 ¼ cups sugar, divided
- ¾ cup vegetable oil
- 4 eggs
- 2 cups flour
- 1 tsp baking powder
- ½ tsp salt
- 1 can (15 oz) lemon pie filling

- 1 ½ tsp cinnamon .

Direction

- In a mixing bowl combine 1 cup sugar and oil; mix well. Add eggs and beat until light and lemon colored. Combine flour, baking powder, and salt. Add to the egg mixture and mix well. Pour half the batter into a greased 13 x 9 x 2 inch baking dish. Spread pie filling over batter. Top with remaining batter.
- Combine the cinnamon and remaining ¼ cup sugar. Sprinkle sugar mixture over top of batter.
- Bake at 350 degrees for 30 minutes or until a toothpick comes out clean

143. Lemon Cream Cheese Coffee Cake Recipe

Serving: 18 | Prep: | Cook: 35mins | Ready in:

Ingredients

- 1 package (8 ounces) cream cheese, softened
- 1 1/4 cups sugar
- 2 eggs
- 1/4 teaspoon McCormick® ground mace
- OR 1/4 teaspoon McCormick® ground nutmeg
- 2 teaspoons McCormick® Pure lemon extract
- 1 3/4 cups sifted flour
- 1 teaspoon baking powder
- 1/2 teaspoon baking soda
- 1/4 teaspoon salt
- 1/4 cup milk
- ....
- Streusel Topping:
- 1/2 cup sugar
- 1/4 cup flour
- 2 teaspoons McCormick® pumpkin pie spice
- 1/4 cup (1/2 stick) cold butter

Direction

- 1. Preheat oven to 350°F. Beat butter, cream cheese and sugar in large bowl with electric mixer until light and fluffy. Add eggs, 1 at a time, beating well after each addition. Stir in mace and lemon extract.
- 2. Sift flour with baking powder, soda and salt. Add alternately with milk to butter mixture. Pour into greased and floured 13x2-inch baking pan.
- 3. For the Streusel Topping, mix sugar, flour and pumpkin pie spice in medium bowl. Cut in butter with pastry blender or 2 knives until mixture resembles coarse crumbs. Sprinkle over batter.
- 4. Bake 35 minutes or until cake pulls away from sides of pan. Cool on wire rack.

144. Lemon Nut Bread Recipe

Serving: 10 | Prep: | Cook: 75mins | Ready in:

Ingredients

- 3/4 cup butter. softened
- 1 1/2 cups sugar
- 3 eggs
- 3/4 cup buttermilk
- 2 1/4 cups flour
- 1/4 tsp baking soda
- 1/8 tsp salt
- lemon zest from one lemon
- 3/4 cup chopped pecans
- Glaze:
- juice of two lemons
- 3/4 cup powdered sugar

Direction

- Cream butter and sugar until light and fluffy.
- Add eggs and beat well.
- Combine dry ingredients.
- Add buttermilk and dry ingredients to sugar mixture, beginning and ending with buttermilk. Stir just until all ingredients are moistened.

- Stir in lemon zest and pecans.
- Spoon batter into a greased 9x5x3-inch loaf pan.
- Bake at 325 degrees for 1 1/4 hours or until toothpick inserted comes out clean.
- Glaze:
- Combine lemon juice and powdered sugar and stir well.
- Punch holes in top of warm bread and pour on glaze.

145. Louisiana Butter Pecan Coffee Cake Recipe

Serving: 8 | Prep: | Cook: 45mins | Ready in:

Ingredients

- 1 cup sugar
- 2 cups sifted all purpose flour
- 3 teaspoons baking powder
- 1 teaspoon salt
- 1/3 cup soft butter
- 1 egg
- 1 cup milk
- ***
- TOPPING
- ***
- 1/2 cup chopped pecans
- 2 tablespoons soft butter
- 1/4 cup brown sugar, packed
- 2 tablespoons flour
- 1 teaspoon cinnamon

Direction

- Preheat oven to 350 degrees F.
- Sift first 4 ingredients together.
- Add butter, egg and milk.
- Beat well, about 2 minutes.
- Pour into greased & floured 9inch square pan.
- Blend topping ingredients and sprinkle over cake mixture.
- Bake for 30 - 45 minutes or when cake tests done.
- ***
- Make peace with imperfection
- ***

146. Low Fat Vegan Coffee Cake Recipe

Serving: 9 | Prep: | Cook: 25mins | Ready in:

Ingredients

- 1/4 cup margarine
- 2 cups applesauce
- 1 cup flour
- 1 1/2 cups wheat bran flakes or oat bran
- 1 cup sugar
- 1 tsp baking soda
- 1 tsp cinnamon
- 1/2 tsp nutmeg
- 1/4 tsp cloves
- 1 cup raisins

Direction

- Pre-heat oven to 350 degrees and grease the bottom of a 9-inch square baking pan.
- In a large saucepan, heat the margarine and applesauce together until margarine is melted. Remove from heat.
- Add the remaining ingredients and mix until well combined, then pour into baking pan.
- Bake for 25-30 minutes, until a toothpick inserted in the center comes out clean.

147. MINCEMEAT COFFEE CAKE Recipe

Serving: 16 | Prep: | Cook: 85mins | Ready in:

Ingredients

- Ingredients:
- 2 packages (¼ -oz each) active dry yeast
- 1 ¼ cups warm milk Temp. (110 to 115) divided
- ½ cup sugar
- ½ cup butter or margarine, softened
- 2 eggs, beaten
- 2 tsp. salt
- 1 tsp. ground cinnamon
- 1/8 tsp. Each ground allspice, ground cloves, mace
- 5 to 5 ½ cups all-purpose flour
- 1 ½ cups prepared mincemeat
- confectioners' sugar

Direction

- Preheat oven at 375.
- In a large bowl, dissolve yeast in ½ cup milk. Add sugar, butter, eggs, salt, cinnamon, allspice, cloves, mace, 2 ½ cups flour and the remaining milk; beat until smooth. Stir in enough remaining flour to form a soft dough. Turn onto a floured board; knead until smooth and elastic, about 6 – 8 minutes. Place in a greased bowl, turning once to grease top. Cover and let rise in a warm place until doubled, about 1 hour. Punch dough down; let rest 10 minutes. Turn onto a lightly floured surface. Roll into a 16-inch x 12-inch rectangle. Spread mincemeat to within 1-inch of edges. Roll up from one long side. Pinch seams; join and seal ends to from a circle. Place in a greased 10-inch fluted tube pan. Cover let rise until nearly doubled, about 30 minutes. Bake at 375 for 40 – 45 minutes or until golden brown. Cool 10 minutes in pan before removing to a wire rack. Just before serving, dust with confectioners' sugar.

148. Make Ahead Orange Coffee Cake Recipe

Serving: 10 | Prep: | Cook: 30mins | Ready in:

Ingredients

- 2 cups all purpose flour
- 3 teaspoons baking powder
- 1/2 teaspoon salt
- 1/2 cup sugar
- 1 teaspoon grated orange rind
- 3/4 cup orange juice
- 1 egg
- 1 teaspoon vanilla
- 1/4 cup vegetable oil
- ***
- TOPPING
- ***
- 2 Tablespoons grated orange rind
- 1/2 cup sugar
- 1 teaspoon cinnamon

Direction

- Preheat oven to 400 degrees F.
- Mix ingredients in order given and stir until well moistened.
- Pour into 10 inch cake pan.
- Mix topping ingredients together.
- Sprinkle topping over batter.
- Dot with 2 tablespoons butter.
- Bake in 400 degree oven for 20 - 30 minutes.
- **
- -Teach love, man will joyously take instruction-
- **

149. Mamon Filipino Sponge Cake Recipe

Serving: 18 | Prep: | Cook: 25mins | Ready in:

Ingredients

- 1 cup   cake flour
- 1 cup white sugar
- 1 teaspoon baking powder
- 1 teaspoon vanilla
- 6 eggyolks
- 1/2 cup vegetable oil
- 6 eggwhites
- 1 teaspoon cream of tartar

Direction

- Preheat oven to 350°F.
- Sift flour and baking powder in bowl; set aside.
- In another large bowl, beat egg white and cream of tartar until meringue-like but not stiff.
- Gradually add sugar while beating.
- Then, add vanilla and vegetable oil.
- Divide sifted cake flour with baking powder into four.
- Add one part of the flour mixture, beat with a spoon until lumps are gone.
- Add egg yolks one at a time and alternately with 1 part of the flour mixture Continue beating until smooth.
- Line small muffin pans (serves 9 big muffin cups) with paper cups and pour mixture about 2/3 full.
- Bake 20-25 minutes or until golden brown. Finished when toothpick comes out clean.

150. Mandarin Chocolate Chip Coffee Cake Recipe

Serving: 12 | Prep: | Cook: 40mins | Ready in:

Ingredients

- coffee Cake:
- 2 large eggs, lightly beaten, at room temperature
- 1 cup freshly squeezed orange juice
- 2 teaspoons vanilla extract
- 3 cups all-purpose flour
- 1 cup granulated sugar
- 1 Tablespoon double acting baking powder
- 1 teaspoon baking soda
- 1 teaspoon salt
- 1/3 cup solid vegetable shortening, chilled and cut into 1/2-inch cubes
- 5 Tablespoons unsalted butter, chilled and cut into 1/2-inch cubes
- Two 11-ounce cans mandarin orange segments in light syrup, drained
- 1 cup semisweet chocolate chips
- Topping:
- 1 cup sweetened flaked coconut
- 1/3 cup granulated sugar
- 2 Tablespoons unsalted butter, melted

Direction

- Coffee Cake: Position a rack in the center of the oven and preheat to 375 degrees. Lightly butter the bottom and sides of a 13 x 19-inch baking pan. Line the bottom of the pan with a rectangular piece of baking parchment or waxed paper. Dust the sides of the pan with flour and tap out the excess. In a small bowl, stir together the eggs, orange juice and vanilla. In a large bowl, stir together the flour, sugar, baking powder, baking soda, and salt. Using a pastry blender or your fingertips, blend the shortening and butter cubes into the flour mixture until the mixture resembles coarse meal. Make a well in the center of the flour ingredients. Using a wooden spoon, stir the egg/juice mixture into the flour/butter mixture until all of the ingredients are moistened. Using a rubber spatula, fold in the mandarin orange segments and chocolate chips. Scrape the coffee cake batter into the prepared pan and smooth the top with a rubber spatula.
- Topping: In a medium bowl, stir together the coconut, sugar, and butter until well combined. Sprinkle the topping mixture evenly over the coffee cake batter. Bake the coffee cake for 35 to 45 minutes, or until a

toothpick inserted into the center of the cake comes out with a few moist crumbs clinging to it. Cool completely in the pan on a wire rack. Run a sharp knife around the edge of the cake. Serve directly from the pan or gently invert the cake onto a large baking sheet and peel off the waxed paper. Re-invert it onto a serving platter.
- Serves: approximately 12

151. Maritime Coffee Cake Recipe

Serving: 12 | Prep: | Cook: 2hours | Ready in:

Ingredients

- Topping:
- ½ cup white whole wheat flour
- ½ cup chickpea flour
- ⅓ cup dark brown sugar
- 2 tsp cinnamon
- ¼ tsp nutmeg
- ¼ tsp allspice
- pinch salt
- 2 tbsp camelina oil or canola oil
- 2 tbsp Amoré almonds + Dairy beverage, whole milk or milk alternative
- Cake:
- 1 cup Amoré almonds + Dairy beverage, whole milk or milk alternative
- 2 tsp apple cider vinegar
- 2 tbsp canola oil
- 2 tbsp camelina oil
- 1 tbsp vanilla
- ¼ tsp nutmeg
- ½ tsp salt
- 1 ¼ cups white whole wheat flour
- 1 tbsp ground flaxseed
- ⅓ cup cup-for-cup stevia (or sugar)
- 2 tsp baking powder
- ¼ tsp baking soda
- 1 cup cooked quinoa

Direction

- Topping:
- Combine the flours, sugar, cinnamon, nutmeg, allspice and salt in a bowl.
- Drizzle in the oil and the milk, tossing with a fork to create a crumbly mixture.
- Set aside while preparing cake.
- Cake:
- Preheat oven to 375F. Grease an 8" square pan and line with parchment paper, leaving overhang on 2 sides for easy removal.
- In a large bowl, combine milk, vinegar, oils, vanilla, nutmeg and salt.
- Add the flour, flaxseed, stevia, baking powder and baking soda, whisking to combine well.
- Fold in the quinoa.
- Pour into the pan and top evenly with the crumb mixture.
- Bake for 30 to 35 minutes. Cool in the pan before removing and slicing.

152. Mississippi Chocolate And Coffee Cake Recipe

Serving: 10 | Prep: | Cook: 75mins | Ready in:

Ingredients

- For the Cake:
- 2 c. all-purpose flour
- 1 t. baking soda
- Pinch of salt
- 1 3/4 c. strong brewed coffee
- 1/4 c. bourbon
- 5 oz. unsweetened chocolate
- 1 c. butter
- 2 c. sugar
- 2 large eggs, lightly beaten
- 1 t. vanilla extract
- For chocolate Icing:
- 6 1/2 oz. semisweet chocolate
- 4 1/2 T. butter

Direction

- For the Cake: Preheat the oven to 350 degrees F. Grease a 9-inch round cake pan. Line pan with parchment paper. Grease sides of cake pan.
- In a mixing bowl, sift together the flour, baking soda, and salt.
- In the top of a double boiler, I use a metal bowl set on top of a pan of simmering water, heat the coffee, bourbon, chocolate, and butter, stirring until the chocolate and butter are melted and the mixture is smooth. Remove the pan from the heat and stir in the sugar. Let the mixture cool for 3 minutes and transfer to an electric mixer. Add the flour mixture to the chocolate mixture, half a cup at a time, and beat medium speed for 1 minute. Add the eggs and vanilla and beat until smooth.
- Pour into the prepared pan and bake for 1 hour and 10 to 15 minutes, or until a skewer inserted in the center comes out clean. Let the cake cool completely in the pan. When cooled, turn out onto a serving plate.
- For Chocolate Icing: Combine the chocolate and butter in the top of a double boiler or bowl resting over a pan of simmering water and stir over low heat until they are melted and combined. Cool slightly and the ice cake.

153. Mochiko Cake Recipe

Serving: 24 | Prep: | Cook: 50mins | Ready in:

Ingredients

- 1 box (16 oz.) Mochiko - sweet rice flour
- 1 tsp kosher salt
- 1 tsp baking soda
- 1 tsp baking powder
- 1 cup (more or less) brown sugar
- 2 1/2 cup milk (or more)
- 1/2 cup chopped mixed nuts (example: pumpkin seeds, walnuts, pecan...)
- 1/2 cup mixed dried fruits (example: blueberries, cranberries, grapes, dates...)
- 1 ~ 2 cups mixed cooked beans (example: kidney beans, green peas, edamame, black beans, red beans...) or steamed & chopped vegetables (example: sweet potatoes, kabocha squash...)
- 1 ~ 2 Tbsp crown daisy powder or green tea powder (matcha powder)

Direction

- Preheat oven to 375 degrees.
- In a large bowl, combine Mochiko flour, baking soda, baking powder, brown sugar, salt, & crown daisy powder and mix well.
- Add milk to flour mixture and mix well.
- Fold in mixed nuts and dried fruits, and cooked beans.
- Pour into greased 8 x 8-inch baking pan.
- Bake at 375 degree for 45 mins till top is golden brown.
- Cool over a wire rack, and then slice and serve with coffee or tea.

154. Monkey Tail Bread Recipe

Serving: 16 | Prep: | Cook: 60mins | Ready in:

Ingredients

- 1/2 Cup shortening
- 1 Cup sugar
- 2 eggs
- 1 cup mashed banana (about 3 medium)
- 2 Cups flour
- 1 tsp baking powder
- 1/2 tsp baking soda
- 1/2 tsp salt
- 1/2 Cup chopped peanuts
- 1/2 Cup miniature chocolate chips
- 2 Tbl ready to spread chocolate frosting
- 1 tbl peanut butter

Direction

- 350 oven.
- Grease bottom only of loaf pan (9x5x3).
- Beat shortening and sugar in a large bowl until light and fluffy.
- Beat in eggs and bananas until smooth.
- Beat in dry ingredients until just mixed.
- Stir in peanuts and chips.
- Pour into loaf pan.
- Bake 1 hour to an hour and 10 minutes or until toothpick inserted in center comes out clean.
- Cool 1 hour.
- Place frosting in a small plastic bag and microwave on high 6 - 10 seconds.
- Add peanut butter to bag; gently squeeze bag until chocolate and peanut butter are well blended.
- Cut off corner of the bag and drizzle mixture over bread.

155. Nana Annas Blueberry Sour Cream Coffee Cake Recipe

Serving: 0 | Prep: | Cook: 60mins | Ready in:

Ingredients

- ½ cup brown sugar
- 1 cup toasted pecans
- 1 ½ teaspoon cinnamon
- ½ cup cake flour
- ½ stick butter, cold, cut in pieces
- In a food processor, pulse brown sugar, pecans, cinnamon and cake flour until combined. Add butter in small pieces and pulse until mixture resembles coarse meal. Divide in half and reserve
- ....
  ....
- Cake:
- 2 ½ cups flour
- 2 ½ teaspoons baking powder
- ½ teaspoon baking soda
- ¼ teaspoon salt
- 2 sticks unsalted butter, room temperature
- 1 ½ cups sugar
- 3 large eggs
- 1 egg yolk
- 2 teaspoons vanilla
- 1 cup sour cream
- Zest of 1 orange
- 1 ½ cups blueberries

Direction

- Preheat oven to 350 degrees. Butter and flour a 10-inch springform pan.
- In a large bowl sift together flour, baking powder, baking soda and salt. Set aside.
- In a large bowl, using an electric mixer, cream butter and sugar until pale and fluffy.
- Add eggs one at a time, mixing well with each addition. Add yolk and mix well. Add vanilla, sour cream and zest, mix until well incorporated.
- Slowly add flour mixture, mixing well. Pour half of batter into prepared pan and top with ¾ cup blueberries and half of topping mixture.
- Spread remaining batter into pan and top with remaining blueberries and topping mixture.
- Bake for 60-70 minutes until a toothpick, inserted in the middle of the cake, comes out clean.
- Let cool in pan on a rack for 5-10 minutes before unmolding.
- Dust with powdered sugar and serve warm.

156. No Knead Coffee Cake Loaf Recipe

Serving: 8 | Prep: | Cook: 45mins | Ready in:

Ingredients

- Sponge:
- 1 pkt active dry yeast
- 1/4 cup warm water
- 1 cup warm milk (or buttermilk)

- 1 cup bread flour
- 1 egg beaten
- 1/2 cup margarine or other shortening softened
- 1 cup sugar
- 1 cup all purpose flour
- 2 tsp baking powder
- 1/4 tsp nutmeg
- 1/4 tsp cinnamon
- 1/4 tsp salt
- 1 cup soft raisins
- Icing:
- 1/2 cup powdered sugar
- f2 Tbs. softened butter or margarine
- 1/4 tsp vanilla or almond extract
- few tsp milk

Direction

- Dissolve yeast in water till foamy.
- Combine with warm milk, flour and mix until combined.
- Cover and let stand in a warm place 1 hour.
- Stir down with egg and margarine.
- Combine dry ingredients and stir well into mixture.
- Blend in raisins.
- Mixture will be a thick batter.
- Place in a greased and floured 9 x 5 loaf pan.
- Bake in a preheated 350 oven 45 minutes or until golden and tested done (toothpick in center will come out clean).
- Remove to rack to cool.
- Cool in pan 5 minutes and carefully remove.
- Blend icing ingredients smooth and drizzle over warm cake.
- Serve warm or at room temperature.
- Note: I often use buttermilk instead of regular milk in the recipe and the texture is softer and the loaf not as tall but still very delicious.

157. Nutty Apricot Coffeecakes Recipe

Serving: 12 | Prep: | Cook: 40mins | Ready in:

Ingredients

- 3/4 cup warm water
- 1 package active dry yeast
- 3/4 cup warm milk
- 2 tablespoons honey
- 2 tablespoons vegetable oil
- 1 teaspoon salt
- 2-1/2 cups all purpose flour
- 2 cups whole wheat flour
- Filling:
- 2 tablespoons butter melted
- 1/2 cup packed light brown sugar
- 1 teaspoon ground cinnamon
- 1 cup chopped dried apricots
- 1 cup chopped pecans toasted
- Glaze:
- 1/4 cup honey
- 1 tablespoon butter

Direction

- Place 1/4 cup warm water in large warm bowl then sprinkle in yeast and stir until dissolved.
- Add remaining water, warm milk, honey, vegetable oil, salt and 1-1/2 cups all-purpose flour.
- Blend well then stir in whole wheat flour and enough remaining flour to make soft dough.
- Knead on lightly floured surface until smooth and elastic about 8 minutes.
- Place in greased bowl turning to grease top then cover and let rise in warm place 45 minutes.
- Punch dough down then remove to lightly floured surface and divide in half.
- Roll each to rectangle and transfer to two greased baking sheets and brush with melted butter.
- In small bowl combine brown sugar, cinnamon, apricots and pecans then stir well.

- Sprinkle half of the brown sugar mixture over center third of each rectangle.
- Along each side of coffeecake cut 1" wide strips from edge of filling to edge of dough.
- Starting at one end alternately fold six strips from each side across filling toward opposite end.
- Repeat from other end using six strips from each side.
- Loosely tie together remaining two center strips on top of loaf.
- Repeat with second coffeecake.
- Cover and let rise in warm draft free place until almost doubled in size about 40 minutes.
- Bake at 375 for 25 minutes and switch positions of sheets halfway through baking.
- Remove from sheets and cool on wire racks then brush with glaze.
- To make glaze stir 1/4 cup honey and 1 tablespoon butter over medium heat until butter melts.

158. Oatmeal Banana Bread Recipe

Serving: 812 | Prep: | Cook: 45mins | Ready in:

Ingredients

- 1/3 cup butter
- 1 cup sugar
- 1 egg
- 1 cup mashed banana (approximately 2 bananas)
- 1 cup plain flour (I use unbleached)
- 1/2 cup old-fashioned type oatmeal (do not use instant or quick cooking!)
- 2 teaspoons baking powder
- 1/4 cup chopped walnuts (or pecans)
- 1/2 teaspoon salt

Direction

- Cream butter, sugar, egg and bananas.
- Add baking powder and salt, mix, then add oatmeal & flour.
- Add the nuts.
- Spread into a greased glass loaf pan and bake at 350 degrees for about 45 minutes. Check middle with a toothpick, if toothpick comes out clean, it is done.
- Take out of oven and cover with a tea cloth until cool.
- Slice and serve.

159. Oh I Knew You Were Coming So I Baked An Almond Cream Cheese Bundt Recipe

Serving: 8 | Prep: | Cook: 45mins | Ready in:

Ingredients

- 24 frozen dinner rolls, thawed but still cold
- 1 c sliced almonds, divided
- 8 oz cream cheese
- 1/2 c sugar
- 1 t cinnamon
- 1 t nutmeg
- 1/2 c butter, melted
- 1 c brown sugar
- Glaze:
- 1 T butter, melted
- 1 c powdered sugar
- 2 T water
- 1/2 t almond extract

Direction

- Sprinkle 1/4 c almonds in a sprayed Bundt pan. Cut cream cheese into 24 equal cubes. In a small bowl mix sugar, cinnamon and nutmeg. Roll cream cheese cubes in sugar mixture and coat completely. Wrap a roll around each cube and completely enclose. Dip each roll in sugar mixture until coated. Place rolls in Bundt pan alternately with 3/4 c almonds. Sprinkle any remaining sugar mixture over rolls. Stir

together butter and brown sugar in a small microwave-safe bowl. Microwave 30 seconds. Stir well and pour over rolls.
- Cover with plastic wrap that has been sprayed and let rise until almost to the top of the pan. Remove wrap and bake at 350 degrees for about 45 minutes. Cover with foil last 15 minutes of baking. Invert immediately onto serving platter (it will settle). Mix glaze ingredients together and drizzle over Bundt while still warm.
- Enjoy!!

160. Old Fashioned Cinnamon Brown Sugar Coffee Cake Recipe

Serving: 12 | Prep: | Cook: 35mins | Ready in:

Ingredients

- For yeast Dough>
- 2 Cups All Purpose flour (Sifted)
- 1 ounce granular yeast
- 6 Tablespoons Scalded milk
- 1 1/2 Tablespoons sugar
- 2 eggs (slightly beaten)
- 1/2 teaspoon salt
- Grated lemon rind of 1/2 of a Lemon
- 1/2 Cup raisins
-
- Filling: 6 Tablespoons flour
- 2 Tablespoons Soft butter
- 1/2 Cup brown sugar
- 1 teaspoon cinnamon
- 1/2 Cup Chopped nuts
-
- Icing: 5 Tablespoons Sifted powdered sugar
- 1 Tablespoon of milk or Cream
- 1/4 teaspoon vanilla
- 1/8 teaspoon salt

Direction

- Preparing Yeast Dough: Cut 1/2 Cup Butter into 2 Cups of All Purpose Flour. Dissolve 1 ounce Granular Yeast (1 small pack of compressed yeast may be substituted) in 2 Tablespoons Warm Water. Add to first mixture with 6 Tablespoons Scalded & Cooled Milk, 1 1/2 Tablespoons Sugar, 2 Eggs, slightly beaten, 1/2 teaspoon Salt, Grated Rind of 1/2 Lemon & 1/2 Cup Raisins. Beat Mixture until Smooth.
- Filling: Sprinkle 6 Tablespoons Flour on Pastry Cloth. Turn dough out on Cloth; knead until Smooth & Elastic. Place in Greased Bowl, cover, let rise in Warm Place until Doubled in Bulk. Roll Dough into a Rectangle, 9 x 18 inches. Spread with 2 Tablespoons Soft Butter; Sprinkle on 1/2 Cup Brown Sugar, 1 teaspoon Cinnamon, & 1/2 Cup Chopped Nuts.
- Roll Dough tightly beginning at Wide side. Place Sealed Edge Down. With Scissors, cut Roll into 2 long strips, do not cut through 1 end. Bring 1 Strip Crosswise over the other, keeping cut side up.
- Cross Strips several times. Bring ends together to form a Ring.
- Place into a 10 Inch Tube Pan. Let Rise until Double in Bulk.
- Bake in Moderate Oven 375 degrees, 35 Minutes.
- Dribble a thin Powdered Sugar Icing on Top of Cake

161. Old Fashioned Pumpkin Bread Recipe

Serving: 810 | Prep: | Cook: 60mins | Ready in:

Ingredients

- 2/3 cup Crisco shortening
- 2 2/3 cup sugar
- 4 eggs or egg substitute
- 1 lb canned pumpkin

- 2/3 cup orange juice /or substitute water (for diabetics)
- 3 1/3 cup flour
- 1/2 tsp baking powder
- 2 tsp baking soda
- 1 1/2 tsp salt
- 1 tsp cinnamon
- 1 tsp ground cloves may be omitted if desired
- 2/3 cup nuts if desired (walnuts or any other)
- 2/3 cup raisins or dates chopped

Direction

- Soak raisins overnight in water or orange juice.
- Prepare batter when raisins are ready after soaking.
- Mix raisins into batter when ready.
- Lightly spray or grease your pans I use non-stick muffin tins.
- Fill about 3/4 full.
- Pre heat oven to 350 degrees.
- Bake at 350 for 1 hour or until tooth pick comes out clean.
- Let cool for approx. 1/2 or serve at your desired temperature and enjoy.
- Serve with Butter if desired.

162. Orange Chocolate Coffee Cake Recipe

Serving: 12 | Prep: | Cook: 30mins | Ready in:

Ingredients

- Streusel
- 1 1/2 cups (packed) golden brown sugar
- 1 tablespoon ground cinnamon
- 6 tablespoons (3/4 stick) chilled salted butter, diced
- 1 1/2 cups coarsely chopped pecans
- 1 cup (6 ounces) semisweet chocolate chips
- cake
- 3 cups all purpose flour
- 1 1/2 teaspoons baking soda
- 1 1/2 teaspoons baking powder
- 1 1/3 cups sugar
- 3/4 cup (1 1/2 sticks) salted butter, room temperature
- 3 large eggs
- 1 1/2 teaspoons grated orange peel
- 1 1/2 teaspoons vanilla extract
- 1 1/2 cups sour cream
- 1/4 cup orange juice
- powdered sugar

Direction

- For streusel:
- Whisk brown sugar and cinnamon in medium bowl to blend. Add butter and rub in with fingertips until mixture holds together in small, moist clumps. Mix in pecans and chocolate chips. (Can be made up to 3 days ahead. Cover and refrigerate.)
- For cake:
- Preheat oven to 350°F. Butter and flour 13x9x2-inch metal baking pan. Sift flour, baking soda, and baking powder into medium bowl. Using electric mixer, beat sugar and butter in large bowl until blended and smooth. Beat in eggs 1 at a time, then orange peel and vanilla extract. Mix in flour mixture in 4 additions alternately with sour cream in 3 additions. Mix in orange juice. Spread half of batter in prepared pan. Sprinkle with half of streusel. Drop remaining batter over by heaping tablespoonfuls; carefully spread batter to make even layer. Sprinkle with remaining streusel. Bake 30-35 minutes.

163. Out With The Old Tea Cake Recipe

Serving: 12 | Prep: | Cook: 2hours | Ready in:

Ingredients

- 1 1/2 cups flour

- 1 1/2 cups whole wheat flour
- 2 tsp baking powder
- 1 tsp baking soda
- 1/3 cup almond meal
- 2 tsp pumpkin pie spice
- 1/4 cup canola oil
- 3 oz chopped dates
- 5 oz raisins
- 2 oz chopped prunes
- 2 oz chopped cashews
- 2 oz chopped walnuts
- 1/2 cup dark brown sugar
- 1/2 cup sugar
- 1/4 cup pureed strawberries
- 1/2 cup 100% fruit juice
- 1/2 cup unsweetened plain almond milk
- 1 tbsp lemon juice

Direction

- Preheat the oven to 300F, grease a 9" springform pan.
- In a small bowl, mix flours, baking powder, baking soda, almond meal and pumpkin pie spice. Set aside.
- Heat oil in a pot over medium heat.
- Add dates, raisins, prunes, cashews and walnuts. Cook just slightly (about 1 minute), stirring well.
- Add sugars, berry puree and fruit juice. Cook until the sugar is dissolved and the mixture is beginning to bubble vigorously.
- Remove from heat and cool 2 minutes, then stir in the almond milk, lemon juice and flour mixture.
- Pour into the prepared pan and bake 1 hour, until it tests done.

164. Overnight Berry Coffee Cake Recipe

Serving: 1216 | Prep: | Cook: 47mins | Ready in:

Ingredients

- 2 cups flour
- 1 cup sugar
- 1/2 cup brown sugar
- 1 tsp baking powder
- 1 tsp soda
- 1 tsp ground cinnamon
- 1/2 tsp salt
- 1 cup buttermilk
- 2/3 cup butter or margarine, melted
- 2 eggs, beaten
- 1 cup fresh or frozen raspberries or blueberries
- Topping:
- 1/2 cup brown sugar
- 1/2 cup chopped nuts
- 1 tsp ground cinnamon

Direction

- In a large bowl, combine flour, sugars, baking powder, baking soda, cinnamon and salt.
- In a separate bowl, combine buttermilk, butter and eggs; add to dry ingredients and mix well until blended.
- Fold in berries.
- Pour into a greased 13 in. x 9 in. 2 in. baking pan.
- Combine topping ingredients; sprinkle over batter.
- Cover and refrigerate several hours or overnight.
- Uncover and bake at 350* for 45-50 minutes.

165. Overnight Coffee Cake Recipe

Serving: 8 | Prep: | Cook: 50mins | Ready in:

Ingredients

- 3 c. all-purpose flour
- 1 1/2 t. baking powder
- 1 1/2 t. baking soda
- 1 t. salt
- 1 c. butter, softened

- 1 1/4 c. sugar
- 3 eggs
- 1 15-ounce carton ricotta cheese
- 3/4 c. chopped nuts (I use pecans)
- 1/2 c. packed dark brown sugar
- 2 T. toasted wheat germ
- 1 T. ground cinnamon
- 1 t. ground nutmeg

Direction

- Grease bottom and 1/2-inch up the sides of a 13x9x2-inch baking pan; set aside.
- In a large bowl, combine flour, baking powder, baking soda and salt; set aside. In a large mixing bowl, beat butter with an electric mixer on medium speed for 30 seconds. Add granulated sugar; beat until combined. Add eggs, one at a time, beating well after each addition. Beat in ricotta cheese. Beat in as much of the flour mixture as you can. Stir in any remaining flour mixture with a wooden spoon. Spread batter into the prepared pan.
- In a bowl, combine nuts, brown sugar, wheat germ, cinnamon and nutmeg. Sprinkle evenly over batter in pan. Cover and refrigerate for up to 24 hours.
- Preheat oven to 350 degrees F. Uncover coffee cake and bake for 50 minutes or until a wooden toothpick inserted near the center comes out clean. Cool slightly in pan on a wire rack. Serve warm.

166. PULL APART COFFEE CAKE Recipe

Serving: 10 | Prep: | Cook: 25mins | Ready in:

Ingredients

- 1/4 C. sugar
- 1/4 C. golden or dark raisins
- 1/4 C. chopped walnuts, almonds or pine nuts
- 2 tsp. grated lemon peel
- 2 Tbs. butter or margarine, melted
- 1 can (12 oz) Pillsbury® Golden Layers® refrigerated buttermilk or original flaky biscuits

Direction

- Heat oven to 375°F.
- Line bottom of 8- or 9-inch round cake pan with waxed paper.
- In large bowl, mix all ingredients except biscuits.
- Separate dough into 10 biscuits.
- Cut each into quarters.
- Place biscuit pieces in sugar mixture; toss to coat.
- Arrange in single layer in waxed paper-lined pan.
- Sprinkle top with any remaining sugar mixture.
- Bake 20 to 25 minutes or until deep golden brown.
- Run knife around side of pan to loosen.
- Place heatproof serving plate upside down over pan; turn plate and pan over.
- Remove pan and waxed paper.
- Cut coffee cake into wedges or pull apart.
- Serve warm.

167. Party Size Coffee Cake Supreme Recipe

Serving: 20 | Prep: | Cook: 90mins | Ready in:

Ingredients

- Streusel topping
- 1 1/4 cups granulated sugar
- 1/4 teaspoon salt (if you use unsalted butter)
- 1 1/2 cups Unbleached all-purpose flour
- 1 tablespoon ground cinnamon
- 6 tablespoons butter, melted
- optional my addition: 1/4 cup finely chopped pecans
- Filling

- 1 cup brown sugar, light or dark
- 1 1/2 tablespoons ground cinnamon
- 2 Tbs unsweetened cocoa powder, Dutch-process or natural
- 1/4 tsp fresh grated black pepper (optional)
- optional my addition: 1/4 cup fine chopped pecans
- cake
- 3/4 cup butter
- 1 teaspoon salt (1 1/4 teaspoons if you use unsalted butter)
- 1 1/2 cups granulated sugar
- 1/3 cup brown sugar
- 2 1/2 teaspoons baking powder
- 2 teaspoons vanilla extract
- 3 large eggs
- 3/4 cup sour cream or plain yogurt (I only use Greek yogurt)
- 1 1/4 cups milk (anything from skim to whole) I used skim
- 3 3/4 cups Unbleached all-purpose flour,

Direction

- Preheat the oven to 350°F. Lightly grease a 9" x 13" pan, or two 9" round cake pans .I used a large tube pan!
- Make the topping by whisking together the sugar, salt, flour, and cinnamon. Add the melted butter, stirring till well combined Stir in nuts if using. Set the topping aside.
- Make the filling by mixing together the brown sugar, cinnamon, and cocoa powder. Note that the cocoa powder is used strictly for color, not flavor; leave it out if you like. Stir in nuts if using. Set it aside. Note: I used more cocoa for the flavor!
- To make the cake: In a large bowl, beat together the butter, salt, sugars, baking powder, and vanilla until well combined and smooth.
- Add the eggs one at a time, beating well after each addition.
- In a separate bowl, whisk together the sour cream or yogurt and milk till well combined. You don't need to whisk out all the lumps.
- Add the flour to the butter mixture alternately with the milk/sour cream mixture, beating gently to combine.
- Pour/spread half the batter (a scant 3 cups) into the prepared pan(s), spreading all the way to the edges. If you're using two 9" round pans, spread 1 1/3 cups batter in each pan.
- Note: I used a large tube pan
- Sprinkle the filling evenly atop the batter.
- Spread the remaining batter atop the filling. Use a table knife to gently swirl the filling into the batter, as though you were making a marble cake. Don't combine filling and batter thoroughly; just swirl the filling through the batter.
- Sprinkle the topping over the batter in the pan.
- Bake the cake until it's a dark golden brown around the edges; medium-golden with no light patches showing on top, and a toothpick or cake tester inserted into the center comes out clean, about 55 to 60 minutes for the 9" x 13" pan, 50 to 55 minutes for the 9" round pans. When pressed gently in the middle, the cake should spring back.
- Note: I baked at 325F and baking time increased in the tube pan to about 80 minutes
- Remove the cake from the oven and allow it to cool for 20 minutes before cutting and serving. Serve cake right from the pan.
- Note: when mine was completely cool, I removed it from the tube pan which had a removable bottom!

168. Party Size Polish Style Coffee Cakes Recipe

Serving: 36 | Prep: | Cook: 40mins | Ready in:

Ingredients

- 2 (.25 ounce) packages active dry yeast
- 1/4 cup warm water (110 degrees F/45 degrees C)
- 3 cups milk

- 1 cup butter
- 10 eggs, beaten
- 1 1/2 cups white sugar
- 1/4 teaspoon ground nutmeg
- 1/4 teaspoon orange extract
- 1 1/2 teaspoons vanilla extract
- 10 cups all-purpose flour
- 1 teaspoon salt
- Topping:
- 1/2 cup butter, cubed
- 2/3 cup white sugar

Direction

- In a small bowl, dissolve yeast in warm water.
- Let stand until creamy, about 10 minutes.
- Warm the milk in a small saucepan until it bubbles, then remove from heat.
- Mix in 1 cup butter until melted.
- Let cool until lukewarm.
- In a large bowl, beat together the eggs and 1 1/2 cups sugar.
- Mix in the nutmeg, orange extract, vanilla extract, and the yeast mixture.
- Stir in 3 cups flour and the salt.
- Stir in 1/3 of the milk mixture.
- Mix in the remaining flour and milk mixture in two alternating additions.
- Cover bowl, and let rise until doubled, about 45 minutes to an hour.
- In a small bowl, prepare the topping by cutting together 1/2 cup butter and 2/3 cups sugar until mixture resembles coarse crumbs.
- Preheat oven to 350 degrees F (175 degrees C).
- Lightly grease 3, 10-inch Bundt pans.
- Divide dough into the prepared pans, and sprinkle with the topping mixture.
- Bake in preheated oven for 30 to 40 minutes, until a toothpick inserted into center comes out clean.
- Best served warm or room temperature.
- Freeze other 2 cakes if desired.

169. Party Size Sour Cream Chocolate Chip Coffee Cake Recipe

Serving: 12 | Prep: | Cook: 60mins | Ready in:

Ingredients

- cake
- 1 stick, butter softened at room temperature
- 1 1/2 cups granulated sugar
- 3 large eggs, separated, room temerature
- 1 1/2 tsp vanilla extract
- 2 cups dairy sour cream
- 3 cups all-purpose flour
- 1 tsp baking powder
- 1 1/2 tsp baking soda
- 1/4 tsp salt
- Filling and Topping
- 2 cups quality semi- sweet or bittersweet chocolate chips
- 1/2 cup granulated sugar
- 1 tsp cinnamon (try the Saigon cinnamon)

Direction

- Preheat oven to 350°F.
- Butter a 9-x-13-inch baking pan or 2, 8 or 9 inch square cake pans or 1 large Bundt or tube pan
- In a large bowl, cream butter and 1 1/2 cups sugar.
- Beat in egg yolks and vanilla.
- Sift flour, baking soda, baking powder and salt together into a separate bowl.
- Alternately mix in sour cream and then dry ingredients into butter mixture until both are used up and the batter is smooth and very thick.
- In a medium bowl, beat eggs whites with clean beaters until stiff, then gently fold into batter.
- In a small dish, whisk together sugar and cinnamon for filling and topping.
- Spread half the cake batter in the bottom of prepared pan(s).
- Sprinkle with half of cinnamon-sugar mixture and 1 cup of chocolate chips.

- Dollop remaining cake batter over filling in spoonfuls.
- Use a rubber spatula or back of a spoon to gently spread it over the filling and smooth the top.
- Sprinkle batter with remaining cinnamon-sugar and sprinkle remaining chocolate chips over cinnamon sugar- do not push them into batter
- Bake for 40 to 50 minutes for oblong pan, 30-40 minutes for square pans and 45-60+ minutes for Bundt pan, OR until a wooden tooth pick inserted into the center of the cake comes out clean.
- Rotating pan(s) halfway through baking.
- Let pan(s) cool completely on rack.
- Serve when completely cooled.
- Also taste wonderful when well chilled.
- Note: I usually freeze one pan if I bake 2 smaller ones.

170. Party Size Strawberry Rhubarb Coffee Cake Recipe

Serving: 20 | Prep: | Cook: 60mins | Ready in:

Ingredients

- 3 cups brown sugar
- 1 cup margarine or butter, softened at room temp
- 4 cups flour
- 2 tsp baking soda
- 1/4 tsp salt
- 2 cups sour cream
- 2 tsp vanilla
- Rhubarb: Mixture
- 3 cups cut up rhubarb
- 2 cups sliced or chopped fresh strawberries
- Topping:
- 1 cup white granulated sugar
- 2 tsp cinnamon
- 2 Tbs cold margarine or butter
- 1 cup chopped walnuts

Direction

- For cake:
- Place all in a large bowl and with beater mix all.
- The mixture will be very thick and you may need to mix remainders by hand if beaters get to slow and stuck.
- If needed thin just a bit with a little milk.
- But mixture should be thick to incorporate the rhubarb and berries as they bake into the batter.
- Combine rhubarb and strawberries and blend into mixture (it will loosen up mixture a bit).
- Grease and flour a 12 inch round wedding cake pan or springform pan (or smaller oblong pans if you wish).
- Spread mixture in pan evenly.
- Prepare topping.
- Mix all with fingers to blend well.
- Sprinkle over cake.
- Bake 350F about one hour or cake tests done in center.
- Cool completely in pan.
- Loosen sides with a knife and remove from pan.
- Place on a large cake plate or platter.
- Garnish as desired.
- Serve warm or cold.
- Freezes well.
- Note: no eggs in the cake.

171. Peaches And Cream Coffee Cake Recipe

Serving: 6 | Prep: | Cook: 60mins | Ready in:

Ingredients

- 2 1/3 cups flour
- 1 1/3 cups sugar
- 3/4 teaspoon salt
- 3/4 cup shortening
- 2 teaspoon baking powder

- 3/4 cup milk
- 2 eggs
- 1 teaspoon vanilla
- 1 3 oz. pkg. cream cheese, softened
- 1 14 oz. can Eagle Brand milk
- 1/3 cup lemon juice
- 2 teaspoon cinnamon
- 1 29 oz. can sliced peaches, well drained
- 1 cup chopped nuts
- 1/3 cup brown sugar

Direction

- In large bowl mix flour, sugar and salt. Cut in shortening till crumbly. Reserve 1 cup of mixture. To the rest of the crumb mixture add baking powder, milk, eggs and vanilla. Beat well.
- Spread into greased 13x9 pan. Bake at 350° for 25 minutes or until set. Meanwhile, in bowl, beat cream cheese till fluffy. Add Eagle Brand milk. Stir in lemon juice and peaches and half of the nuts and cinnamon.
- In another bowl combine reserved crumbs and remaining nuts and cinnamon and brown sugar. Spoon peach mixture on top of cake and sprinkle crumb mixture on top. Bake 35 minutes longer or until set. Serve warm.

172. Peachy Morning Coffeecake Recipe

Serving: 12 | Prep: | Cook: 45mins | Ready in:

Ingredients

- Coffeecake:
- ¾ cup white sugar
- ½ cup brown sugar
- ½ cup butter, softened
- 1 cup sour cream
- 1 teaspoon vanilla extract
- ½ teaspoon almond extract
- 2 eggs, lightly beaten
- 2 cups all-purpose flour
- 1½ teaspoons baking powder
- ½ teaspoon baking soda
- ½ teaspoon salt
- 4 cups peeled, sliced fresh peaches, tossed in a little flour (about 2 tablespoons) to coat them just a bit
- NOTE: canned peaches tend to make this a bit too mushy - fresh will give you the best texture results
- Topping:
- ¼ cup all-purpose flour
- ¼ cup white sugar
- 1 teaspoon ground cinnamon
- 4 tablespoons cold butter
- ¼ cup chopped pecans (or chopped almonds taste nice in this, too)

Direction

- In a large bowl, cream together both sugars and the butter.
- Beat in sour cream, extracts, and eggs.
- Mix in flour, baking powder, baking soda, and salt.
- Spread ½ the batter into a greased 9x13 pan.
- Layer with peaches, and top with remaining ½ of batter.
- Prepare the topping by mixing the flour, sugar, and cinnamon in a small bowl; cut in cold butter until the mixture becomes crumbly, then stir in chopped pecans.
- Sprinkle topping evenly over the batter.
- Bake at 325 degrees for 45 minutes, or until a knife inserted in the center comes out clean.

173. Peanut Butter Coffee Cake Recipe

Serving: 16 | Prep: | Cook: 30mins | Ready in:

Ingredients

- 1/2 cup brown sugar, packed
- 1/2 cup all-purpose flour
- 1/4 cup peanut butter

- 3 tbsp margarine or butter
- 2 cups all purpose flour
- 1 cup brown sugar, packed
- 2 tsp baking powder
- 1/2 tsp baking soda
- 1/4 tsp salt
- 1 cup milk
- 1/2 cup peanut butter
- 2 eggs
- 1/4 cup margarine or butter

Direction

- Preheat oven to 375 degrees.
- For topping, in a bowl, stir together, 1/2 cup brown sugar and 1/2 cup all-purpose flour. Cut in 1/4 cup peanut butter and 3 tbsps. margarine or butter until crumbly. Set aside.
- In a bowl, stir together 2 cups flour, 1 cup brown sugar, baking powder, baking soda and salt. Add milk, 1/2 cup peanut butter, eggs and 1/4 cup margarine or butter. Beat with an electric mixer on low speed until blended. Beat on high speed for 3 minutes, scraping sides of bowl.
- Pour batter into a greased 13x9x2 baking pan, spreading evenly. Sprinkle with topping mixture. Bake in 375 oven for about 30 minutes or until toothpick inserted in middle comes out clean.

174. Pecan Coffee Cake Recipe

Serving: 6 | Prep: | Cook: 25mins | Ready in:

Ingredients

- 1 3/4 cups all- purpose flour
- 2 pkgs. rapid rise yeast
- 1 Tbsp. sugar
- 1/2 tsp. salt
- 3/4 cup very warm water
- 2 Tbsp. melted butter
- cinnamon sugar Topping:

- 1/4 cup sugar
- 1 tsp. cinnamon
- caramel pecan Topping:
- 1/3 cup light or dark corn syrup
- 1/3 cup brown sugar
- 2 Tbsp. melted butter
- 1/2 cups pecans

Direction

- Mix batter ingredients in a greased deep dish pie plate.
- Stir together corn syrup, brown sugar, and butter in a small bowl, add pecans and mix well.
- Combine sugar, cinnamon topping ingredients together in small bowl.
- Top batter with cinnamon/sugar topping; then spoon caramel/pecan topping evenly over the batter.
- Bake by placing in a COLD oven; set temp. to 350. Bake 25 mins. until lightly browned and firm in center. Cool slightly and serve warm.

175. Pecan Roll Monkey Bread Recipe

Serving: 12 | Prep: | Cook: 60mins | Ready in:

Ingredients

- For the Dough:
- PROOF:
- 1 packet (2 1/4 t.) active dry yeast
- 1 c. warm water (100-110 degrees)
- WARM; ADD:
- 3/4 c. whole milk
- 1/2 c. buttermilk
- 3 T. sugar
- 2 T. unsalted butter, room temperature
- 5 c. all-purpose flour, divided
- 1 1/2 t. kosher salt...okay I am on a kosher kick. Regular salt is fine.
- FOR THE FILLING---

- SOFTEN AND BLEND:
- 3/4 c. unsalted butter, room temperature
- 1 1/4 c. sugar
- 1/4 c. cinnamon
- toast AND CHOP:
- 1 1/2 c. pecans; divided
- For the caramel topping ---
- COMBINE; ADD:
- 1 1/2 c. brown sugar
- 1/2 c. heavy cream
- 1/4 c. pure maple sytrup
- 1 T. bourbon
- 1 t. kosher salt (I know, again with the kosher salt - you can use regular salt)
- Remaining pecans

Direction

- BUTTER a 12-cup Bundt pan; set aside.
- PREPARE dough and filling.
- PROOF the yeast for the dough in warm water in the bowl of a stand mixer for 5 minutes, or until foamy. (You can proof in a regular large bowl to do this recipe if you do not have a stand mixer but your arm will fall off working the dough.)
- WARM the milk to 100 degrees in a saucepan over low heat while yeast is proofing. Add warmed milk, buttermilk, 3 T. sugar, 2 T. butter, 3 1/2 cups flour, and salt to the proofed yeast. With a paddle attachment, mix on low speed until combined, then increase speed to high; beat for 2 more minutes.
- SWITCH to the dough hook and add the remaining 1 1/2 cups of flour. Mix on low speed until incorporated, then increase speed to medium. Mix for 5-7 minutes, or until dough pulls away from the sides of the bowl. (It will still be stuck to the bottom of the bowl, so don't worry.) Cover bowl with plastic and let dough rise in a warm place for 1-1 1/2 hours, or until doubled. Butter two 9" square pans. (I know, 9" is not a regular size that many have but it is better just because they get BIG)
- SOFTEN 3/4 cup butter for the filling in a bowl in a microwave for 30 seconds. Use a hand mixer to blend in the sugar and cinnamon; set aside (do not chill).
- TOAST pecans in a non-stick skillet until golden and fragrant; chop and set aside. While dough rises make caramel topping.
- COMBINE brown sugar, cream, maple syrup, bourbon, and salt in a saucepan. Bring to a boil over medium-low heat (DO NOT STIR, and keep an eye on it--there's a tendency for it to boil over).
- Simmer for 10 minutes, then pour 1 cup caramel into the prepared Bundt pan. Set aside.
- ONCE the dough has risen, hook your fingers under the edges to release the dough from the bowl. Scrape it onto a well-floured surface, sprinkle flour over the top, and press gently to remove air bubbles. Divide the dough in half and roll one portion into a 10 x 16" rectangle.
- SPREAD half of the filling onto the dough, and sprinkle with 1/2 c. pecans, pressing them lightly into the dough. Cut each rectangle into thirds and roll the rectangles long ways - jelly-roll style- into logs. (Remember that you want miniature cinnamon rolls to pile on top of each other in the Bundt pan.)
- TRANSFER to a baking sheet, freeze 10 minutes, and then slice into 1" rolls with a serrated knife.
- ARRANGE rolls in the prepared pan in circles, building two layers. (Another words, pile the miniature cinnamon rolls on top of each other all the way around the Bundt pan.) Cover with foil that's been coated with non-stick spray, then let rise for 1 hour; preheat oven to 350 degrees. Bake bread, covered with foil, for 30 minutes, then remove foil and bake an additional 25-30 minutes. Allow the bread to rest for 15 minutes.
- MEANWHILE, bring the remaining caramel to a simmer, then add the remaining 1/2 c. pecans. Invert bread onto a plate, then drizzle with caramel.
- A LONG PROCESS, but great eating. So many people enjoy this when I make it. I love the aroma I get in the whole house. Yum!

176. Pecan Streusel Coffee Cake Recipe

Serving: 12 | Prep: | Cook: 45mins | Ready in:

Ingredients

- Streusel:
- 2/3 cup (packed) dark brown sugar
- 2/3 cup all purpose flour
- 3/4 teaspoon ground cinnamon
- 6 tablespoons (3/4 stick) unsalted butter, melted, cooled slightly
- 1/2 cup pecans, toasted, coarsely chopped
- Cake:
- 2 cups all purpose flour
- 1 1/4 teaspoons baking soda
- 1 teaspoon ground nutmeg
- 1/2 teaspoon salt
- 1 1/3 cups (packed) golden brown sugar
- 1/2 cup (1 stick) unsalted butter, room temperature
- 1 teaspoon vanilla extract
- 2 large eggs
- 1 cup whole-milk or reduced-fat
- (2%) plain Greek-style yogurt*

Direction

- For streusel:
- Combine brown sugar, flour, and cinnamon in medium bowl. Add melted butter; toss with fork to blend. Using fingertips, rub mixture together until small clumps form. Mix in pecans. DO AHEAD: Can be made 1 day ahead. Cover and chill.
- For cake:
- Position rack in center of oven and preheat to 350°F. Butter 9x9x2-inch metal baking pan. Combine flour, baking soda, nutmeg, and salt in medium bowl; whisk to blend. Using electric mixer, beat brown sugar, butter, and vanilla in large bowl until well blended, about 2 minutes. Add eggs 1 at a time, beating well after each addition and scraping down sides of bowl occasionally. Add half of flour mixture; beat just until blended. Add yogurt; beat just until blended. Beat in remaining flour mixture just until blended.
- Spoon half of batter into prepared baking pan; spread evenly. Sprinkle half of streusel evenly over batter. Spoon remaining batter in dollops over streusel, then spread evenly over with offset spatula. Sprinkle remaining streusel evenly over top.
- Bake cake until streusel topping is brown and tester inserted into center of cake comes out clean, about 45 minutes. Cool cake in pan on rack 30 minutes. Cut into squares and serve slightly warm or at room temperature.
- * A thick yogurt; sold at some supermarkets and at specialty foods stores and Greek markets. If unavailable, spoon regular yogurt into cheesecloth-lined strainer set over large bowl. Cover and refrigerate overnight to drain.

177. Peek A Boo Fig Coffeecake Recipe

Serving: 8 | Prep: | Cook: 45mins | Ready in:

Ingredients

- 1/2 cup shortening
- 1/2 cup granulated sugar
- 1/2 teaspoon vanilla
- 1 egg beaten
- 1-1/2 cups all purpose flour
- 1/2 teaspoon salt
- 1-1/2 teaspoons baking powder
- 1/2 cup milk
- Filling:
- 1/2 cup dried figs chopped fine
- 1/4 cup chopped walnuts
- 1/2 cup brown sugar
- 1/4 cup melted butter
- 1 tablespoon cinnamon

Direction

- Cream shortening then add sugar and vanilla and cream thoroughly.
- Add beaten egg and mix thoroughly.
- Sift dry ingredients and add alternately with milk.
- Spread half the batter in a greased square cake pan then cover with fig filling.
- Add remaining batter than bake at 350 for 45 minutes.
- For the filling rinse figs with hot water then chop fine.
- Blend with remaining filling ingredients and spread over bottom half of batter.

178. Perfect Apple Cream Coffee Cake Recipe

Serving: 8 | Prep: | Cook: 40mins | Ready in:

Ingredients

- 1 stick margarine
- 1 c. sugar
- 2 eggs
- 1 tsp. soda
- 1 tsp. baking powder
- 1 tsp. cinnamon
- 2 apples, peeled and finely chopped
- 1/2 tsp. salt
- 1 c. sour cream
- 1 tsp. vanilla
- 2 c. flour
- Cream margarine and sugar together. Add eggs
- and beat well add vanilla. Sift all dry ingredients
- together add alternately with sour cream to the
- creamed mixture. Fold in apples. Pour into a
- greased and floured bundt pan.
- Sprinkle with this mixture before baking:
- 1/2 c. brown sugar
- 1 tbsp. margarine
- 1 tsp. cinnamon
- 1/2 c. chopped nuts
- Bake 40 minutes at 375 degrees.

Direction

- Cream margarine and sugar together.
- Add eggs and beat well add vanilla.
- Sift all dry ingredients together add alternately with sour cream to the creamed mixture.
- Fold in apples.
- Pour into a greased and floured Bundt pan.
- Sprinkle with this mixture before baking:
- 1/2 c. brown sugar
- 1 tbsp. margarine
- 1 tsp. cinnamon
- 1/2 c. chopped nuts
- Bake 40 minutes at 375 degrees.
- ***
- -A true friend never gets in your way - unless you are on your way down -
- ***

179. Pineapple Macadamia Coffeecakes Recipe

Serving: 8 | Prep: | Cook: 30mins | Ready in:

Ingredients

- 3/4 cup warm water
- 1 package active dry yeast
- 3/4 cup warm milk
- 2 tablespoons honey
- 2 tablespoons vegetable oil
- 1 teaspoon salt
- 2-1/2 cups all purpose flour
- 2 cups whole wheat flour
- Filling:
- 2 tablespoons butter melted
- 1/2 cup packed light brown sugar

- 1 teaspoon ground cinnamon
- 1 cup chopped dried pineapple
- 1 cup chopped toasted macadamia nuts
- Glaze:
- 1/4 cup honey
- 1 tablespoon butter

Direction

- Place 1/4 cup warm water in large warm bowl then sprinkle in yeast and stir until dissolved.
- Add remaining water, warm milk, honey, vegetable oil, salt and 1-1/2 cups all-purpose flour.
- Blend well then stir in whole wheat flour and enough remaining flour to make soft dough.
- Knead on lightly floured surface until smooth and elastic about 8 minutes.
- Place in greased bowl turning to grease top then cover and let rise in warm place 45 minutes.
- Punch dough down then remove to lightly floured surface and divide in half.
- Roll each to rectangle and transfer to two greased baking sheets and brush with melted butter.
- In small bowl combine brown sugar, cinnamon, pineapple and macadamia nuts then stir well.
- Sprinkle half of the brown sugar mixture over center third of each rectangle.
- Along each side of coffeecake cut 1" wide strips from edge of filling to edge of dough.
- Starting at one end alternately fold six strips from each side across filling toward opposite end.
- Repeat from other end using six strips from each side.
- Loosely tie together remaining two center strips on top of loaf.
- Repeat with second coffeecake.
- Cover and let rise in warm draft free place until almost doubled in size about 40 minutes.
- Bake at 375 for 25 minutes and switch positions of sheets halfway through baking.
- Remove from sheets and cool on wire racks then brush with glaze.

- To make glaze stir 1/4 cup honey and 1 tablespoon butter over medium heat until butter melts.

180. Pioneer Ladies Coffee Cake Recipe

Serving: 12 | Prep: | Cook: 52mins | Ready in:

Ingredients

- FOR THE CAKE:
- 1-1/2 stick butter, Softened
- 2 cups sugar
- 3 cups flour, Sifted
- 4 teaspoons baking powder
- 1 teaspoon salt
- 1-1/4 cup whole milk (I used skim milk)
- 3 whole egg whites, (note no egg yolks in recipe)
- Note: no yolks in the recipe
- 2 tsp vanilla (my addition)
- FOR THE TOPPING:
- 1-1/2 stick butter, Softened
- 3/4 cups flour
- 1-1/2 cup brown sugar
- 2 Tablespoons cinnamon
- 1-1/2 cup pecans, Chopped

Direction

- Preheat oven to 350 degrees.
- Sift together flour, baking powder, and salt.
- Beat egg whites to soft peaks and set aside.
- Cream butter and sugar.
- Add flour mixture and milk alternately until combined but don't over beat.
- Fold in beaten egg whites with a rubber spatula.
- Spread in a well-greased 9 x 13 or 10 x 14 inch baking pan esp. with high sides.
- In a separate bowl, combine topping ingredients with a pastry cutter until crumbly.
- Sprinkle evenly all over the top.

- Bake for 40 to 45 minutes, or until no longer jiggly.
- Serve warm or at room temperature.

181. Polish Coffee Cake Recipe

Serving: 36 | Prep: | Cook: 40mins | Ready in:

Ingredients

- 2 (.25 ounce) packages active dry yeast, (not in the original recipe but 3 pkgs yeast may be better!
- 1/4 cup warm water (110 degrees F/45 degrees C)
- 3 cups milk
- 1 cup butter
- 10 eggs, beaten
- 1 1/2 cups white sugar
- 1/4 teaspoon ground nutmeg
- 1/4 teaspoon orange extract
- 1 1/2 teaspoons vanilla extract
- 10 cups all-purpose flour
- 1 teaspoon salt
- Topping:
- 1/2 cup butter, cubed
- 2/3 cup white sugar

Direction

- In a small bowl, dissolve yeast in warm water.
- Let stand until creamy, about 10 minutes.
- Warm the milk in a small saucepan until it bubbles, then remove from heat.
- Mix in 1 cup butter until melted.
- Let cool until lukewarm.
- In a large bowl, beat together the eggs and 1 1/2 cups sugar.
- Mix in the nutmeg, orange extract, vanilla extract, and the yeast mixture.
- Stir in 3 cups flour and the salt.
- Stir in 1/3 of the milk mixture.
- Mix in the remaining flour and milk mixture in two alternating additions.
- Cover bowl, and let rise until doubled, and light.
- In a small bowl, prepare the topping by cutting together 1/2 cup butter and 2/3 cups sugar until mixture resembles coarse crumbs.
- Preheat oven to350 degrees F (175 degrees C).
- Lightly grease 3 10-inch Bundt pans.
- Lightly divide dough into the prepared pans, and sprinkle with the topping mixture. Let rise till doubled.
- Bake in preheated oven for 30 to 40 minutes, or until a toothpick inserted into center comes out clean.
- Note: as with any yeast coffee cake, these taste best the day baked and freeze leftover.

182. Praline Apple Bread Recipe

Serving: 8 | Prep: | Cook: 65mins | Ready in:

Ingredients

- Praline-Apple bread
- Makes 1 loaf Prep: 20 min.
- Bake:1 hr. Cool: 1 hr 10 min.
- Cook: 5 min.
- 1 1/2 cups chopped pecans, divided
- 1 (8oz.) container sour cream
- 1 cup granulated sugar
- 2 large eggs
- 1 tbsp. vanilla extract
- 2 cups all-purpose flour
- 2 tsp. baking powder
- 1/2 tsp. baking soda
- 1/2 tsp salt
- 1 1/2 cups finely chopped, peeled granny smith apples(about 3/4 pound)
- 1/2 cup butter
- 1/2 cup firmly packed light brown sugar

Direction

1. Preheat oven to 350*. Bake 1/2 cup pecans in a single layer in a shallow pan 6 to 8 min. or until toasted and fragrant, stirring after 4 min.
2. Beat sour cream and next 3 ingredients at low speed with an electric mixer 2 minutes or until blended.
3. Stir together flour and next 3 ingredients. Add to sour cream mixture, beating just until blended. Stir in apples and 1/2 cup toasted pecans. Spoon batter into a greased and floured 9-x5-inch loaf pan. Sprinkle with remaining 1 cup chopped pecans; lightly press pecans into batter.
4. Bake at 350* for 1 hour to 1 hour and 5 minutes or until wooden pick inserted into center comes out clean, shielding with aluminum foil after 50 minutes to prevent excessive browning. Cool in pan on a wire rack 10 minutes; remove from pan to wire rack.
5. Bring butter and brown sugar to boil in a 1-qt. heavy saucepan over medium heat, stirring constantly; boil 1 minute. Remove from heat, and spoon over top of bread; let cool completely (about 1 hour)
- Note: To freeze, cool bread completely; wrap in plastic wrap, then in aluminum foil. Freeze up to 3 months. Thaw at room temperature.
- Recipe: Adapted from Southern Living

183. Pull Apart Or Monkey Coffee Cake Recipe

Serving: 12 | Prep: | Cook: 30mins | Ready in:

Ingredients

- 1 pkg active dry yeast
- 1/4 cup warm water
- 1/2 tsp salt
- 1/4 cup sugar
- 1/4 cup oil
- 3/4 cup warm milk
- 1 large egg
- 3 1/2 cups flour or more as needed
- 1 cup raisins
- 1 cup sugar
- 2 tsp cinnamon
- 1/2 cup melted butter

Direction

- Dissolve yeast in water until foamy.
- Stir in salt, sugar, oil, milk and egg to blend.
- Stir in 3 1/4 cups flour until smooth.
- Knead dough smooth and elastic on floured surface, adding additional flour if needed to prevent stickiness.
- If using a dough hook in mixer, beat high speed about 5 minutes.
- Knead in raisins by hand.
- Divide dough into 3 portions.
- Cut each portion into 16 small pieces.
- Shape pieces into balls.
- Roll dough balls in 1/2 cup melted butter and then in the sugar/cinnamon mixture.
- Stagger balls barely touching in a greased and floured 9 inch Bundt or tube pan.
- Sprinkle on any remaining sugar mixture and drizzle on any remaining melted butter.
- Cover lightly with plastic wrap and let rise puffy in a warm place about 45 minutes to 1 hour.
- Or you can chill the dough and let it rise puffy in the refrigerator about 16 to 18 hours.
- Bake in a preheated 350F oven about 30 minutes or golden and done.
- This particular recipe needs to cool in the pan about 10 minutes before removing so the warmed sugar and butter firms up.
- Carefully run a blade of knife around pan to loosen and carefully invert onto serving platter to serve.
- Serve warm.
- Advice guests to pull off pieces.
- Note: for the cake, I made slices of dough and not balls.
- Use portions of dough and roll out as you would for cinnamon rolls: roll up jelly roll style and slice off pieces and proceed with the remainder of the recipe.

- I also added a powder sugar icing over the warm cake with some nuts for decoration.
- TIP: Make cinnamon rolls/buns into a cake!
- Use your favorite cinnamon bun/roll recipe and when the pieces are cut into individual rolls (slices) pile them loosely in a tube pan after they have been dipped in the melted butter& sugar to make the bubble cake.
- Let them rise puffy and bake.

184. Pull Apart Coffee Cake Recipe

Serving: 12 | Prep: | Cook: 35mins |Ready in:

Ingredients

- 1 can (16.3 oz.) refrigerated buttermilk biscuits
- 1 pkg. (3.4 oz.) JELL-O vanilla flavor Instant Pudding
- 1 tsp. orange zest
- 1/4 tsp. ground cinnamon
- 2 Tbsp. butter, melted
- 1/4 cup PHILADELPHIA cream cheese spread
- 1/4 cup powdered sugar
- 2 tsp. milk
- 2 Tbsp. chopped toasted PLANTERS pecans

Direction

- HEAT oven to 350°F.
- SEPARATE biscuits; cut into quarters.
- Mix dry pudding mix, zest and cinnamon in medium bowl.
- Add biscuit pieces; toss to coat.
- Drizzle with butter; toss lightly.
- Place in 9-inch round pan sprayed with cooking spray.
- BAKE 20 min.
- Cool 5 min.; remove from pan.
- MICROWAVE cream cheese spread in small microwaveable bowl on HIGH 15 sec.; stir in sugar and milk. Drizzle over cake; top with nuts.

185. Pull Apart Caramel Coffee Cake

Serving: 16 | Prep: | Cook: 35mins |Ready in:

Ingredients

- 2 tubes (12 ounces each) refrigerated buttermilk biscuits
- 1 cup packed brown sugar
- 1/2 cup heavy whipping cream
- 1 teaspoon ground cinnamon

Direction

- Preheat oven to 350°. Cut each biscuit into four pieces; arrange evenly in a 10-in. fluted tube pan coated with cooking spray. In a small bowl, mix remaining ingredients until blended; pour over biscuits.
- Bake 25-30 minutes or until golden brown. Cool in pan 5 minutes before inverting onto a serving plate.
- Nutrition Facts
- 5 pieces : 204 calories, 8g fat (3g saturated fat), 10mg cholesterol, 457mg sodium, 31g carbohydrate (16g sugars, 0 fiber), 3g protein.

186. Pumpkin Coffeecake Recipe

Serving: 6 | Prep: | Cook: 45mins |Ready in:

Ingredients

- 1 package yellow cake mix
- 1 pound can pumpkin
- 1/2 cup brown sugar
- 1/2 cup oil
- 3 eggs
- 1/2 cup chopped nuts

- 1 teaspoon pumpkin pie spice
- Topping:
- 1/2 cup sugar
- 1/2 cup flour
- 1/4 cup butter softened
- 1 teaspoon cinnamon

Direction

- Preheat oven to 350.
- In large bowl combine cake mix, pumpkin, brown sugar, oil, eggs, nuts, and pumpkin pie spice.
- Blend at low speed until completely moistened about 1 minute.
- Beat 2 minutes at medium speed then spread batter in greased and floured rectangular pan.
- In medium bowl combine sugar, flour, softened butter and cinnamon and stir with a fork.
- Sprinkle evenly over batter then bake at 350 for 45 minutes.

187. Pumpkin Spice Coffee Cake Recipe

Serving: 8 | Prep: | Cook: 70mins | Ready in:

Ingredients

- 1 pkg. of spice cake mix
- 3 eggs
- 1 Cup Libby's 100% pumpkin
- 2/3 Cup evaporated milk
- 1/3 Cup vegetable oil
- 1 Cup white chocolate morsels
- butter Cream Frosting:
- ½ Cup margarine
- ½ Cup shortening
- 1/8 tsp. salt
- 1 ½ vanilla extract
- 5 Cups of confectioner's sugar
- ¼ Cup of milk

Direction

- Pre-heat oven to 350 F.
- Combine cake mix, eggs, pumpkin, evaporated milk and vegetable oil in a large mixing bowl. Beat at low speed until moistened.
- Beat at medium speed for two minutes; stir in the morsels. Pour into a well-greased and floured bunt cake pan.
- Bake for 40-45 minutes or until a wooden toothpick is inserted into the center and comes out clean. Cool on a wire rack for 25 minutes.
- Frosting:
- In a large bowl, cream margarine and shortening until light and fluffy.
- Add salt, vanilla and confectioner's sugar and milk. Beat well.

188. Quick Bread Dry Mix Recipe

Serving: 0 | Prep: | Cook: | Ready in:

Ingredients

- 1 1/2 cups whole-wheat pastry flour (see ingredient note) or whole-wheat flour
- 1 cup flour
- 1 1/2 tsp. baking powder
- 1/2 tsp. baking soda
- 1 tsp. cinnamon
- 1/4 tsp. salt

Direction

- Whisk together all the ingredients
- TIPS:
- Stores nicely in a freezer bag in the freezer for up to 6 months
- Ingredient Note: Whole-wheat pastry flour, lower in protein than whole-wheat flour, has less gluten-forming potential, making it a better choice for tender baked goods. You can find it in the natural foods section of large supermarkets and natural-foods stores. Store in the freezer.

189. Quickie Sticky Buns Recipe

Serving: 8 | Prep: | Cook: 30mins | Ready in:

Ingredients

- 1 cup packed brown sugar, divided
- 10 tablespoons butter, softened and divided
- 1 package hot roll mix
- 2 Tablespoons granulated sugar
- 1 cup hot water(120 - 130 degrees F)
- 1 egg
- 1 2/3 cups (10 oz. package) Hershey's cinnamon chips

Direction

- Lightly grease 2-9inch round baking pans.
- Combine 1/2 cup brown sugar and 4 tablespoons softened butter in a small bowl with pastry blender; sprinkle mixture evenly on bottom of prepared pan.
- Set aside.
- Combine contents of hot roll mix package, including yeast packet, and granulated sugar in large bowl.
- Using spoon, stir in water, 2 tablespoons butter and egg until dough pulls away from sides of bowl.
- Turn dough onto lightly floured surface.
- With lightly floured hands, shape into ball.
- Knead 5 minutes or until smooth, using additional flour if necessary.
- To shape: using lightly floured rolling pin, roll into 15 X 12-inch rectangle.
- Spread with remaining 4 tablespoons butter.
- Sprinkle with remaining 1/2 cup brown sugar and cinnamon chips, pressing lightly into dough.
- Starting with 12-inch side, roll tightly as for jelly roll; seal edges.
- Cut into 1-inch wide slices with floured knife.
- Arrange 6 slices, cut sides down, in prepared pan.
- Cover with towel; let rise in warm place about 30 minutes
- Heat oven to 350 degrees F.
- Uncover rolls.
- Bake 25 to 30 minutes or until golden brown.
- Cool 2 minutes in pan; with knife, loosen around edges of pan.
- Invert onto serving plate.
- Serve warm or at room temperature.
- Don't sweat the small stuff.

190. RASPBERRY CREAM CHEESE COFFEE CAKE Recipe

Serving: 1 | Prep: | Cook: 55mins | Ready in:

Ingredients

- 2 1/4 cups flour
- 3/4 cup sugar
- 3/4 cup chilled unsalted butter. cut into pieces
- 1/2 tsp baking powder
- 1/2 tsp baking soda
- 1/2 tsp salt
- 3/4 cup sour cream
- 1 large egg, beaten
- 1 1/2 ts almond extract
- FILLING
- 1 (8 oz) pkg cream cheese, softened
- 1/2 cup sugar
- 1 large egg
- 1/2 cup raspberry jam
- 1/2 cup slivered almonds

Direction

- Preheat oven to 350°.
- In a large bowl, combine flour and sugar. Cut in butter until mixture is crumbly. Remove 1 cup and set aside. To remaining crumbs, add baking powder, baking soda, salt, sour cream,

egg and almond extract; mix well. Spread in bottom and 2 inches up the sides of a greased 9 inch springform pan.
- Combine the cream cheese, sugar and egg in small bowl; beat well. Spoon over batter in pan. Top with raspberry jam. Sprinkle with almonds and reserved crumb mixture.
- Bake for 55 to 60 min. Cool on a wire rack for 15 min. Carefully run a knife around edge of pan to loosen. Remove sides of the pan. Cool completely on rack. Store wrapped in the refrigerator.

191. RICH COFFEE CAKE DOUGH Recipe

Serving: 4 | Prep: | Cook: 30mins | Ready in:

Ingredients

- 2 packages dry active yeast (4 1/2 scant teaspoons)
- 1/4 cup water (warm, 110 to 115 degrees)
- 1/2 cup granulated sugar
- 4 large eggs
- 2 tablespoons milk
- 1 teaspoon vanilla extract
- 4 1/4 cups unbleached all-purpose flour
- 2 1/4 teaspoons table salt
- 1/2 pound unsalted butter (2 sticks), cut into 1-inch pieces and slightly softened
- egg wash
- 1 large egg
- 1 teaspoon heavy cream (preferably) or whole milk
- Streusel Topping (optional)
- 1/3 cup packed light brown sugar
- 1 tablespoon granulated sugar
- 1/2 cup unbleached all-purpose flour
- 1/2 teaspoon ground cinnamon
- 1/4 teaspoon table salt
- 5 tablespoons butter (cold), cut into 8 pieces
- coffee cake icing (optional)
- 3/4 cup confectioners' sugar , sifted
- 3 1/2 teaspoons milk
- 1/2 teaspoon vanilla extract
- Sweet cheese Filling
- 8 ounces cream cheese
- 1/4 cup granulated sugar
- 2 1/2 tablespoons unbleached all-purpose flour
- pinch table salt
- 2 teaspoons grated lemon zest from 1 lemon
- 1 large egg
- 1/2 teaspoon vanilla extract
- .

Direction

- Note: The finished cakes made from this dough freeze beautifully, so we like to make the full amount of dough, bake two smaller cakes (as the smaller pieces of dough are easier to work with), and freeze one for later. You can use the full quantity of dough to make one large cake if you prefer (increase the baking time to 35 to 40 minutes if you go this route), or the recipe can be halved, as it must be if you opt to mix the dough in a food processor rather than a standing mixer. Between rising, shaping, and proofing, preparing these cakes is time-consuming, though not at all labor-intensive. An early morning start will let you make, rise, shape, proof, and bake the dough all in one day. Alternatively, you can refrigerate the shaped, proofed loaf overnight and bake it the next morning for breakfast.
- 1. Sprinkle yeast over warm water in bowl of standing mixer fitted with paddle; stir to dissolve. With mixer set on lowest possible speed, mix in sugar, eggs, milk, and vanilla until well combined. Add 3 1/4 cups flour and salt, mixing at low speed until flour is incorporated, about 1 minute. Increase mixer speed to medium-low and add butter pieces one at a time, beating until incorporated, about 20 seconds after each addition (total mixing time should be about 5 minutes). Replace paddle with dough hook and add remaining 1 cup flour; beat at medium-low speed until soft and smooth, about 5 minutes longer. Increase

speed to medium and beat until dough tightens up slightly, about 2 minutes longer.

- 2. Scrape dough (which will be too soft to pick up with hands) into straight-sided plastic container or bowl using plastic dough scraper. Cover container tightly with plastic wrap and let dough rise at warm room temperature until doubled in size, 3 to 4 hours. Punch dough down, replace plastic, and refrigerate until thoroughly chilled, at least 4 or up to 24 hours. Alternatively, for a quick chill, spread dough about 1-inch thick on baking sheet, cover with plastic, and refrigerate until thoroughly chilled, about 2 hours.
- 3. For the egg wash: Beat egg and cream or milk in small bowl until combined. Cover with plastic wrap and refrigerate until ready to use.
- 4. For the streusel topping (optional): Mix brown and granulated sugars, flour, cinnamon, and salt in small bowl. Add butter; toss to coat. Pinch butter chunks and dry mixture between fingertips until mixture is crumbly. Chill thoroughly before using. (Can be refrigerated in an airtight container up to 2 weeks).
- 5. For the icing (optional): Whisk all ingredients in medium bowl until smooth. (Can be refrigerated in an airtight container up to 1 week. Thin with a few drops of milk before using, if necessary.)
- 6. For the filling: Beat cream cheese, sugar, flour, and salt with hand-held electric mixer or in work bowl of standing mixer fitted with paddle at high speed until smooth, 2 to 4 minutes. Add lemon zest, egg, and vanilla; reduce beater speed to medium and continue beating, scraping down sides of bowl at least once, until incorporated, about 1 minute. Scrape mixture into small bowl and chill thoroughly before using. (Can be refrigerated in an airtight container up to 3 days).
- 7. For the cakes: Turn chilled dough, scraping container sides with rubber spatula if necessary, onto lightly floured work surface. Roll, shape, and top or fill following illustrations for Lattice Top or Twisted Coil cakes.
- 8. Cover loosely with plastic wrap on parchment-covered baking sheet and let cakes rise until slightly puffed (will not increase in volume as dramatically as a leaner bread dough), about 1 1/2 to 2 hours. (After this final rise, unbaked cakes can be refrigerated overnight and baked the next morning.)
- 9. Adjust oven rack to middle position and heat oven to 350 degrees. Working with and baking one coffee cake at a time, brush Egg Wash evenly on exposed dough. Sprinkle evenly with streusel topping, if using. Slide baking sheet onto a second baking sheet to prevent bottom crust from overbrowning and bake until deep golden brown and/or an instant-read thermometer inserted in center of cake registers 190 degrees, 25 to 30 minutes. Slide parchment with coffee cake onto rack and cool at least 20 minutes. Drizzle icing over cake, if using, and serve
- Notes: Coffee Cakes - Lattice Top
- 1. Working with a half recipe of cold dough at a time, shape dough into a 5-by-6-inch rectangle, then roll into an 8-by-12-inch rectangle (dough should be about 1/3-inch thick). Straighten with a pastry scraper to keep the sides even.
- 2. Place on a prepared pan. Spread a 3-inch-wide strip of filling down the center of the dough, leaving a 1 1/2-inch border at each short end.
- 3. Using a knife, cut a 1 1/2-inch square out of each corner of the dough.
- 4. Using scissors, cut a triangle with 1 1/2-inch sides in the center of each long side of the dough. Cut two more triangles (leaving a 1-inch strip of dough between each triangle) to the right and two to the left of the center triangle. Set aside dough scraps. Repeat with second long side.
- 5. Fold the ends over the filling, pinching the corner edges together to seal.
- 6. Bring the sections of dough from the long sides together in the center, overlapping the ends and pinching tightly to secure.
- 7. Cover lightly with plastic and proof until slightly puffed, 1 1/2 to 2 hours. Brush with

egg wash and sprinkle streusel topping down the center, leaving a 1-inch border down each side. Bake as directed.

- Remove from oven and let cool 5 minutes before inverting and placing on wire rack to cool.

192. Rage Of The Town Raspberry Coffeecake Recipe

Serving: 8 | Prep: | Cook: 45mins | Ready in:

Ingredients

- 2 cups all purpose flour
- 1 cup granulated sugar
- 2 teaspoons baking powder
- 1/2 teaspoon salt
- 1/2 cup milk
- 1 stick butter melted
- 2 large eggs
- 1 teaspoon raspberry extract
- 2 cups fresh raspberries
- Topping:
- 1/2 cup all purpose flour
- 1/2 cup granulated sugar
- 4 tablespoons butter softened
- 1 teaspoon ground cinnamon

Direction

- Preheat oven to 350 then spray angel food cake pan with non-stick cooking spray.
- Lightly dust pan with flour.
- In medium mixing bowl sift together flour, sugar, baking powder and salt.
- In large bowl beat together milk, butter, eggs and extract.
- Beat in flour mixture a little at a time then gently fold in berries and pour into prepared pan.
- To prepare topping combine flour, sugar, butter and cinnamon in small bowl until a crumbly.
- Sprinkle topping over cake batter then bake 45 minutes.

193. Ramona Cafe Cinnamon Rolls Recipe

Serving: 12 | Prep: | Cook: 15mins | Ready in:

Ingredients

- Dough Mixture:
- 4 eggs
- 6 ounces sugar
- 1 teaspoon fine salt
- 2 cups milk, lukewarm
- 4 ounces margarine
- 8 cups all-purpose flour, divided
- 2 tablespoons yeast
- Filling:
- 4 ounces margarine
- 2 cups brown sugar
- 3 tablespoons ground cinnamon
- 1 cup pecans, chopped
- Icing:
- 4 cups powdered sugar
- 4 ounces margarine
- 1 cup milk
- 1 tablespoon almond extract

Direction

- In a large mixing bowl beat the eggs, sugar, and salt for the dough mixture. Combine the warm mile and margarine and add to the egg mixture. Slowly add 4 cups flour and beat well. Add the yeast and mix thoroughly. Add the remaining 4 cups flour and mix on medium speed for 7 minutes. Place the dough in an oiled bowl and cover with plastic wrap. Let the dough rise to double its size, about 1 hour.
- Roll the dough into a 1 1/2 by 2-foot rectangle.
- For the filling:

- Spread 4 ounces of margarine over the dough and sprinkle entire surface with brown sugar, cinnamon, and chopped pecans. Roll the dough into a cylinder shape starting with the bottom edge, and then cut into 12 slices. Place the slices onto an oiled pan and bake at 350 degrees F for 15 minutes. Cool and cover with icing.
- For the icing:
- Stir all 4 icing ingredients until thoroughly combined.
- I saw Ramona who owns the restaurant and this recipe put the icing ingredients into a squirt bottle and then she just squirted it on, which was pretty cool & easy!
- Makes 12 rolls.

194. Raspberry Cheese Coffee Cake Recipe

Serving: 10 | Prep: | Cook: 75mins | Ready in:

Ingredients

- 2 1/2 cups flour
- 3/4 cup sugar
- 3/4 cup butter, cold
- 1/2 teaspoon baking powder
- 1/2 teaspoon baking soda
- 1/4 teaspoon salt
- 3/4 cup dairy sour cream
- 1 large egg
- 1 1/2 teaspoons almond flavoring
- 1 – 8 ounce package cream cheese
- 1/4 cup sugar
- 1 large egg
- 1/2 cup raspberry jam
- 1/2 cup almonds, slice
- 2 teaspoons flour

Direction

- Oven Temp: 375°
- Recipe Cooking Time: 75 minutes
- Pan Type: 9" springform pan
- ....
- Preheat oven, spray and flour pan.
- In a large mixing bowl combine the flour and sugar, mix well and add in the cold butter.
- Use a fork to mix butter into flour mixture until it resembles coarse crumbs.
- Remove 1 cup of crumb mixture and set aside for later use.
- Add to the remaining mixture the baking powder, baking soda, salt, sour cream, egg and almond flavoring, mix until well blended.
- Spread the batter into bottom of your pan, trying to leave the sides higher than the middle.
- In a mixing bowl beat the cream cheese and sugar until fluffy, add the egg and blend well.
- Pour cream cheese mixture over the crust.
- Carefully spoon jam over cream cheese mixture.
- Mix the reserved crumb mixture with the almonds.
- Sprinkle over the top of cheese mixture.
- Bake raspberry cheese coffee cake until it sets up and crust is golden brown.
- Cool 15 minutes on wire rack remove sides of pan.
- Serve up coffee cake while it is warm. Refrigerate raspberry cake leftovers.
- Recipe Serves: about 10

195. Raspberry Coffee Cake Recipe

Serving: 12 | Prep: | Cook: 60mins | Ready in:

Ingredients

- 2 sticks butter
- 2 cups sugar
- 2 eggs
- 1/4 teaspoon salt
- 2 cups flour
- 1 teaspoon baking powder

- 1 cup sour cream
- 1/2 teaspoon vanilla
- FILLING
- 1 (10 ounce) package frozen raspberries
- 1-3 ounce package cream cheese
- 1 tablespoon flour
- 1 egg
- 1/4 cup sugar

Direction

- In large mixer bowl, with an electric mixer, cream butter and sugar until fluffy.
- Add eggs. 1 at a time, beating well after each addition.
- Add flour, baking powder and salt.
- Fold in sour cream and vanilla.
- FILLING
- Thaw and drain raspberries.
- Blend cream cheese, egg, sugar and flour.
- Lightly mix in raspberries.
- Pour 1/2 batter into a greased and floured tube pan.
- Then add filling, then top with rest of batter.
- Bake at 350 degrees for 60-70 minutes, or until toothpick inserted in center comes out clean.

196. Raspberry Cream Cheese Coffee Cake Recipe

Serving: 1 | Prep: | Cook: 55mins | Ready in:

Ingredients

- 2 1/2 cups all-purpose flour
- 3/4 cup sugar
- 3/4 cup butter
- 1/2 teaspoon baking powder
- 1/2 teaspoon baking soda
- 1/4 teaspoon salt
- 3/4 cup dairy sour cream
- 1 egg
- 1 teaspoon almond extract
- Filling:

- 1 package (8 oz.) cream cheese, softened
- 1/4 cup sugar
- 1 egg
- 1/2 cup raspberry jam
- Topping:
- 1/2 cup sliced almonds

Direction

- In a large bowl, combine flour and sugar; cut in the butter using a pastry blender until mixture resembles coarse crumbs. Remove 1 cup crumbs for topping. To remaining crumb mixture, add baking powder, soda, salt, sour cream, egg and almond extract; blend well.
- Spread batter over bottom and 2 inches up side of greased and floured 9-inch springform pan. (Batter should be 1/4 inch thick on sides.)
- In small bowl, combine cream cheese, 1/4 cup sugar and egg; blend well. Pour over batter in the pan. Carefully spoon jam evenly over cheese filling.
- In a small bowl, combine 1 cup of reserved flour mixture and almonds; sprinkle over top.
- Bake at 350° for about 55-60 minutes or until cream cheese filling is set and crust is a deep golden brown. Cool 15 minutes. Remove sides of pan. Serve warm or cool. Cover and refrigerate leftovers. Yield: 16 servings

197. Raspberry Crunch Coffeecake Recipe

Serving: 8 | Prep: | Cook: 30mins | Ready in:

Ingredients

- 1/4 cup butter
- 1/2 cup granulated sugar
- 1 large egg
- 1 cup all purpose flour
- 1 teaspoon baking powder
- 1/4 teaspoon salt
- 1/3 cup milk
- 1/2 teaspoon vanilla extract

- 2 cups fresh raspberries
- Topping:
- 1/4 cup butter
- 1/2 cup sugar
- 1/3 cup flour
- 1/2 teaspoon ground cinnamon

Direction

- Preheat oven to 350 then grease a square baking pan and set aside.
- Cream butter, sugar and egg together until light and fluffy.
- Combine dry ingredients and stir by hand into creamed mixture alternately with milk and vanilla.
- Spread batter in prepared baking pan and top with berries.
- Combine topping ingredients using pastry blender until mixture resembles coarse crumbs.
- Sprinkle over the berries then bake for 30 minutes.
- Cool slightly before serving.

198. Raspberry Marzipan Coffee Cake Recipe

Serving: 12 | Prep: | Cook: 50mins | Ready in:

Ingredients

- Almond Streusel:
- 1/4 c. firm stick butter (or margarine)
- 1/3 c. all-purpose flour
- 1/4 c. sugar
- 1/3 c. slivered or sliced almonds
- Cake:
- 2 c. all-purpose flour
- 3/4 c. sugar
- 1/4 c. stick butter (or margarine), softened
- 1 c. milk
- 2 tsp. baking powder
- 1 tsp. vanilla
- 1/2 tsp. salt
- 1 large egg
- 1/2 of an 8 oz. package almond paste, finely chopped
- 1 c. fresh or unsweetened (thawed and drained) raspberries

Direction

- Preheat oven to 350 degrees F. Grease bottom and sides of square pan, 9 x 9 x 2 inches, with shortening.
- Prepare Almond Streusel: Cut butter into flour and sugar in medium bowl, using pastry blender or crisscrossing two knives, until crumbly. Stir in almonds. Set aside.
- Beat together cake ingredients, except almond paste and raspberries, in medium bowl with electric mixer on low speed 30 seconds. Beat on medium speed 2 minutes, scraping bowl occasionally.
- Spread half of the batter in prepared pan. Sprinkle with half each of the almond paste, raspberries, and Almond Streusel. Repeat with remaining batter, almond paste, raspberries, and Streusel.
- Bake about 40 - 50 minutes or until toothpick inserted in center comes out clean.

199. Raspberry Almond Coffee Cake Recipe

Serving: 12 | Prep: | Cook: 45mins | Ready in:

Ingredients

- 1/4 cup butter, softened
- 2 cups self-rising flour
- 1 cup sugar 1/2 cup brown sugar
- 1/4 cup butter, melted
- 4 oz. almond paste, chopped
- 1 egg
- 1/3 cup slivered almonds
- 1 cup milk
- 1 cup raspberries

- 2 teaspoons vanilla or almond extract

Direction

- Preheat the oven to 350° F and grease a 9 x 9 x 2-inch pan.
- In a medium-sized bowl, beat the softened butter, sugar, egg, milk, and extract at low speed until smooth.
- Add the flour; beat at low speed for 4 minutes.
- Spread half the batter in the baking dish.
- Mix the melted butter, brown sugar, almond paste, almonds, and raspberries.
- Sprinkle half the brown sugar mixture on top of the batter.
- Spread the rest of the batter; top with the remaining brown sugar mixture. Bake until a knife inserted near the middle comes out clean, about 45 minutes.
- Yields 12 pieces
- **
- Note: If you are not using self-rising flour, add 3 teaspoons baking powder and 1 teaspoon salt.
- **
- Variation Strawberries, blueberries, or cranberries may be substituted for the raspberries in this recipe. Cranberries may need additional sweetening.
- **
- Magical Attributes Happiness, celebration, romance; well-being of body, mind, and spirit.
- **
- Celebrations Hand fasting or courtship rituals, Valentine's Day, Sweetest Day, Anniversaries, and May Day.

200. Raspberry Marzipan Coffee Cake Recipe

Serving: 12 | Prep: | Cook: 50mins | Ready in:

Ingredients

- buttery Streusel
- 1/3 cup Gold Medal® all-purpose flour
- 1/4 cup sugar
- 1/4 cup firm butter or margarine
- 1/3 cup slivered almonds
- coffee cake
- 2 cups Gold Medal® all-purpose flour
- 3/4 cup sugar
- 1/4 cup butter or margarine, softened
- 1 cup milk
- 2 teaspoons baking powder
- 1 teaspoon vanilla
- 1/2 teaspoon salt
- 1 egg
- 1/2 package (7- or 8-oz size) almond paste, finely chopped
- 1 cup fresh or unsweetened frozen (thawed) raspberries

Direction

- 1. Heat oven to 350°F. Grease 9-inch square pan. In small bowl, mix 1/3 cup flour and 1/4 cup sugar. Cut in firm butter, using pastry blender (or pulling 2 table knives through ingredients in opposite directions), until crumbly. Stir in almonds.
- 2. In large bowl, beat all coffee cake ingredients except almond paste and raspberries with electric mixer on low speed 30 seconds. Beat on medium speed 2 minutes, scraping bowl occasionally.
- 3. Spread half of batter in pan. Sprinkle with half each of the almond paste, raspberries and streusel. Repeat with remaining batter, almond paste, raspberries and streusel.
- 4. Bake about 50 minutes or until toothpick inserted in center comes out clean. Serve warm or cool.

201. RaspberryCheese Coffee Cake Recipe

Serving: 16 | Prep: | Cook: 30mins | Ready in:

Ingredients

- 1 8-oz. pkg cream cheese, softened
- ½ cup butter
- 1-3/4 cups flour
- 1 cup granulated sugar
- 2 eggs
- ¼ cup milk
- 1 tsp. baking powder
- ½ tsp. baking soda
- ½ tsp. vanilla
- ½ cup seedless red raspberry or strawberry preserves
- powdered sugar (optional)

Direction

- Preheat oven to 350F. Grease a 13x9-inch baking pan; set aside.
- In a large mixing bowl, beat cream cheese and butter with an electric mixer on medium to high speed for about 30 seconds or until combined. Add about half of the flour to the cream cheese mixture.
- Add the granulated sugar, eggs, milk, baking powder, baking soda, and vanilla to the cream cheese mixture. Beat on low speed until thoroughly combined. Beat on medium speed for 2 minutes. Beat in remaining flour just until combined.
- Spread batter evenly into prepared pan. Spoon preserves in small spoonfuls on top of the batter. Using a small narrow spatula or knife, gently swirl preserves into the batter to create a marble effect.
- Bake at 350F for 30-35 minutes, or until a toothpick inserted near the center comes out clean.

202. Reillys Monkey Bread Recipe

Serving: 10 | Prep: | Cook: 30mins | Ready in:

Ingredients

- 2 cans Pillsbury Grands! Homestyle refrigerated buttermilk biscuits
- 1½ teaspoons of cinnamon
- ½ cup of white sugar
- ¾ cup of butter
- 1 cup of brown sugar, firmly packed into the measuring cup
- ½ cup pecans

Direction

- Pre-heat the oven to 350o and lightly butter the Bundt pan.
- Pour white sugar and cinnamon into a large Zip Lock bag.
- Cut each biscuit into 4 pieces. Add biscuit pieces, several at a time to the bag; shake to coat well. Begin placing the biscuit pieces in the Bundt pan. Sprinkle layers with the pecans.
- Ask Mom for help to melt the brown sugar and butter in saucepan. Cool 10 minutes, then CAREFULLY pour over the top of the biscuit pieces.
- Bake 28-32 minutes, until no longer doughy in center. Allow the Monkey Bread to cool 15 minutes before removing from pan. Turn upside down on a plate and pull apart to serve.

203. Rhubarb Coffee Cake Recipe

Serving: 1 | Prep: | Cook: 50mins | Ready in:

Ingredients

- 1 cup coarsely chopped pecans
- 1/2 cup firmly packed brown sugar
- 1 teaspoon cinnamon
- 2-1/2 cups flour
- 1 teaspoon vanilla
- 1 teaspoon baking powder
- 12-oz package fresh or frozen rhubarb
- 1/2 teaspoon salt

- 1/4 cup butter
- 1 cup sour cream
- 1-1/2 cups sugar
- 2 eggs

Direction

- Heat oven to 350.
- Grease 10-inch Bundt pan.
- In medium bowl, combine pecans, brown sugar and cinnamon. Sift together flour, baking powder, baking soda and salt.
- Cream butter and sugar together. Add eggs and vanilla. Stir flour mixture into butter mixture and fold in rhubarb and sour cream.
- Sprinkle 1/3 nut mixture over bottom of pan. Spread 1/2 batter. Sprinkle with remaining mixture and batter.
- Bake 50-55 minutes. Cool 10 minutes and invert on wire rack. Serve warm or cooled.

204. Roses Overnight Coffee Cake Recipe

Serving: 8 | Prep: | Cook: 40mins | Ready in:

Ingredients

- 1/3 cup butter, softened
- ½ cup sugar
- 1/4 cup packed brown sugar
- 1 egg, beaten
- 1 cup flour
- ½ tsp. baking powder
- 1/4 tsp. baking soda
- ½ tsp. ground cinnamon
- ½ cup buttermilk
- Topping 1/4 cup packed brown sugar
- 1/4 cup finely chopped pecans
- 1/4 tsp. ground cinnamon
- 1/8 tsp. ground nutmeg

Direction

- In a mixing bowl, cream butter and sugars. Add egg; mix well. Combine flour, baking powder, baking soda and cinnamon; add to creamed mixture alternately with buttermilk. Beat well. Spread into a greased 8" square baking pan. Combine topping ingredients; sprinkle over batter. Cover and refrigerate overnight. Bake, uncovered, at 350 F for 40 to 45 minutes or until the cake tests done. Serves 6 to 8.

205. Russian Honey Coffee Cake Loaf Recipe

Serving: 12 | Prep: | Cook: 45mins | Ready in:

Ingredients

- 1/2 c sugar
- 2 eggs, well beaten
- 3/4 c honey
- 2 tb oil
- 1/2 c Hot dark tea
- 2 tb whiskey
- 2 c Sifted flour
- 1 ts cinnamon
- 1/2 ts baking powder
- 1/2 ts baking soda
- 3/8 c Chopped nuts
- Grated rind of one lemon

Direction

- Mix all ingredients together and beat well.
- Pour into greased loaf pan which has been lined with waxed paper on the bottom.
- Bake at 325 degrees for 45 minutes to an hour or until tested done.
- If browning too fast, cover with foil last 15 minutes of baking.
- Cool completely.
- Wrap overnight before slicing.
- Freezes well.

206. Russian Nut Roll Bread Recipe

Serving: 20 | Prep: | Cook: 25mins | Ready in:

Ingredients

- 1 package(1/4 oz.) active dry yeast
- 1/4 cup warm water
- 1 cup butter, melted and slightly cooled
- 1/2 cup warm milk
- 3 egg yolks
- 2 tbsp. sugar
- 1/2 tsp. salt
- 3 cups all-purpose flour
- FOR FILLING:
- 3 egg whites
- 1 tsp. vanilla extract
- 3/4 cup sugar
- 2 1/2 cups ground nuts (walnuts or pecans work best)
- FOR GLAZE:
- 3/4 cup confectioners' sugar
- 1 tsp. butter, softened
- 1 tsp. vanilla extract
- 4 tsp. milk

Direction

- In a large bowl, dissolve yeast in warm water. Stir and let sit for 3 minutes.
- Add the melted butter (warm, not hot), milk, egg yolks, sugar, salt and flour. Beat until smooth. Do not knead the dough. Cover and refrigerate for 6 hours or overnight.
- FOR FILLING:
- In a small bowl beat egg whites until soft peaks form. Gradually beat in sugar, a little at a time, until stiff glossy peaks form and sugar is dissolved.
- Stir in vanilla. Fold in ground nuts, set aside.
- Place dough onto a lightly floured surface. Let it relax for 10 minutes. Divide the dough in half. Roll each half into a thin rectangle.
- Spread nut filling over rectangles to within 1/2 inch from the edges. Roll up jelly-roll style, starting with a long side and tucking in the edges. Brush the seams with water to help seal. Pat the bread loaves gently, flattening them slightly.
- Place seam side down on greased baking sheets. Cover and let rise in a warm place until doubled in size, for about 45 minutes.
- Bake at 350F for 25 minutes, or until golden brown. Remove from pans and let cool for about 10 minutes.
- Meanwhile, for the glaze, combine confectioners' sugar, vanilla and milk. Spread the glaze over the nut bread, or drizzle in a desirable pattern.
- This recipe makes 2 nut loaves. Delicious warm, or cold. Makes great dessert or breakfast food.

207. SOUR CREAM COFFEE CAKE Recipe

Serving: 1 | Prep: | Cook: 45mins | Ready in:

Ingredients

- 2 cups flour
- 1 tsp baking soda
- 3/4 tsp salt
- 1/2 tsp baking powder
- 1 cup walnuts, toasted
- 2 tsp cinnamon
- 1 1/4 cups sugar
- 3/4 cup unsalted butter softened plus 2 Tbsp melted
- 2 large eggs, room temperature
- 1 cup sour cream
- 1 tsp vanilla

Direction

- Preheat oven to 350°. Generously butter 10-inch (10 cup capacity) Bundt pan and dust with flour, knocking out excess.

- Whisk together flour, baking soda, salt and baking powder in bowl.
- Pulse walnuts, cinnamon, 1/4 cup sugar and pinch of salt in food processor until nuts are chopped. Add melted butter and pulse once to combine.
- Beat together remaining butter and 1 cup sugar in large bowl with electric mixer at high speed until pale and fluffy, 3 to 5 min. Reduce speed to medium and add eggs 1 at a time, beating well after each addition, then beat in sour cream and vanilla until light and fluffy, about 2 to 4 min more. Reduce speed to low and add flour mixture, scraping down side of bowl occasionally and mixing until just combined.
- Sprinkle 1/2 of nut mixture evenly in bottom of Bundt pan. Spoon 1/2 of batter over nuts and smooth with a rubber spatula. Sprinkle with remaining nut mixture and top with remaining batter, smoothing top.
- Bake in middle of oven until cake begins to pull away from side of pan and tester comes out clean, 45 to 50 min.
- Cool cake in pan on rack 1 hour, run a knife around outer and inner edges. Place rack on top of pan, flip to invert cake onto rack. Cool completely.

208. Save The Day Quick Cake Recipe

Serving: 10 | Prep: | Cook: 55mins | Ready in:

Ingredients

- 1 cup flour
- 1 tbsp mesquite flour
- 1 tsp cocoa powder
- 1/2 tsp baking powder
- 3/4 tsp baking soda
- pinch salt
- pinch nutmeg
- 2 oz low-fat cream cheese
- 2/3 cup sugar
- 1 egg
- 1 tsp vanilla
- 1/3 cup buttermilk
- 1/4 cup miniature chocolate chips

Direction

- Preheat oven to 375F, grease a 9" springform pan.
- In a medium bowl, whisk together flour, mesquite flour, cocoa, baking powder, baking soda, salt and nutmeg.
- In a large bowl, cream cream cheese and sugar.
- Add egg and vanilla, beating well.
- Add half the flour mixture to the creamed ingredients, blending in slightly, then add buttermilk. Follow with remaining dry ingredients.
- Spread batter in prepared pan, smoothing to the edges.
- Top with chocolate chips.
- Bake for 35 minutes, cool completely in the pan before unmoulding.

209. Sinfully Delicious Strawberry Coffeecake Recipe

Serving: 8 | Prep: | Cook: 45mins | Ready in:

Ingredients

- 2 cups all purpose flour
- 1 cup granulated sugar
- 2 teaspoons baking powder
- 1/2 teaspoon salt
- 1/2 cup milk
- 1 stick butter melted
- 2 large eggs
- 1 teaspoon strawberry extract
- 2 cups fresh strawberries sliced thin
- Topping:
- 1/2 cup all purpose flour

- 1/2 cup granulated sugar
- 4 tablespoons butter softened
- 1 teaspoon ground cinnamon

Direction

- Preheat oven to 350 then spray angel food cake pan with non-stick cooking spray.
- Lightly dust pan with flour.
- In medium mixing bowl sift together flour, sugar, baking powder and salt.
- In large bowl beat together milk, butter, eggs and extract.
- Beat in flour mixture a little at a time then gently fold in berries and pour into prepared pan.
- To prepare topping combine flour, sugar, butter and cinnamon in small bowl until a crumbly.
- Sprinkle topping over cake batter then bake 45 minutes.
- Remove from oven and let cool 5 minutes before inverting and placing on wire rack to cool.

210. Sour Cream Apple Coffee Cake Squares Recipe

Serving: 11 | Prep: | Cook: 40mins | Ready in:

Ingredients

- coffee CAKE:
- 1/2 cup butter, softened
- 1 cup sugar
- 2 eggs
- 2 tablespoons instant coffee
- 1 teaspoon vanilla
- 1 cup sour cream
- 2 cups unbleached flour
- 1 teaspoon baking powder
- 1 teaspoon baking soda
- 1 pinch salt
- FILLING:
- 1/4 cup brown sugar
- 1 tablespoon unbleached flour
- 1 teaspoon cinnamon
- 1 tablespoon butter, melted
- 3 granny smith apples, peeled cored and sliced

Direction

- Preheat oven to 350 F.
- Cream butter and sugar until smooth.
- Add eggs one at a time, mixing well after each addition.
- Add vanilla and stir in sour cream.
- In a separate bowl, combine dry ingredients and stir into wet ingredients until just mixed.
- In another bowl, combine all ingredients for topping except the apples.
- Toss the topping with the sliced apples.
- Scrape the cake batter into a 9x12 inch cake pan and level.
- Arrange the apple topping over the batter.
- Bake for 35 to 40 minutes or until a toothpick inserted in the centre of the cake comes out clean.
- Cut into squares and serve warm or at room temperature.

211. Sour Cream Coffee Cake Recipe

Serving: 8 | Prep: | Cook: 55mins | Ready in:

Ingredients

- Cake:
- 12 T. unsalted butter, softened at room temperature
- 1 1/2 c. sugar
- 3 extra-large eggs, at room temperature
- 1 1/2 t. vanilla extract
- 1 1/4 c. sour cream
- 2 1/2 c. cake flour (not self-rising)
- 2 t. baking powder
- 1/2 t. baking soda

- 1/2 t. salt
- For the Streusel:
- 3/4 c. light brown sugar, packed
- 1/2 c. all-purpose flour
- 1 1/2 t. ground cinnamon
- 1/4 t. kosher salt
- 3 T. cold unsalted butter, cut into pieces
- 3/4 c. chopped walnuts (optional)
- For the Glaze:
- 1 c. powdered sugar
- 5 T. real maple syrup

Direction

- Preheat the oven to 350 degrees F. Grease and flour a 10-inch tube pan.
- Cream the butter and sugar in the bowl of an electric mixer fitted with the paddle attachment for 4 to 5 minutes, until light. Add the eggs 1 at a time, then add the vanilla and sour cream. In a separate bowl, sift together the flour, baking powder, baking soda, and salt. With the mixer on low, add the flour mixture to the batter until just combined. Finish stirring with a spatula; to be sure the batter is completely mixed.
- For the streusel, place the brown sugar, flour, cinnamon, salt, and butter in a bowl and pinch together with your fingers until it forms a crumble. Mix in the walnuts, if desired.
- Spoon half the batter into the pan and spread it out with a knife. Sprinkle with 3/4 cup streusel. Spoon the rest of the batter in the pan, spread it out, and scatter the remaining streusel on top. Bake for 50 to 60 minutes, until a cake tester comes out clean.
- Let cool on a wire rack for at least 30 minutes. Carefully transfer the cake, streusel side up, onto a serving plate. Whisk the confectioners' sugar and maple syrup together, adding a few drops of water if necessary, to make the glaze runny. Drizzle as much as you like over the cake with a fork or spoon.

212. Sour Cream Coffee Cake Trifle Recipe

Serving: 12 | Prep: | Cook: | Ready in:

Ingredients

- By butterflydog
- 1 8 or 9 inch sour cream coffee cake with cinnamon
- nut streusel - loaf, tube or bundt variety
- (home made or store bought)
- 1, 16 oz can Hershey's chocolate syrup
- 32 oz frozen strawberries in sugar syrup, thawed
- 1 large container of whipped topping or one pint cream whipped
- 1 small jar of maraschino cherries in juice
- mint leaves for garnish

Direction

- When cake is completely cold, tear up in coarse chunks. Or use a store bought coffee cake.
- In a glass bowl layer the cake, berries with juice, chocolate syrup, cut of maraschino and juice and repeat layers again.
- Spread whipped topping or cream over the trifle. Cover and chill well.
- Serve individual portions in glass bowls or dishes.
- Note: variations: eggnog pound cake would also work well in the recipe for New Year's

213. Sour Cream Coffee Cake With Brown Sugar Pecan Streusel Recipe

Serving: 16 | Prep: | Cook: 60mins | Ready in:

Ingredients

- Streusel

- 3/4 cup unbleached all-purpose flour (3 3/4 ounces)
- 3/4 cup granulated sugar (5 1/4 ounces)
- 1/2 cup packed dark brown sugar (3 1/2 ounces)
- 2 tablespoons ground cinnamon
- 2 tablespoons unsalted butter , cold, cut into 2 pieces
- 1 cup pecans , chopped
- cake
- 12 tablespoons unsalted butter (1 1/2 sticks), softened but still cool, cut into 1/2-inch cubes, plus 2 tablespoons softened butter for greasing pan
- 4 large eggs
- 1 1/2 cups sour cream
- 1 tablespoon vanilla extract or almond extract
- 2 1/4 cups unbleached all-purpose flour (11 1/2 ounces)
- 1 1/4 cups granulated sugar (8 3/4 ounces)
- 1 tablespoon baking powder
- 3/4 teaspoon baking soda
- 3/4 teaspoon table salt

Direction

- Note: Refer to the illustrations below when layering the batter and streusel in the pan. A fixed-bottom, 10-inch tube pan (with 10-cup capacity) is best for this recipe. Note that the streusel is divided into two parts — one for the inner swirls, one for the topping.
- 1. For the streusel: In food processor, process flour, granulated sugar, 1/4 cup dark brown sugar, and cinnamon until combined, about 15 seconds. Transfer 1 1/4 cups of flour/sugar mixture to small bowl; stir in remaining 1/4 cup brown sugar and set aside to use for streusel filling. Add butter and pecans to mixture in food processor; pulse until nuts and butter resemble small pebbly pieces, about ten 1-second pulses. Set aside to use as streusel topping.
- 2. For the cake: Adjust oven rack to lowest position and heat oven to 350 degrees. Grease 10-inch tube pan with 2 tablespoons softened butter. Whisk eggs, 1 cup sour cream, and vanilla in medium bowl until combined.
- 3. Combine flour, sugar, baking powder, baking soda, and salt in bowl of standing mixer; mix on low speed for 30 seconds to blend. Add butter and remaining 1/2 cup sour cream; mix on low speed until dry ingredients are moistened and mixture resembles wet sand, with few large butter pieces remaining, about 1 1/2 minutes. Increase to medium speed and beat until batter comes together, about 10 seconds; scrape down sides of bowl with rubber spatula. Lower speed to medium-low and gradually add egg mixture in 3 additions, beating for 20 seconds after each and scraping down sides of bowl. Increase speed to medium-high and beat until batter is light and fluffy, about 1 minute.
- 4. Using rubber spatula, spread 2 cups batter in bottom of prepared pan, smoothing surface. Sprinkle evenly with 3/4 cup streusel filling (without butter or nuts). Repeat with another 2 cups batter and remaining 3/4 cup streusel filling (without butter or nuts). Spread remaining batter over, then sprinkle with streusel topping (with butter and nuts).
- 5. Bake until cake feels firm to touch and long toothpick or skewer inserted into center comes out clean (bits of sugar from streusel may cling to tester), 50 to 60 minutes. Cool cake in pan on wire rack 30 minutes. Invert cake onto rimmed baking sheet (cake will be streusel-side down); remove tube pan, place wire rack on top of cake, and reinvert cake streusel-side up. Cool to room temperature, about 2 hours. Cut into wedges and serve. (Cake can be wrapped in foil and stored at room temperature for up to 5 days.)
- Variation: add 1 cup chocolate chips. Or 1 cup frozen blueberries and 1 tsp. grated zest tossed in a bowl set aside until ready to alternate with streusel. Or 1/2 cup apricot jam.
- Note: Layering the Batter and Streusel
- 1. Using rubber spatula, spread 2 cups batter in bottom of prepared pan, smoothing surface. 2. Sprinkle evenly with 3/4 cup streusel filling without butter or nuts. 3. Repeat steps 1 and 2

with 2 cups batter and remaining streusel without butter or nuts. 4. Spread remaining batter over, then sprinkle with streusel topping with butter and nuts.

214. Sour Cream Coffee Cake With Pears And Pecans Recipe

Serving: 1 | Prep: | Cook: 50mins | Ready in:

Ingredients

- TOPPING
- 1 1/2 cups pecans
- 1/3 cup (packed) golden brown sugar
- 2 Tbsp flour
- 1 tsp cinnamon
- 2 Tbs chilled unsalted butter, cut into 1/2-inch cubes
- Blend first 4 ingredients in processor until nuts are coarsely chopped. Add butter; using on/off turns, blend until coarse crumbs form
- cake
- 2 3/4 cups flour
- 2 tsp baking powder
- 1/2 tsp salt
- 1/2 tsp baking soda
- 1 cup unsalted butter, room temperature
- 1 cup sugar
- 3/4 cup (packed) golden brown sugar
- 3 large eggs
- 1 tsp grated lemon peel
- 1 tsp vanilla
- 1/2 cup sour cream
- 1/2 cup whole milk
- 1 1/2 cups 1/2-inch cubes peeled pears

Direction

- Preheat oven to 350°.
- Butter and flour 13x9x2-inch metal baking pan.
- CAKE:
- Sift flour baking powder, salt and baking soda into medium bowl. Using electric mixer, beat butter in large bowl until fluffy. Gradually add both sugars and beat until well blended. Beat in eggs, 1 at a time, then lemon peel and vanilla. Blend sour cream and milk in small bowl. Beat in sour cream mixture alternately with dry ingredients in 3 additions each.
- Spread half of batter in prepared pan. Sprinkle half of topping over; cover with pears. Spread remaining batter over; sprinkle with remaining topping.
- Bake until top is brown and tester inserted into center comes out clean, about 50 min. Cool cake completely in pan on rack. (Can be made 1 day ahead. Cover and store at room temperature.)

215. Sour Cream Coffee Cake With Apples Recipe

Serving: 12 | Prep: | Cook: 50mins | Ready in:

Ingredients

- Topping
- 1 1/2 cups pecans
- 1/3 cup (packed) golden brown sugar
- 2 tablespoons all purpose flour
- 1 teaspoon ground cinnamon
- 2 tablespoons chilled unsalted butter, cut into 1/2-inch cubes
- cake
- 2 3/4 cups all purpose flour
- 2 teaspoons baking powder
- 1/2 teaspoon salt
- 1/2 teaspoon baking soda
- 1 cup unsalted butter, room temperature
- 1 cup sugar - I use 50-50 spenda and sugar
- 3/4 cup (packed) golden brown sugar
- 3 large eggs
- 1 teaspoon grated lemon peel
- 1 teaspoon vanilla extract
- 1/2 cup sour cream

- 1/2 cup whole milk
- 1 cups, 1/2-inch cubes, peeled apples
- 1/2 cup dried cherries

Direction

- For topping:
- Blend first 4 ingredients in processor until nuts are coarsely chopped. Add butter; using on/off turns, blend until coarse crumbs form.
- For cake:
- Preheat oven to 350°F. Butter and flour 13x9x2-inch metal baking pan. Sift flour, baking powder, salt, and baking soda into medium bowl. Using electric mixer, beat butter in large bowl until fluffy. Gradually add both sugars and beat until well blended. Beat in eggs, 1 at a time, then lemon peel and vanilla. Blend sour cream and milk in small bowl. Beat in sour cream mixture alternately with dry ingredients in 3 additions each. Spread half of cake batter in prepared pan. Sprinkle half of topping over; cover with apples and cherries. Spread remaining batter over; sprinkle with remaining topping.
- Bake until top is brown and tester inserted into center comes out clean, about 50 minutes. Cool cake completely in pan on rack. (Can be made 1 day ahead. Cover and store at room temperature.)

216. Sour Cream Coffeecake Recipe

Serving: 8 | Prep: | Cook: 50mins | Ready in:

Ingredients

- 1-1/2 cup shortening
- 1 cup sugar
- 1 cup sour cream
- 1 teaspoon grated orange peel
- 2 cups flour
- 1-1/2 teaspoon baking powder
- 1-1/2 teaspoon baking soda
- 1/4 teaspoon salt
- 1 cup pecans
- 1/2 cup brown sugar
- 1/2 teaspoon cinnamon
- 3/4 cup raisins

Direction

- Beat shortening, sugar and eggs until fluffy then blend in sour cream and orange peel.
- Sift together flour, baking powder, baking soda and salt then gradually add to mixture.
- Mix nuts, brown sugar and cinnamon in separate bowl.
- Spread half the batter into greased and floured 9" pan.
- Sprinkle with raisins and half the nut mixture.
- Spoon on remaining batter and spread evenly.
- Sprinkle with remaining nut mixture.
- Bake at 350 degrees for 50 minutes.

217. Sour Cream Pumpkin Coffeecake Recipe

Serving: 8 | Prep: | Cook: 30mins | Ready in:

Ingredients

- 1/2 cup butter
- 3/4 cup sugar
- 1 teaspoon vanilla
- 3 eggs
- 2 cup flour
- 1 teaspoon baking powder
- 1 teaspoon baking soda
- 1 cup sour cream
- 16 ounce can pumpkin
- 1 slightly beaten egg
- 1/3 cup sugar
- 1 teaspoon pumpkin pie spice
- Streusel:
- 1 cup packed brown sugar
- 1/3 cup butter
- 2 teaspoons cinnamon

- 1 cup chopped pecans

Direction

- Cream together butter, sugar and vanilla then add 3 eggs beating well.
- Combine flour, baking powder and soda then add to butter mixture alternately with sour cream.
- Combine pumpkin, slightly beaten egg, sugar and pumpkin pie spice.
- Spoon half of batter into rectangular baking dish and spread to corners.
- For streusel combine brown sugar, butter and cinnamon together and mix well then stir in nuts.
- Sprinkle half of streusel over batter then spread pumpkin mixture over streusel.
- Carefully spread remaining batter over pumpkin mixture then sprinkle with remaining streusel.
- Bake at 325 for 35 minutes.

218. Sour Cream Rhubarb Coffee Cake Recipe

Serving: 10 | Prep: | Cook: 35mins | Ready in:

Ingredients

- 2 cups diced rhubarb(could be apples, peaches etc.)
- 1 1/2 cups sugar
- 1 tsp baking soda
- 1 cup sour cream
- dash salt
- 2 cups flour
- dash nutmeg to taste
- butter to taste

Direction

- Mix rhubarb and 1/2 cup sugar and let stand 30 minutes.
- Stir baking soda into sour cream.
- Sift, flour, salt and 1 cup sugar.
- Combine everything together, mixture will be thick.
- Spread mixture in a 9 inch pan.
- Sprinkle with extra sugar, nutmeg and some pats of butter.
- Bake 350F for 30 to 40 minutes or tested done.
- Serve warm or at room temperature.

219. Spiced Brown Sugar Pecan Coffee Cake Recipe

Serving: 8 | Prep: | Cook: 55mins | Ready in:

Ingredients

- For the spiced pecan crumb topping:
- 1/4 cup light brown sugar
- 1/4 cup granulated sugar
- 1/2 cup unbleached all-purpose flour
- 1/2 teaspoon ground cinnamon
- 1/2 teaspoon ground mace
- 1/2 teaspoon ground ginger
- 6 tablespoons (3/4 stick) cold unsalted butter, cut into small pieces
- 2 cups (8 ounces) pecans, coarsely chopped
- ....
- For the coffee cake:
- 4 tablespoons (1/2 stick) unsalted butter, at room temperature
- 1/2 cup packed light brown sugar
- 1/2 cup granulated sugar
- 2 large eggs
- 2 teaspoons vanilla
- 2 cups unbleached all-purpose flour
- 1 teaspoon baking powder
- 1 teaspoon baking soda
- 1/4 teaspoon salt
- 1 cup buttermilk

Direction

- 1. Heat oven to 350 degrees. Line the bottom of an 8-inch springform pan or a 2-inch-deep

removable-bottom tart pan with parchment paper. Butter the sides of the pan.
- 2. Prepare the crumb topping: Combine the sugars, flour and spices in a small bowl or food processor fitted with the metal blade. Work the butter into the flour with your fingers (or process if using the food processor) until mixture forms coarse crumbs (do not over process or it will turn to dough). Add the pecans; mix and set aside.
- 3. Make the coffee cake: In a bowl using a wooden spoon, or in a heavy-duty electric mixer, beat the butter and sugars until light and fluffy. Add eggs and vanilla, beating until smooth.
- 4. In another bowl, combine the flour, baking powder, baking soda and salt; stir with a whisk to combine. In small batches, add the flour mixture to the butter mixture alternately with small amounts of the buttermilk. Beat hard or at high speed until batter is creamy, about 1 minute.
- 5. Scrape half of the batter into the prepared pan. Sprinkle evenly with half of the crumb topping. Spoon remaining batter on top and sprinkle with remaining topping.
- 6. Bake in the center of the oven until a wooden toothpick or a cake tester inserted in the center of the cake comes out clean, about 45 to 55 minutes (baking times vary depending on the type of pan used).
- 7. Remove cake from oven. Let cool in pan on a cooling rack. To serve, remove sides of pan and peel off parchment paper.

220. Starbucks Blueberry Coffee Cake Recipe

Serving: 6 | Prep: | Cook: 45mins | Ready in:

Ingredients

- For the Cake:
- 1 egg
- 1 cup milk
- 1/4 cup unsalted butter, melted
- 2 cups all-purpose flour
- 1/2 cup granulated sugar
- 2 1/2 tsps baking powder
- 1/2 tsp salt
- 1/2 tsp ground mace
- 1 cup fresh blueberries
- For the Topping:
- 2 tbsps unsalted butter
- 1/3 tsp ground cinnamon
- 1/4 cup granulated sugar
- 1/2 cup all-purpose flour

Direction

- To make the topping, combine cinnamon, sugar and flour in a small bowl.
- Add butter and beat with a pastry blender until the mixture is crumbly.
- Set aside.
- To make the cake, beat together the egg, milk and butter in a large bowl.
- Sift flour, sugar, baking powder, salt and mace into a bowl.
- Add the egg mixture and beat together until well blended.
- Stir in blueberries.
- Lightly butter a 9-inch-diameter cake pan.
- Evenly spread the cake batter in the pan and sprinkle with the topping.
- Bake in a preheated 350° F oven for about 40 - 45 minutes.

221. Strawberry Coffee Cake With Crumb Topping Recipe

Serving: 8 | Prep: | Cook: 35mins | Ready in:

Ingredients

- • 1 cup sifted all-purpose flour
- • 1/2 cup sugar
- • 2 teaspoons baking powder

- 1/2 teaspoon salt
- 1/2 cup milk
- 1 egg
- 2 tablespoons melted butter
- 1 1/2 cups strawberries, sliced
- .
- Crumb Topping:
- 1/2 cup flour
- 1/2 cup sugar
- 1/4 cup butter

Direction

- Sift together the 1 cup flour, 1/2 cup sugar, baking powder, and salt. Add milk, egg, and melted butter; beat 2 minutes. Spoon batter into a greased and floured 8-inch square baking pan. Top with sliced strawberries. Combine 1/2 cup flour and 1/2 cup sugar; cut in butter until mixture resembles coarse crumbs. Add chopped pecans or walnuts. Sprinkle crumb topping over the strawberries. Bake at 375° for 30 to 35 minutes. Serves 8.

222. Strawberry Cream Coffeecake Recipe

Serving: 8 | Prep: | Cook: 45mins | Ready in:

Ingredients

- 1-3/4 cups all purpose flour
- 1/2 cup granulated sugar
- 3/4 cup butter softened
- 2 eggs
- 1/2 teaspoon baking powder
- 1/2 teaspoon baking soda
- 1/4 teaspoon salt
- 1 teaspoon vanilla
- 1/4 cup granulated sugar
- 8 ounces cream cheese softened
- 1 egg
- 1 teaspoon grated lemon peel
- 10 ounce jar strawberry preserves
- 1/3 cup powdered sugar
- 3 teaspoons lemon juice

Direction

- Preheat oven to 350.
- Grease and flour bottom and sides of a spring form pan.
- Combine flour, sugar, butter, eggs, baking powder, baking soda, salt and vanilla.
- Beat at medium speed scraping bowl often until well mixed about 2 minutes.
- Spread batter on bottom and 2" up sides of prepared pan.
- Combine 1/4 cup sugar, cream cheese, egg and lemon peel in large mixer bowl.
- Beat at medium speed scraping bowl often until smooth about 3 minutes.
- Pour over batter in pan then spoon preserves evenly over filling.
- Bake 45 minutes then cool for 20 minutes.
- Loosen sides of cake from pan by running knife around inside of pan then remove side of pan.
- Stir together powdered sugar and lemon juice until smooth then drizzle over warm coffeecake.
- Serve warm or cold.

223. Strawberry Delight Coffee Cake Recipe

Serving: 9 | Prep: | Cook: 35mins | Ready in:

Ingredients

- 1 tablespoon cornstarch
- 10 ounce package frozen sweetened sliced strawberries
- ¼ teaspoon cinnamon (if you've never tried Saigon cinnamon, do try it!)
- ¼ teaspoon vanilla or almond extract (use the real thing – you'll get more flavor than the artificial)
- 2⅓ cups flour

- ¾ cup white sugar
- ¼ cup brown sugar
- ¾ cup butter, chilled (best if you do not substitute margarine)
- ½ teaspoon baking powder
- ½ teaspoon baking soda
- a couple pinches of salt
- ¾ cup buttermilk
- 1 egg, beaten

Direction

- In a large saucepan, combine the cornstarch and strawberries until well blended.
- Over medium heat, bring the mixture to a boil, stirring continually. Continue to cook and stir for another 2 minutes, or until thickened. Remove pan from heat and stir in the cinnamon and extract; set aside.
- In a large bowl, combine flour and both sugars.
- Cut in the cold butter until mixture is the consistency of crumbs. Take out ½ cup of the crumb mixture and save it for the topping.
- Add baking powder, baking soda and salt to the remaining crumb mixture.
- Stir in buttermilk and egg until moist and blended.
- Spread about 1½ cups of batter into a greased 8" square pan. Carefully spread the strawberry mixture over the batter.
- Drop remaining batter by spoonfuls over the strawberry layer. Sprinkle top with reserved crumb mixture.
- Bake at 350 degrees for 35 to 40 minutes, or until golden brown. Serve warm (or cool pan on a wire rack before wrapping coffee cake up to freeze).

224. Strawberry Poppy Seed Coffeecake Recipe

Serving: 8 | Prep: | Cook: 50mins | Ready in:

Ingredients

- 2/3 cup sugar
- 1/2 cup butter softened
- 2 teaspoons grated lemon peel
- 1 egg
- 1-1/2 cups all purpose flour
- 2 tablespoons poppy seeds
- 1/2 teaspoon baking soda
- 1/4 teaspoon salt
- 1/2 cup dairy sour cream
- Filling:
- 2 cups fresh strawberries
- 1/3 cup granulated sugar
- 2 teaspoons flour
- 1/4 teaspoon nutmeg
- Glaze:
- 1/3 cup powdered sugar
- 1 teaspoon milk

Direction

- Preheat oven to 350 then grease and flour a spring form pan and set aside.
- Beat sugar and butter until light and fluffy then add peel and egg and beat 2 minutes at medium.
- Combine flour, poppy seeds, baking soda and salt.
- Add to butter mixture alternately with sour cream.
- Spread batter over bottom and up sides of prepared pan making sure batter on sides is 1/4" thick.
- Combine all filling ingredients then spoon over batter and bake 50 minutes.
- Cool slightly on wire rack then remove sides of pan.
- Combine powdered sugar and enough milk for desired consistency then drizzle over warm cake.

225. Strawberry Rhubarb Coffee Cake Recipe

Serving: 16 | Prep: | Cook: 45mins | Ready in:

Ingredients

- FILLING:
- 3 cups sliced fresh or frozen rhubarb (1-inch pieces)
- 1 quart fresh strawberries, mashed
- 2 tablespoons lemon juice
- 1 cup sugar
- 1/3 cup cornstarch
- CAKE:
- 3 cups all-purpose flour
- 1 cup sugar
- 1 teaspoon baking powder
- 1 teaspoon baking soda
- 1/2 teaspoon salt
- 1 cup butter, cut into pieces
- 1-1/2 cups buttermilk
- 2 eggs
- 1 teaspoon vanilla extract
- TOPPING:
- 1/4 cup butter
- 3/4 cup all-purpose flour
- 3/4 cup sugar

Direction

- In a large saucepan, combine rhubarb, strawberries and lemon juice.
- Cover and cook over medium heat about 5 minutes.
- Combine sugar and cornstarch; stir into saucepan.
- Bring to a boil, cook and stir for 2 minutes or until thickened.
- Remove from heat and set aside.
- In a large bowl, combine flour, sugar, baking powder, baking soda and salt.
- Cut in butter until mixture resembles coarse crumbs.
- Beat buttermilk, eggs and vanilla; stir into crumb mixture.
- Spread half of the batter evenly into a greased 13-in. x 9-in. baking dish.
- Carefully spread filling on top.
- Drop remaining batter by tablespoonfuls over filling.
- For topping, melt butter in a saucepan over low heat.
- Remove from heat; stir in flour and sugar until mixture resembles coarse crumbs.
- Sprinkle over batter.
- Lay foil on lower rack to catch any juice fruit spill overs.
- Place coffee cake on middle rack; bake at 350° for 40-45 minutes. Cool in pan.
- Cut in squares.
- Yield: 16-20 servings.

226. Strawberry Rhubarb Filled Coffee Cake Recipe

Serving: 10 | Prep: | Cook: 45mins | Ready in:

Ingredients

- • Filling:
- • 3 cups sliced rhubarb, (1 inch pieces) fresh or frozen
- • 2 pints fresh strawberries, mashed
- • 2 tablespoons lemon juice
- • 1 cup sugar
- • 1/3 cup cornstarch
- • .
- • Cake:
- • 3 cups all-purpose flour
- • 1 cup sugar
- • 1 teaspoon baking powder
- • 1 teaspoon baking soda
- • 1/2 teaspoon salt
- • 1 cup butter or margarine, cut in small pieces
- • 1 1/2 cups buttermilk
- • 2 eggs
- • 1 teaspoon vanilla extract
- • .

- • Topping:
- • 1/4 cup butter or margarine
- • 3/4 cup all-purpose flour
- • 3/4 cup sugar

Direction

- In a large saucepan combine rhubarb, strawberries and lemon.
- Cover and cook over medium heat for about 5 minutes. Combine sugar and cornstarch; stir into strawberry rhubarb mixture. Bring to a boil over medium heat, stirring constantly until thickened; remove from heat.
- In a large bowl, combine flour, sugar, baking powder, baking soda and salt. Cut in butter with a pastry blender until mixture resembles coarse crumbs. In a separate bowl, beat together buttermilk, eggs and vanilla; stir into crumb mixture. Spread half of the batter evenly into a greased 9x13x2-inch baking dish. Carefully spread filling over the batter. Drop remaining batter evenly over filling with a tablespoon.
- Directions for Topping
- In a small saucepan over low heat, melt butter. Remove saucepan from heat; stir in flour and sugar until mixture is crumbly then sprinkle over batter. Lay foil on lower rack to catch any juicy fruit spill overs. Bake at 350° for about 45 minutes, or until cake is done. Cool cake in pan on rack. Cut rhubarb coffee cake into squares to serve.

227. Streusel Coffee Cake A Delectable Cake For Tea Or Dessert Recipe

Serving: 15 | Prep: | Cook: 60mins | Ready in:

Ingredients

- flour – 1 ¾ cups
- baking powder – 1 tsp
- baking soda – ½ tsp
- sugar – 2/3 cup (original recipe has 3/4 cup)
- eggs – 2 / large
- vanilla essence – 1 tsp
- butter – 1/2 cup
- yogurt – 4 tbsp
- Cream – 2 tbsp (25% fat)
- juice of ½ lime
- Zest of 1 orange
- Streusel:
- flour – 1 tbsp
- brown sugar – ¼ cup
- toasted walnuts – ½ cup (toasted in oven for 8-10minutes. Keep an eye on them or they will brown too fast & burn).
- Regular chocolate chips – ½ cup (I used Ghirardelli bittersweet)
- mini chocolate chips – ½ cup

Direction

- Line & grease & dust the bottom of a 9" spring form baking tin. Grease and dust the sides.
- Preheat the oven to 180 degrees C.
- Prepare the streusel by mixing the 1 tbsp. of flour + brown sugar + toasted walnuts in a bowl. Divide into 2; mix big chocolate chips in one, and the mini chips in the other. (Use only 1 size/variety of chips if you like.)
- Stir together the flour + baking powder + baking soda in a bowl.
- Mix the yogurt + cream + lime juice in a small bowl. (You can use sour cream instead)
- Beat the butter + sugar until light.
- Beat in the eggs one by one, and then the vanilla essence + orange zest.
- Beat in the 1/3 of the flour mixture; then 1/3 of the yogurt/cream mixture. Repeat twice & beat until just mixed in properly.
- Put half the batter in the tin; level out. Sprinkle the half streusel mix with the regular Ghirardelli chips evenly over this.
- Top with the remaining batter; then sprinkle the other half of the streusel mix evenly.
- Bake for approximately 60 minutes/ till done.
- Leave to cool in tin on rack for 10 minutes, and then remove the sides.

- I took the bottom lining parchment off about an hour later; peeled it off carefully as I couldn't invert the cake, else the topping may have fallen off.
- Serve warm as it is…OR with whipped cream or a dollop of vanilla ice-cream!

228. Super Moist Pumpkin Bread Recipe

Serving: 20 | Prep: | Cook: 75mins | Ready in:

Ingredients

- 3 1/2 cups all-purpose flour
- 2 cups packed dark brown sugar
- 2/3 cup white sugar
- 2 cups pumpkin puree
- 1 cup vegetable oil
- 2/3 cup coconut milk
- 2 teaspoons baking soda
- 1 teaspoon salt
- 1 teaspoon ground nutmeg
- 1 1/2 teaspoons ground cinnamon
- 2/3 cup flaked coconut
- 1 cup toasted walnuts

Direction

- Preheat oven to 350 degrees F (175 degrees C). Grease and flour two 8x4 inch loaf pans.
- In a large bowl combine the flour, brown sugar, white sugar, pumpkin puree, oil, coconut milk, baking soda, salt, ground nutmeg and ground cinnamon. Mix until all of the flour is gone. Fold in the nuts and flaked coconut. Pour batter into the prepared pans.
- Bake at 350 degrees F (175 degrees C) for 1 hour and 15 minutes or until a toothpick inserted in the center comes out clean. Remove from oven and cover loaves with foil tightly. Allow to steam for 10 minutes. Remove foil and turn out onto a cooling rack. Tent lightly with the foil and allow to cool completely.

229. Swedish Scorpa Recipe

Serving: 16 | Prep: | Cook: 45mins | Ready in:

Ingredients

- 1 package active dry yeast
- 1/4 cup warm water (105 to 115 degrees)
- 3/4 cup milk
- 1/2 cup (1 stick) butter, melted
- 1 teaspoon saffron threads (a good pinch or two)
- 1/2 to 3/4 teaspoon ground cardamom (optional)
- 1/2 cup sugar
- 1/2 teaspoon salt
- 1/2 cup currants
- 2 eggs, warmed
- 4 to 4 1/2 cups flour
- 1 large egg, beaten
- sugar sprinkles, optional
- 1 cup raisins (optional)
- ** This authentic recipe is from Beatrice Ojakangas's "Scandinavian Feasts" (University of Minnesota Press)
- http://www.beatrice-ojakangas.com/
- St. Lucia's Day (my birthday, Dec. 13th) is a world wide tradition for swedes as well as this Saint Lucia Wreath recipe is a standard among the Swedish culture.

Direction

- (Similar to Biscotti)
- To make the dough: In a large bowl, sprinkle the yeast over the warm water. Add a pinch of sugar. Heat the milk and add the melted butter to it; cool until the mixture is lukewarm.
- Pulverize the saffron with 1 teaspoon of the sugar, using a mortar and pestle or with the back of a spoon in a small dish. Add 1 tablespoon of the warm milk-and-butter mixture and allow the saffron to steep for 5 minutes.
- Add the saffron mixture, milk-and-butter mixture, sugar, salt, currants and eggs to the

yeast. Using an electric blender on medium speed, beat until blended. Add 2 cups flour and beat on medium speed for 2 minutes. Add 2 cups of the remaining flour and mix with a wooden spoon to make a medium-stiff dough. Let dough rest for 15 minutes.

- Turn the dough out onto a lightly floured board. Knead for 8 minutes or until the dough is smooth and satiny. Place the dough in a clean, lightly oiled bowl. Turn the dough over to lightly oil the top. Cover and let rise in a warm place until doubled in size, about 1 hour.
- To make a braided wreath: Punch the dough down and divide into 3 parts. With the palms of your hands, roll and shape each part into a rope-like strand about 36 inches long. Braid the strands by aligning them vertically and alternately crossing each outer strand over the center strand. Shape the braid into a circle and place on a greased or parchment-covered baking sheet. Pinch the ends together where they meet to seal the strands and to conceal the beginning and end of the braid.
- Transfer to the baking sheet. Brush with the beaten egg. Sprinkle with sugar sprinkles if using. Let rise for about 45 minutes or just until puffy.
- Preheat oven to 375 degrees. Bake for 20 to 25 minutes, until lightly browned, or until a wooden skewer inserted into the center of the dough comes out clean and dry.
- Cool on a wire rack for 15 minutes. Reduce heat to 300 degrees F. Carefully cut each rectangle into 1/2-in. slices. Place slices with cut side down on baking sheet. Bake 8-10 minutes longer.
- Note: To make two smaller wreaths: Divide the dough into 2 parts and braid as above. Place each wreath on a baking sheet, allow to rise and bake for about 20 minutes.

230. Sweet Lemon Coffeecake Recipe

Serving: 0 | Prep: | Cook: 30mins | Ready in:

Ingredients

- 1 cup milk
- 1 cup butter or margarine
- 2 packages active dry yeast
- 1/4 cup warm water (105 degrees F to 115 degrees F)
- 3/4 cup sugar
- 1 teaspoon salt
- 2 eggs, beaten
- 1 teaspoon vanilla
- 1 tablespoon lemon peel
- 3 tablespoons lemon juice
- 6 to 6-1/2 cups all-purpose flour
- Filling
- 1 cup sugar
- 1 cup chopped walnuts
- 1 tablespoon lemon peel
- 3 tablespoons lemon juice
- Combine ingredients in a medium bowl until well mixed.
- glaze
- 1 cup powdered sugar
- 1 tablespoon vanilla
- 2 tablespoons milk
- Combine ingredients in a small bowl until well mixed.

Direction

- Combine milk and butter in a saucepan. Heat over low heat until butter melts. Cool to 110 degrees F. Dissolve yeast in warm water in warmed bowl. Add milk mixture, sugar, salt, eggs, vanilla, lemon peel, lemon juice, and 5 cups flour. Attach bowl and dough hook. Turn to speed 2 and mix 2 minutes.
- Continuing on speed 2, add remaining flour, 1/2 cup at a time, until dough clings to hook and cleans sides of bowl. Knead on speed 2 for 2 minutes longer.

- Place in greased bowl, turning to grease top. Cover; let rise in warm place, free from draft, until doubled in bulk, about 1 hour.
- Punch dough down. Roll to a 16 x 8 x 1/4-inch rectangle. Spread filling on dough. Roll dough tightly from 16-inch side, pinching seam to seal. Place on greased baking sheet, seam side down. Pinch ends together to form a ring. Cut 2/3 the way into ring with scissors at 1-inch intervals. Turn each section on its side. Repeat with remaining dough. Cover; let rise in warm place, free from draft, until doubled in bulk, about 1 hour.
- Bake at 375 degrees F for 30 to 35 minutes. Remove from baking sheets immediately and cool on wire racks. Drizzle glaze over top of each coffee cake.
- Yield: 2 coffee cakes.

231. Sweet Potato Caramel Coffee Cake Recipe

Serving: 6 | Prep: | Cook: 45mins | Ready in:

Ingredients

- 1/3 cup butter
- 1/2 cup packed brown sugar
- 1/4 cup corn syrup
- 1/2 cup chopped pecans
- 2 1/2 cups Original Bisquick mix
- 2/3 cup mashed vacuum-pack sweet potatoes
- 1/3 cup milk
- 2 tablespoons butter, softened
- 3 tablespoons packed brown sugar

Direction

- Heat oven to 400 degrees. Melt 1/3 cup butter in ungreased square pan, 9x9x2 inches, in oven. Stir in 1/2 cup brown sugar and the corn syrup. Sprinkle with pecans. Mix Bisquick mix, sweet potatoes and milk until dough forms a ball. Turn dough onto surface dusted with Bisquick mix.
- Knead lightly 10 times. Roll or pat into 12-inch square. Spread 2 tablespoons butter over dough. Sprinkle 3 tablespoons brown sugar over butter. Fold dough into thirds; press edges together to seal. Cut crosswise into twelve 1-inch strips.
- Twist ends of each strip in opposite directions. Arrange twists on pecans in pan. Bake 25 to 30 minutes or until golden brown. Immediately turn upside down onto heatproof serving plate; leave pan over coffee cake 1 minute. Serve warm. Makes 12 twists.

232. Sweet Potato Coffee Cake With Pecan Topping Recipe

Serving: 12 | Prep: | Cook: 60mins | Ready in:

Ingredients

- • 2/3 cup melted butter
- • 3/4 cup granulated sugar
- • 2 large eggs
- • 1 teaspoon vanilla
- • 1 cup sour cream
- • 3/4 cup cooked, mashed sweet potatoes
- • 2 cups all-purpose flour
- • 1 teaspoon baking powder
- • 1/2 teaspoon baking soda
- • 1/4 teaspoon salt
- • ....
- • Topping
- • 1 cup chopped pecans
- • 1/2 cup light brown sugar, firmly packed
- • 1/2 cup all-purpose flour
- • 3 tablespoons margarine
- • 2 teaspoons vanilla

Direction

- Heat oven to 325°. Grease a 9 to 10-inch springform pan. In mixing bowl, combine butter, sugar, eggs, and vanilla; add sour cream and mashed sweet potatoes. In large mixing bowl, combine flour, baking powder, baking soda and salt. Stir first mixture into the flour mixture, stirring just until blended. Spread batter in prepared pan. Combine topping ingredients until crumbly and sprinkle over the batter. Bake coffee cake for about 1 hour to 1 hour and 10 minutes, or until a wooden toothpick inserted near center comes out clean. Let cool, loosen edges, and remove sides of pan.

233. Sweet Potatoe Praline Coffee Cake Recipe

Serving: 12 | Prep: | Cook: 30mins | Ready in:

Ingredients

- 4 tablespoons butter or margarine
- 2/3 cup brown sugar
- 2 tablespoons light corn syrup
- 3 tablespoons brown sugar
- 1/2 cup chopped pecans
- 2 and 1/2 cups biscuit baking mix
- 1 15 oz can sweet potatoes drained and mashed
- 1/3 cup milk
- 14 cup dried carnberries

Direction

- Preheat oven to 400 degrees.
- Using a 9 by 9 inch square non-stick baking pan melt the butter in the oven.
- Stir in the 2/3 cup brown sugar and the light corn syrup.
- Spread the mixture evenly in the pan.
- Sprinkle with the pecans.
- In large bowl mix the baking mix sweet potatoes and milk until the dough forms a ball.
- Turn dough out onto a surface dusted with the baking mix and knead several times.
- Roll or pat into a 12 inch rectangle.
- Sprinkle with the 3 tablespoons of brown sugar and the cranberries.
- Roll up jellyroll style and cut into one inch pieces.
- Arrange atop the butter mix in the pan.
- Dough will spread when baking.
- Bake for 25 to 30 minutes until golden brown.
- Turn upside down onto serving platter immediately.

234. Sweetly Cinnamon Coffee Cake Recipe

Serving: 16 | Prep: | Cook: 60mins | Ready in:

Ingredients

- ---Batter---
- 1 3/4 cups flour
- 1 cup spelt flour
- 1 tbsp baking powder
- 3/4 tsp baking soda
- 1/3 cup unsalted butter
- 1/2 cup Splenda granular
- 1/2 cup brown sugar
- 5 oz silken tofu, pureed
- 1 tbsp vanilla
- 1 tsp maple extract
- 3/4 cup pure apple butter
- 1 1/2 cups plain nonfat yogurt
- ---Filling---
- 2 tbsp brown sugar
- 1 tbsp chopped pecans
- 1 tbsp ground cinnamon

Direction

- Preheat oven to 350F. Grease a tube pan with cooking spray and set aside.
- Whisk together flours, baking powder, and baking soda and set aside.
- Cream the butter, Splenda and brown sugar until fluffy.
- Add pureed tofu, vanilla and maple extracts, beat well.

- Add apple butter and half the yogurt, beating smooth.
- Add the flour mixture alternating with remaining yogurt and beat until batter is smooth.
- Place 1/3 the cake batter into a small bowl. Add brown sugar, pecans and cinnamon, stirring well.
- Place 1/2 the plain batter into pan.
- Top with cinnamon-nut batter, swirling in with the tip of a knife.
- Top with remaining plain batter.
- Bake 60 minutes, or until tests done.

235. Tea Braised Beef With Apples Recipe

Serving: 4 | Prep: | Cook: 80mins | Ready in:

Ingredients

- 500 g beef
- 3 tbs olive oil
- 1/2 teaspoon nutmeg
- 1 teaspoon cumin
- 1 onion
- 2 garlic cloves
- 1 jalapeño
- 1/2 cup strongly brewed black tea
- 1 green apple
- 10 prunes
- 2 tbs chopped cilantro for garnish
- salt, pepper to taste

Direction

- Add oil to a pan and once heated add the finely chopped onion, cumin and nutmeg, sauté for 5 minutes, add garlic, jalapeño, sauté for 3 minutes, add meat, brown for a 3-5 min, add 1/3 cup tea, cover the pan and cook until ready. Add the remaining tea, salt, pepper, chopped prunes and apple and stew for 10 minutes more. Garnish with cilantro.

236. The Best Pumpkin Bread Ever Recipe

Serving: 12 | Prep: | Cook: 60mins | Ready in:

Ingredients

- 2 cups of canned pumpkin
- 1 cup Canolla oil
- 3 cups sugar
- 4 eggs,beaten
- 31/4 cups unbleached flour
- 1 tsp.baking powder
- 1 tsp.baking soda
- 1 tsp. nutmeg
- 2 tsp. cinnamon
- 2 tsp. salt
- 1 cup chopped walnuts or pecans (optional)OR MORE IF DESIRED

Direction

- Mix ingredients well.
- Pour into 2 greased bread pans.
- Bake for 1 hour in pre-heated 350 degree oven.
- Cool and slice.
- Makes 2 loaves.

237. The Manly Coffee Cake Recipe

Serving: 12 | Prep: | Cook: 30mins | Ready in:

Ingredients

- 3/4 cup dried apricots, soaked in hot water, drained and chopped
- 1 cup flour
- 1 cup whole-wheat flour (pastry if you have it, regular if not)
- 2 teaspoons baking powder
- 1/4 teaspoon salt
- 4 eggs, at room temperature

- 1 1/2 cups granulated sugar
- 2 tsp almond extract
- 1 tsp vanilla extract
- 2 Tbsp apricot or apple puree
- 1 cup McAuslan Apricot Wheat ale (or other fruited beer)

Direction

- Preheat oven to 375 degrees F.
- Grease and flour a Bundt cake pan.
- Sprinkle 1/2 of the apricots along the bottom of the cake pan.
- In a medium bowl, whisk together flours, baking powder, and salt, set aside.
- Beat eggs on high speed until thick and light in color, about 3 to 5 minutes.
- Beat in sugar until combined, then add almond and vanilla extracts.
- Fold flour mixture into egg and sugar mixture.
- Heat beer just until bubbles begin to rise around the edge of the pan. Add fruit puree and remove from heat.
- Add batter, stirring gently to combine.
- Pour 1/2 the batter into the prepared pan.
- Sprinkle 1/2 the remaining apricots over batter.
- Top with last of batter.
- Sprinkle the chopped apricots over the top of the batter.
- Bake 30 minutes. Do not over-bake.
- Cool on rack for 30 minutes.
- Invert onto a large platter and let cool to room temperature.

238. Triple Chocolate Coffee Cake Recipe

Serving: 9 | Prep: | Cook: 25mins | Ready in:

Ingredients

- 1 (18.25 oz) pkg devil's food cake mix
- 1 (3.9) oz pkg. chocolate instant pudding mix
- 2 c sour cream
- 1 c butter, softened
- 5 large eggs
- 1 tsp vanilla
- 3 c semi-sweet chocolate morsels, divided
- 1 c white chocolate morsels
- 1 c chopped pecans, toasted

Direction

- Preheat oven to 350 degrees. Beat first 6 ingredients at low speed with electric mixer 30 seconds or just till moistened; beat at medium speed 2 mins. Stir in 2 c semisweet chocolate morsels; pour batter evenly into 2 greased and floured 9" square cake pans.
- Bake for 25-30 mins or until a wooden pick comes out clean. Let cool completely in pans on wire racks.
- Microwave white chocolate morsels in glass bowl at high 30-60 seconds or till morsels melt, stirring at 30 second intervals until smooth. Drizzle evenly over cakes; repeat procedure with remaining 1 c semisweet morsels. Spoon pecans over cakes. Cut in squares or wedges.
- Makes 2 cakes. 9 pieces per cake.

239. Turkish Coffee Cake Recipe

Serving: 6 | Prep: | Cook: 45mins | Ready in:

Ingredients

- 1 c. yogurt
- 1 tsp. nutmeg
- 1/2 c. vegetable oil
- 1 c. honey
- 1/8 c. extra fine, ground Turkish coffee, sift some OR Turkish coffee spice mix
- 3/4 tsp. salt
- 2 1/4 c. whole wheat flour
- 2 1/4 tsp. cinnamon
- 1 1/8 tsp. soda
- TOPPING:

- 3/4 c. honey
- 3/8 c. melted butter
- 1/2 c. poppy seeds
- 5/8 c. raisins

Direction

- Use 2 bowls, one for dry ingredients and one for wet ingredients.
- Stir each bowl of ingredients, then pour all together into a buttered 9 x 13 inch baking dish. Bake at 350 degrees for 45 minutes. After 35 minutes remove and top with topping and return to bake another 10 minutes.
- TOPPING:
- Mix all ingredients together.

240. Unbelievable Coffee Cake Recipe

Serving: 6 | Prep: | Cook: 30mins | Ready in:

Ingredients

- 2 1/2 cups all-purpose flour
- 3/4 cup sugar
- 1 cup brown sugar
- 1/8 teaspoon nutmeg
- 1 teaspoon cinnamon
- 3/4 cup vegetable oil
- 2/3 cup crushed pecans
- 1 egg
- 1/2 teaspoon salt
- 2 teaspoons soda
- 1 cup buttermilk (may substitute 1 tablespoon lemon juice or vinegar plus milk to make 1 cup. Let stand 5 minutes before adding to batter

Direction

- Preheat oven to 350.
- Combine first 6 ingredients till crumbs are formed.
- Remove 1/3 cup crumbs.
- In a separate bowl, mix 2/3 cup crushed pecans and crumbs.
- Set aside for topping.
- Add remaining ingredients and mix well.
- Pour into a greased 8" x 11.5" .glass baking dish.
- Sprinkle topping over batter.
- Bake for 30 minutes or until seems firm on top.
- Serve warm.

241. VELVET DEVILS FOOD LAYER CAKE WITH COFFEE BUTTERCREAM FROSTING Recipe

Serving: 12 | Prep: | Cook: 30mins | Ready in:

Ingredients

- Velvet Devil's Food cake
- 1/2 cup natural cocoa powder
- 2 teaspoons instant espresso powder , or instant coffee
- 1 cup boiling water
- 2 teaspoons vanilla extract
- 12 tablespoons unsalted butter (1 1/2 sticks), softened
- 1 1/4 cups granulated sugar
- 2 large eggs , at room temperature
- 1 1/4 cups unbleached all-purpose flour
- 1/2 teaspoon baking soda
- 1/2 teaspoon table salt
- coffee buttercream frosting
- 1 tablespoon instant espresso powder , or instant coffee
- 1 tablespoon coffee liqueur
- 1 tablespoon vanilla extract
- 1/2 pound unsalted butter (2 sticks), softened
- 2 cups confectioners' sugar
- 1 egg yolk (beaten) , or 2 tablespoons beaten egg

Direction

- Note: This cake's texture is both soft and dense, similar to chocolate pound cake, only softer and lighter. Its flavor is intensely chocolate, yet pleasantly sweet. The substantial coffee-flavored buttercream stands up to the cake's dense texture and balances the rich chocolate flavor.
- 1. For the Cake: Adjust oven rack to center position and heat oven to 350 degrees. Grease two 8-by-1 1/2-inch round baking pans with shortening. Line pan bottoms with waxed or parchment paper; grease paper as well. Dust pans with flour; tap out excess.
- 2. Mix cocoa and instant coffee in small bowl; add boiling water and mix until smooth. Cool to room temperature, then stir in vanilla.
- 3. Beat butter in bowl of electric mixer set at medium-high speed until smooth and shiny, about 30 seconds. Gradually sprinkle in sugar; beat until mixture is fluffy and almost white, 3 to 5 minutes. Add eggs one at a time, beating 1 full minute after each addition.
- 4. Whisk flour, baking soda and salt in medium bowl. With mixer on lowest speed, add about 1/3 of dry ingredients to batter, followed immediately by about 1/3 of cocoa mixture; mix until ingredients are almost incorporated into batter. Repeat process twice more. When batter appears blended, stop mixer and scrape bowl sides with rubber spatula. Return mixer to low speed; beat until batter looks satiny, about 15 seconds longer.
- 5. Divide batter evenly between pans. With rubber spatula, run batter to pan sides and smooth top. Bake cakes until they feel firm in center when lightly pressed and skewer comes out clean or with just a crumb or two adhering, 23 to 30 minutes. Transfer pans to wire racks; cool for 20 minutes. Run knife around perimeter of each pan, invert cakes onto racks, and peel off paper liners. Reinvert cakes onto additional racks; cool completely before frosting.
- 6. For the Buttercream Frosting: Mix instant coffee, coffee liqueur, and vanilla in small cup until coffee dissolves; set aside. Beat butter in bowl of electric mixer at medium-high speed until fluffy, about 1 minute. Add sugar and beat 3 minutes longer. Add coffee mixture and egg to frosting; beat until frosting mounds around beaters in a fluffy mass, 3 to 5 minutes longer. Apply frosting onto first cake layer and spread with a long metal spatula, top with second cake layer, top second layer with frosting, spread and then frost sides.

242. Vegan Rhubarb Cake Recipe

Serving: 24 | Prep: | Cook: 1hours | Ready in:

Ingredients

- 3 c flour
- 1 3/4 c sugar
- 1 1/2 t soda
- 1/4 t salt
- 4-5 c chopped rhubarb
- 1 1/2 c soy milk
- 2 t vinegar
- 1/3 c oil
- 3 T warm water
- 1 t vanilla
- egg replacer for 2 eggs (optional)
- 1/2 c margarine
- 1 c brown sugar
- 2 t cinnamon

Direction

- 1. Grease and flour 9" x 13" pan. Preheat oven to 350F.
- 2. Mix together margarine, brown sugar, and cinnamon, and set aside.
- 3. Sift together flour, sugar, soda, and salt.
- 4. Stir rhubarb into dry ingredients.
- 5. Mix together liquid ingredients, and stir into dry ingredients.
- 6. Spread evenly in pan and sprinkle cinnamon mixture over top.
- 7. Bake until toothpick comes out clean (about 40 minutes).

243. Vegan Sour Creme Coffeecake Recipe

Serving: 16 | Prep: | Cook: 45mins | Ready in:

Ingredients

- ¼ c. water
- 1 T. egg replacer, dry
- 1/3 c. smooth, unsweetened applesauce
- 3 T. oil
- ¼ c. soymilk
- 1 c. sugar
- 1 tsp. vanilla extract
- 1 ¼ c. whole wheat pastry flour
- ¾ c. unbleached flour
- 1 tsp baking powder
- 1 tsp baking soda
- ½ tsp. salt
- ½ c. extra-firm silken tofu
- ½ c. soymilk
- 1 T. lemon juice
- 1 c. chopped pecans
- 1/3 c. melted good-tasting margarine
- 2/3 c. brown sugar
- 1 tsp. cinnamon

Direction

- Preheat oven to 350 degrees F. Grease and flour a 10" tube cake pan.
- In a blender, blend the water and egg replacer.
- Add applesauce, oil, soymilk, sugar and vanilla and process well.
- Pour into a medium mixing bowl.
- Whisk together the flours, baking powder, baking soda and salt in another bowl.
- In the blender (no need to wash it out after blending the Wet Mix) blend the silken tofu, soymilk, and lemon juice until VERY smooth.
- Add the dry ingredients and the tofu mix alternately to the wet ingredients, starting and ending with the dry.
- Mix the remaining ingredients together well in a small bowl. Sprinkle half of the topping into the bottom of the pan.
- Top with half the batter.
- Sprinkle the rest of the topping over that and end with the remaining batter.
- Bake 45 minutes.
- Let the cake sit on a rack for 5 minutes, then loosen it carefully with a butter knife and invert carefully onto a serving plate.
- Cool on a rack.

244. White Chocolate Banana Bread Recipe

Serving: 10 | Prep: | Cook: 55mins | Ready in:

Ingredients

- 3 very ripe bananas
- 2 tbsp soft butter
- 1 cup sugar
- 1 ½ cups flour
- 1 tsp baking soda
- 1 cup white chocolate chips and /or coarsely chopped nuts
- pecans or walnuts work well (optional)

Direction

- Preheat oven to 375°/190°C.
- Mash bananas in a bowl and add rest of the ingredients. Stir just until blended. It seems as if there is not enough liquid but don't be fooled. The very ripe bananas add all the moisture needed. Mixing the ingredients together with a fork for 2-3 minutes is all you need to create the batter.
- .Pour into greased 9"x5" loaf pan and bake for 45 minutes or until toothpick comes out dry (unless of course you hit a chocolate chip).
- Cool for 10 minutes on a cake rack before removing from pan.
- Instead of chocolate chips (or with them, if you prefer) try:

- Chopped walnuts or pecans
- Dried cranberries or cherries
- Just make sure these ingredients add up to one cup. More than that will lose the bread/cake texture.
- YOU CAN TWEAK THIS RECIPE TO YOUR CHOICE OF FRUITS, NUTS, ETC... MAKE SURE TO USE THE WHITE CHOCOLATE!

245. Cheese And Apricot Coffee Cake Recipe

Serving: 10 | Prep: | Cook: | Ready in:

Ingredients

- cake Ingredients:
- 1 stick of butter, softened
- 1/2 cup sugar
- grated rind of one lemon
- 2 eggs
- 1 teaspoon vanilla
- 1/2 teaspoon salt
- 1 teaspoon baking powder
- 1 heaping cup unbleached flour
- cake Topping:
- 10 halved and pitted apricots (or prune plums)
- 4 oz. cream cheese
- 1/2 cup sugar
- 2 Tablespoons sour cream
- 1 egg
- 1 teaspoon vanilla

Direction

- Cream together butter and sugar with lemon rind. Add eggs, one at a time, and then the vanilla. Beat.
- Add salt, baking powder, and flour.
- Beat together and spread into the bottom of a 9 inch springform pan (greased).
- Place apricots skin side down on top of cake batter.
- In same mixing bowl (don't bother to wash) beat cream cheese and sugar until smooth.
- Add sour cream, vanilla, and egg. Continue to beat.
- Pour on top of cake spreading over the apricots.
- Bake in 350 degrees (F) oven until top is completely set and begins to brown.

246. Choco Choco Coffee Dream Cake Recipe

Serving: 1012 | Prep: | Cook: 45mins | Ready in:

Ingredients

- FOR THE cake
- 200 grs. butter
- 200 grs. sugar
- 150 grs. flour
- 200 grs. semi-sweet chocolate (or milk chocolate) melted
- 65 grs. milk
- 6 egg whites
- 6 egg yolks
- 1 tbsp. powder coffee (diluted in 1 tbsp. of water)
- FOR THE GANACHE
- 250 grs. semi-sweet chocolate
- 150 grs. milk
- 20 grs. butter

Direction

- FOR THE CAKE
- Preheat oven 350 degrees.
- 1. Cream the butter until it has a lighter color, then add the sugar, egg yolks, beat for one minute, then the chocolate, give this 2 minutes and add milk and coffee.
- 2. In another bowl whisk the egg whites until stiff, then add it to the cake batter with soft revolving movements.
- 3. Grease a pan, this is a medium cake, so any medium to big cake pan will do.

- 4. Put the cake batter in the oven and bake for 35 to 45 min. or until it's done.
- FOR THE GANACHE
- 1. Heat the milk, and add the melted chocolate beat for 2 minutes and add the butter.
- Cover the cake.
- DECORATIONS
- If you want to put chocolate decorations just melt chocolate, put it into a decorating pipe and do whatever you want.

247. Chocolate Cinnamon Nut Filled Coffee Cake Recipe

Serving: 12 | Prep: | Cook: 55mins | Ready in:

Ingredients

- • Filling:
- • 1/2 cup granulated sugar
- • 1 teaspoon ground cinnamon
- • 1 tablespoon unsweetened cocoa powder
- • 1/2 cup finely chopped pecans or walnuts
- • ....
- • 1 cup butter
- • 1 1/3 cups granulated sugar
- • 3 large eggs
- • 3 cups flour
- • 3 teaspoons baking powder
- • 1 teaspoon baking soda
- • 8 ounces sour cream
- • 1/4 cup cream or milk

Direction

- Combine filling ingredients; set aside.
- Grease and flour a 10-inch tube cake pan. Heat oven to 350°.
- In a mixing bowl with mixer at high speed, beat butter with sugar until light. Beat in eggs, one at a time, and beating after each addition.
- Combine the flour, baking powder, and soda in a medium bowl. Combine sour cream and milk or cream in a small bowl.
- Slowly beat in flour mixture, alternating with the sour cream mixture. Beat until smooth. Spoon half of the batter into the prepared pan. Sprinkle the filling mixture over the batter. Spoon remaining batter evenly over the filling. Carefully spread to cover.
- Bake for 55 to 60 minutes, or until a wooden pick or cake tester inserted in center comes out clean. Cool on a rack in the pan for 10 minutes. Remove the sides of the pan and cool completely on rack.

248. Cup Of Coffee Cake Recipe

Serving: 1 | Prep: | Cook: 2mins | Ready in:

Ingredients

- one cake mix   you pick the flavor
- one pudding mix...yup you pick the flavor
- 1 egg white
- Pam cookin spray
- 1 tsp oil
- 1 tsp water

Direction

- Mix the two mixes with a whisk.
- Separate evenly into eight zip lock bags.
- Get a microwave safe cup that holds a cup and half.
- Spray cup insides with Pam.
- Add the egg white oil and water mix for 20 secs.
- Micro on high for 2 minutes. Check with a toothpick.

249. Mango Coffee Cake Recipe

Serving: 1216 | Prep: | Cook: 42mins | Ready in:

Ingredients

- 2 cups allpurpose flour
- 2 cups sugar
- 1 1/2 tsp. baking powder
- 1/2 tsp. baking soda
- 1/2 tsp. ground nutmeg
- 1/2 cup butter
- 1 cup buttermilk or sour milk
- 2 eggs, beaten
- 1 tsp. vanilla
- 3 cups coarsely chopped, seeded and peeled mangoes (about 3)
- 1/3 cup sugar
- 3/4 tsp. ground cinnamon
- sweetened wipped cream

Direction

- Preheat oven to 350, grease a 13x9x2 baking pan; set aside. In a large bowl combine flour, the 2 cups sugar, baking powder, soda, nutmeg, and 1/4 teaspoon salt. Using a pastry blender or two knives, cut in butter until mixture resembles coarse crumbs.
- In a small bowl combine buttermilk, eggs, and vanilla. Add to flour mixture all at once; stir just until moistened. Fold in mangoes. Spread in prepared pan. Combine the 1/3 cup sugar and cinnamon. Sprinkle evenly over batter. Bake for 40 to 45 minutes or until a wooden pick inserted near center comes out clean; break crust slightly when inserting pick. (Mango pieces will sink to bottom of coffee cake.) Cool slightly. Serve warm with sweetened whipped cream.

250. Traditional Cape Koeksisters Recipe

Serving: 60 | Prep: | Cook: 30mins | Ready in:

Ingredients

- 4 cups cake flour
- 250g potatoes
- 90g soft butter
- 1/4cup sugar
- 1/2 tsp salt
- 2 eggs
- 10g(1sachet) instant yeast
- 20ml mixed spice
- 20ml fine ginger powder
- 20ml fine cinnamon powder
- 15ml grated naartjie peel(optional)
- 1 cup lukewarm milk
- oil for deep frying
- dessicated coconut
- syrup ingredients:-
- 2&1/2 cups sugar
- 1&1/2 cups water

Direction

- Peel potatoes, boil in water until soft, drain & mash until smooth.
- Beat eggs slightly & mix with butter.
- Sift flour, mixed spice, salt, ginger, cinnamon& naartjie peel (optional) together, add sugar& instant yeast.
- Add egg mixture to mashed potato add warm milk.
- Add to dry ingredients.
- Make a soft dough.
- Knead for +- 10 minutes.
- Leave dough covered in dish in warm place to rise until double +- 2hrs.
- Shape into 36-40 balls elongating slightly.
- Place on greased sheet let rise for another +- 1/2 hr.
- Fry koeksisters on medium heat in deep oil turn to brown evenly.
- Drain on absorbent paper.
- Make syrup by boiling sugar with water under 10 mins.
- Stir in hot syrup.
- Hot tip; fry koeksisters, store stir in hot syrup before serving.
- Roll in desiccated coconut.
- Enjoy with your favourite cup of coffee or tea.

Index

A
Ale 4,70

Almond 3,4,5,8,9,15,35,52,89,113

Apple 3,4,5,6,10,11,12,13,14,15,23,66,79,101,103,119,122,134

Apricot 3,5,6,15,16,88,135,139

B
Baking 24,48

Banana 3,5,6,17,18,19,20,34,89,138

Beef 6,134

Berry 5,92

Biscotti 130

Blackberry 3,21,22

Blueberry 3,4,5,6,23,24,25,26,27,28,58,62,87,125

Bran 3,29,97

Bread 3,4,5,6,20,27,28,31,40,44,45,46,48,49,70,75,81,86,89,90,98,103,106,115,117,130,134,138

Brown sugar 7

Buns 4,5,46,72,107

Butter 3,4,5,18,19,29,30,31,44,45,71,72,75,82,87,90,91,95,97,99,100,122,123,125,137

C
Cake 1,3,4,5,6,7,9,10,11,13,14,15,17,18,19,20,21,22,23,24,25,26,27,28,29,30,34,35,36,37,38,39,40,41,42,43,44,47,48,51,52,53,54,55,56,57,58,59,60,61,62,64,65,66,68,69,71,72,73,74,75,76,77,78,79,80,81,82,83,84,85,86,87,90,91,92,93,94,95,96,97,98,100,101,102,103,104,105,106,109,111,112,113,114,115,116,118,119,120,121,122,124,125,126,128,129,132,133,134,135,136,137,139,140

Caramel 3,4,5,6,7,35,65,105,132

Carrot 4,77

Cashew 3,37

Caster sugar 42

Cheese 3,4,5,6,14,24,25,26,27,28,36,42,49,60,61,66,79,81,89,111,112,114,139

Cherry 3,37,38,39

Chocolate 3,4,5,6,16,17,18,40,41,42,43,44,45,46,47,56,68,84,85,86,91,95,135,138,140

Cinnamon 3,4,5,6,10,31,40,48,49,50,51,72,77,90,110,133,140

Cocoa powder 42

Coconut 4,52

Coffee 1,3,4,5,6,7,9,10,11,12,13,14,15,16,17,18,19,20,21,22,23,25,26,27,28,29,30,31,34,35,36,37,38,39,41,42,44,47,48,50,51,52,53,54,55,56,57,58,59,60,61,62,65,66,67,68,69,71,72,73,74,75,76,77,78,80,81,82,83,84,85,87,88,90,91,92,93,94,95,96,97,98,100,101,102,103,104,105,106,109,110,111,112,113,114,115,116,118,119,120,122,123,124,125,126,127,128,129,131,132,133,134,135,136,138,139,140

Cranberry 4,58,59,60

Cream 3,4,5,6,12,14,17,20,21,22,23,24,25,26,28,36,39,42,47,49,51,54,55,60,61,62,63,65,68,71,74,78,79,81,87,89,90,95,96,101,102,106,112,113,116,119,120,122,123,124,126,129,133,139

Crumble 51,60

Custard 3,12

E
Egg 90,109

F

Fat 4,33,79,82
Fig 5,100
Flour 90
Fruit 3,4,9,69
Fudge 3,4,42,57

G

Gin 3,4,11,70,71

H

Hazelnut 3,11,42
Honey 3,4,5,29,75,116

I

Icing 85,86,88,90,110

J

Jus 12,43,72,83,139

L

Lemon 3,4,6,9,16,75,80,81,90,131
Liqueur 4,52

M

Macadamia 4,5,43,101
Mandarin 5,84
Mango 6,140,141
Marshmallow 4,55
Marzipan 5,113,114
Mascarpone 4,56,62
Milk 76,90
Muffins 4,44,53

N

Nut 3,4,5,6,14,35,42,44,48,54,55,56,81,88,90,105,117,140

O

Oatmeal 3,4,5,11,75,89
Oats 4,65
Orange 4,5,57,83,91

P

Pastry 3,4,36,64,90
Peach 4,5,63,96,97
Pear 3,5,17,122
Pecan 3,4,5,6,7,20,51,52,58,65,82,98,100,120,122,124,132
Peel 14,32,141
Pineapple 5,101
Potato 3,6,35,132,133
Praline 5,6,103,133
Pulse 60,118
Pumpkin 3,4,5,6,40,49,70,90,105,106,123,130,134

R

Raisins 4,51,90
Raspberry 3,4,5,35,45,62,66,71,110,111,112,113,114
Rhubarb 3,5,6,10,39,96,115,124,128,137
Ricotta 3,17,27,42
Rum 3,12

S

Salt 90
Squash 3,30,31
Strawberry 4,5,6,10,71,96,118,125,126,127,128
Sugar 5,6,71,90,120,124

T

Tea 4,5,6,46,83,91,129,134

V

Vegan 4,6,82,137,138

W

Walnut 3,4,13,19,48

Y

Yeast 90

Z

Zest 8,87,129

Conclusion

Thank you again for downloading this book!

I hope you enjoyed reading about my book!

If you enjoyed this book, please take the time to share your thoughts and post a review on Amazon. It'd be greatly appreciated!

Write me an honest review about the book – I truly value your opinion and thoughts and I will incorporate them into my next book, which is already underway.

Thank you!

If you have any questions, **feel free to contact at:** *author@bisquerecipes.com*

Angela Haas

bisquerecipes.com

Made in United States
Orlando, FL
13 May 2024